I0809990

IMAGES
of America

TOBACCO VALLEY

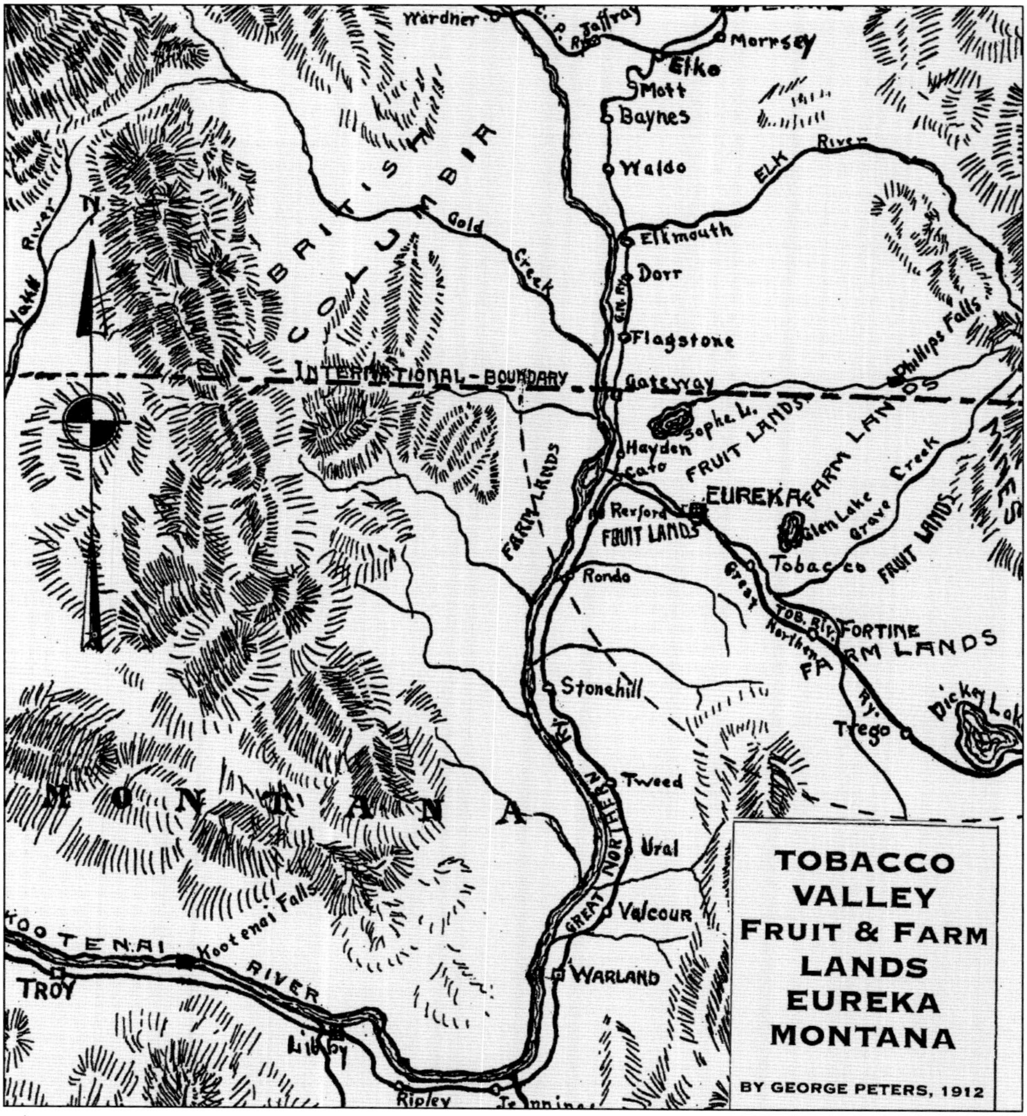

This 1912 map of the Tobacco Valley region shows the small towns along the Kootenai River long before the Libby Dam created Lake Koocanusa. Today that narrow lake covers about 90 miles of territory along the old Kootenai route, split between the United States and Canada (note the international boundary). (Drawn by George Peters; courtesy of Tobacco Valley Board of History.)

ON THE COVER: In 1897, Amine Blanche Dewey came to Columbia Falls with two brothers and two sisters at the age of 21. Two years later she married Elzeor Demers, one of the prime movers and shakers in Tobacco Valley. The house he built for her was located where the new high school sits today. Mounted on her horse (left) in front of that house, she and her sister Grace, one of the area's first teachers, appear to be out for a ride. Demers named Dewey Avenue to honor his wife's maiden name after failing to secure the name of Dewey for the new town. Amine bore Demers three children and was raising an adopted child when she died at the age of 40. (Courtesy of Tobacco Valley Board of History.)

IMAGES
of America

TOBACCO VALLEY

Gary Montgomery and the
Tobacco Valley Board of History

ARCADIA
PUBLISHING

ISBN 978-0-7385-7088-4

Published by Arcadia Publishing
Charleston, South Carolina

Printed in the United States of America

Library of Congress Control Number: 2009924711

For all general information contact Arcadia Publishing at:
Telephone 843-853-2070
Fax 843-853-0044
E-mail sales@arcadiapublishing.com
For customer service and orders:
Toll-Free 1-888-313-2665

Visit us on the Internet at www.arcadiapublishing.com

To Clara Brock Fewkes, née Enden, who inspired my interest in the history of Tobacco Plains country.

To Cathryn Schroeder, whose tireless effort has resulted in the Historical Village, a crown jewel of the Tobacco Valley.

To Elsie Helms, a genuine daughter of Montana (December 11, 1909, to July 13, 2009).

To Lincoln County, Montana, on its 100th birthday, 1909–2009

CONTENTS

ACKNOWLEDGMENTS

The work of other dedicated historians who have gone before me was essential to this effort. Without *The Story of the Tobacco Plains Country*, published in 1950 by Olga Weydemeyer and the Pioneers of Tobacco Plains Country, I would have spent months searching through boxes and file cabinets, and even then, much local history would have already been lost. *Early Flathead and Tobacco Plains* by Marie Cuffe Shea, 1977, was also an important reference. Thanks to Madeline Utter and her book, *Pinkham Pioneers*, for information on Pinkham Creek people. Nancy Anderson provided information on early-day U.S. Forest Service pictures. Darris Flanagan, who has published a number of books on specific aspects of Tobacco Valley history, was forthcoming with both photographs and fact checking. Thanks to old-timers like Pete Klinke, Wylie Osler, Tom Price, Larry Curtiss, Marie Purdy, and Joan Shirley for their consultation and help in finding photographs. Most of all, thanks to the Tobacco Valley Board of History, whose vote of confidence and permission to use its archives was of critical importance. Unless otherwise noted the images in this book are from those archives.

INTRODUCTION

One of the most curious aspects regarding the history of the area named on the cover of this book is that it somehow involves tobacco. Clearly, northwest Montana is not tobacco-producing country. Why then is there a river, a valley, a former settlement, and several thousand acres of prairie country carrying this moniker?

The name goes back 200 years to when explorer David Thompson first descended the Kootenai River (he called it the McGillivray River) out of Canada and arrived at the confluence of the Tobacco River (he called it Fine Meadow Creek). There he found a pristine expanse of relatively open land ringed with rugged mountains that for the past 9,000 years or so had been the heart of the country over which the Kutenai people ranged.

There Thompson learned that the Native Americans used a variety of wild tobacco mixed with kinnikinnick for ceremonial purposes. It was he, so far as it is known, who first used the word tobacco for any geographical feature in this area, referring to the expanse as Tobacco Meadow on one of his early maps. Tobacco Plains came into the lexicon on an 1819 Arrowsmith map produced in London. An early French map named the area Prairie du Tubac. Fr. Jean DeSmet, a Jesuit coming from Belgium in 1845, referred to it by that name.

In the succeeding 50 years, the Kutenai Indians continued to hold sway over the Tobacco Plains as well as the larger Tobacco Valley, which drained to the plains from the south, its total length being about 30 miles as the crow flies. In that span of years, a few trappers and prospectors probed the surrounding mountains. Many more saw the country as hopeful travelers passing through on their way to the Wild Horse goldfields in British Columbia. But the land remained the domain of the Native Americans, and they completely disregarded the fact that the United States and Canada established an arbitrary border (by treaty) that transected the Tobacco Plains in 1846. David, who in 1887 was the Kutenai chief, in a meeting with an official from the Canadian government regarding border issues asked, "What is the meaning of this boundary line? It runs through the middle of my house. My home is on both sides. Why should you, without talking with me or considering me, divide my property in two and also divide my children? I have many people and where are they to hunt?"

It was not until the late 1880s that pressure came to bear on the indigenous population when cattlemen found the isolated Tobacco Plains. There were some incidents. In 1889, a contingent of buffalo soldiers rode to the Tobacco Plains from Fort Missoula in what amounted to little more than a show of force. By and large, the Kutenais stepped peacefully aside and took up land immediately north of the border that the Canadian government allotted them as a reservation.

Then as now, there were only two practical ways to reach the Tobacco Valley. One could travel along the Kootenai River as it transected the Tobacco Plains from north to the southwest or on the ancient Native American trail. Running for hundreds of miles along the Rocky Mountain Trench, the Kalispell/Fort Steele Trail was called the Tobacco Plains Trail only when one was going there and no farther. Heavy freight wagons plied the difficult trail well before the beginning of the 20th century, but at the time the cattlemen came in, and the supplies and their relatives who followed, they found that the easiest way to get to the Tobacco Plains was by riverboat.

The Great Northern Railroad pushed over the Continental Divide and on to the West Coast in the early 1890s. Initially, the tracks were routed through Kalispell, then over Haskell Pass into the Fisher River drainage, and on to Libby. Near the confluence of the Fisher and Kootenai Rivers, some 15 miles upriver and east of Libby, the small town of Jennings sprang up.

Jennings became the terminus for a succession of small stern-wheelers that plied the often-treacherous waters of the Kootenai River to Fort Steele and the Wild Horse goldfields of British Columbia, with stops at Tobacco Plains along the way. For nine years, gutsy boatmen hauled supplies and adventurous travelers upriver and gold ore downriver. All that ended in 1901 when the Great Northern extended its tracks along the Kootenai River to Rexford at the western edge of Tobacco Plains and then on into Canada to the extensive coalfields around Fernie, British Columbia.

A momentous change came in 1904 when Jim Hill abandoned the Kalispell/Libby connection. He rerouted his railroad from Columbia Falls to Whitefish and then to the Tobacco Valley, connecting with the spur line that ran from Jennings to Rexford.

Up to that time, the settlements of Tobacco and Mills Springs were the focus of social and business life for the cattle ranchers and a few prospectors who were combing the mountains to the east for signs of minerals and precious metals. The railroad tracks never came closer than a mile to Tobacco and Mills Spring, and as a result, a new town was born at the most southern tip of the Tobacco Plains at the only suitable spot possible before the Tobacco River drops into the Kootenai Valley. For a short while, the new town was called Dewey, but unable to secure that name with the U.S. Post Office, early movers and shakers settled on the name Eureka.

As it was all across the west, the coming of the railroad changed everything. Not only did it provide access to the Tobacco Valley for businessmen and homesteaders, but it provided an opportunity to move timber products to outside markets, and it was not long before logging established the basis for an economy. South of Eureka, the small towns of Stryker, Trego, and Fortine sprung up. Fortine in particular dreamed big, but none of the three towns have ever been much larger or smaller than they are right now.

The Eureka Lumber Company was founded in 1906. At one time it claimed to be the largest mill in Montana, and workers came from far and wide. Camps were established upstream, and winters were spent decking logs along the Tobacco River and its tributaries. In the spring with high water, so-called river rats brought the logs to Eureka. The sawmill ran day and night to process the harvest, and the town prospered. During World War I, when paranoia reigned over the influence of the Workers of the World, also known as the Wobblies, federal troops were brought in to guard the infrastructure.

In 1920, Prohibition became the law of the land, but as the Canadians still manufactured and sold various forms of alcohol, there was ample opportunity for enterprising bootleggers to move contraband liquor on down the line. It came across the border on coal trains, under the seats of family sedans, in broken down Ford Model Ts belonging to Native Americans, specially equipped rumrunner cars, and even floated down the Kootenai River by a variety of means, including rafts disguised as floating brush. The Pinkham Creek area, having been settled by several Appalachian families who knew how to distill moonshine, developed a reputation for making good whiskey.

In the thick of it all was Sheriff Frank Baney, a local legend. He was the law for 40 years and is the nexus for many stories that not only involve bootleggers and moonshiners, but desperados that moved through the area, first by train and then by automobile when roads reached the valley from the outside world in the mid-1920s.

Various attempts were made to supplement the economy with something other than the Big Mill. One of them was the chemical plant, which was built to process the butts of large tamarack trees. The bell-like butts had been sawed off and left in the woods as waste. But eastern investors learned that large amounts of mucic acid were concentrated in those butts. Given that mucic acid was a product in demand for making baking soda, an extraction plant was built next to the

Big Mill. Although it occupied the imagination of investors and local workers from 1922 to 1929, the plant never operated for very long at any one time and scarcely at all after 1924.

In decline as the easy pickings along the Tobacco River and its tributaries were run through the mill, and after an effort to supply the mill with a logging railroad that ran up into the surrounding mountains to Frank Lake, the big lumber mill, which had been the mainstay of the Tobacco Valley economy for 18 years, closed down. It was with considerable apprehension about the future that Eureka people saw their mill loaded onto flatcars and moved to points west.

Following the demise of the lumber company in 1924, Eureka entered a dormant period and remained to a great extent below the radar line. Those who remained quietly plugged away in the woods, making railroad ties and especially two-by-fours for a burgeoning construction market following World War II. Tractor crawlers were manufactured instead of tanks, and heavy military transport trucks became log haulers. The log harvest was on again once loggers were able to reach new stands of timber that were neither close to the railroad nor standing along the river. It was during this period that Christmas tree harvesting became important to the area's economy, the Christmas trees being abundant in the regrowth after logging. The accolade, "Christmas Tree Capital of the World," was no joke as each autumn, workers—many of them women—cut, bundled, and loaded out hundreds of carloads of Christmas trees from the 1940s through the 1960s.

As the Christmas tree business waned, primarily the result of competition from plantation trees and the once logged-over land recovering into stands of timber, the Tobacco Valley took another run at a timber-based economy. By 1975, two major, and a number of minor, sawmills began turning out impressive amounts of lumber. Within the last few years, both large mills have closed, mainly because of the inability to secure enough logs to make the operations profitable.

Tobacco and Kootenai Valley history changed forever when Congress funded the building of Libby Dam, which eventually backed up water in Lake Koocanusa for 90 miles in the United States and Canada, inundating all the small towns that were situated along the banks of the Kootenai River. Many construction jobs came to the area to build the dam itself as well as a 7-mile tunnel to reroute the mainline of the Great Northern Railroad. These events provide a perfect end point for a historical book on the Tobacco Valley because these events ushered in a new era.

One

The Native People

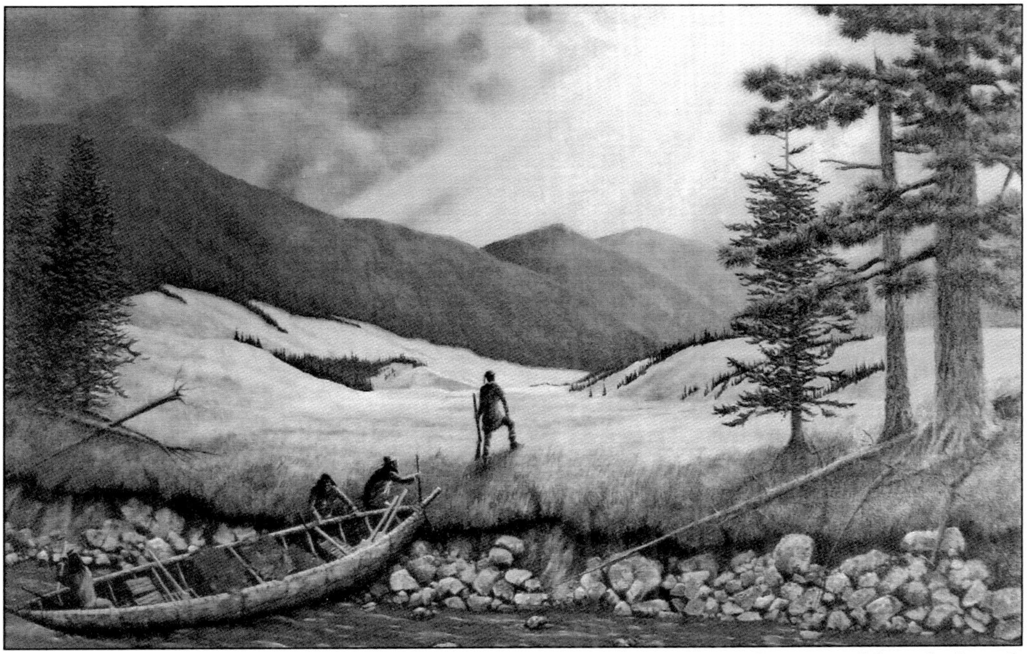

David Thompson descended the Kootenai River out of Canada in April 1808 and found a broad, relatively treeless expanse inhabited by Kutenai Indians. He learned they grew a form of wild tobacco for ceremonial use and named the area Tobacco Meadows. Thompson, a navigator and geographer, was in the employ of the Hudson's Bay Company. He traveled extensively with his Irish-Chippewa wife, Charlotte Small. Incredibly, she bore him 13 children, the entire retinue traveling with Thompson as he mapped vast portions of the northwest. (Painting by Jim Snow.)

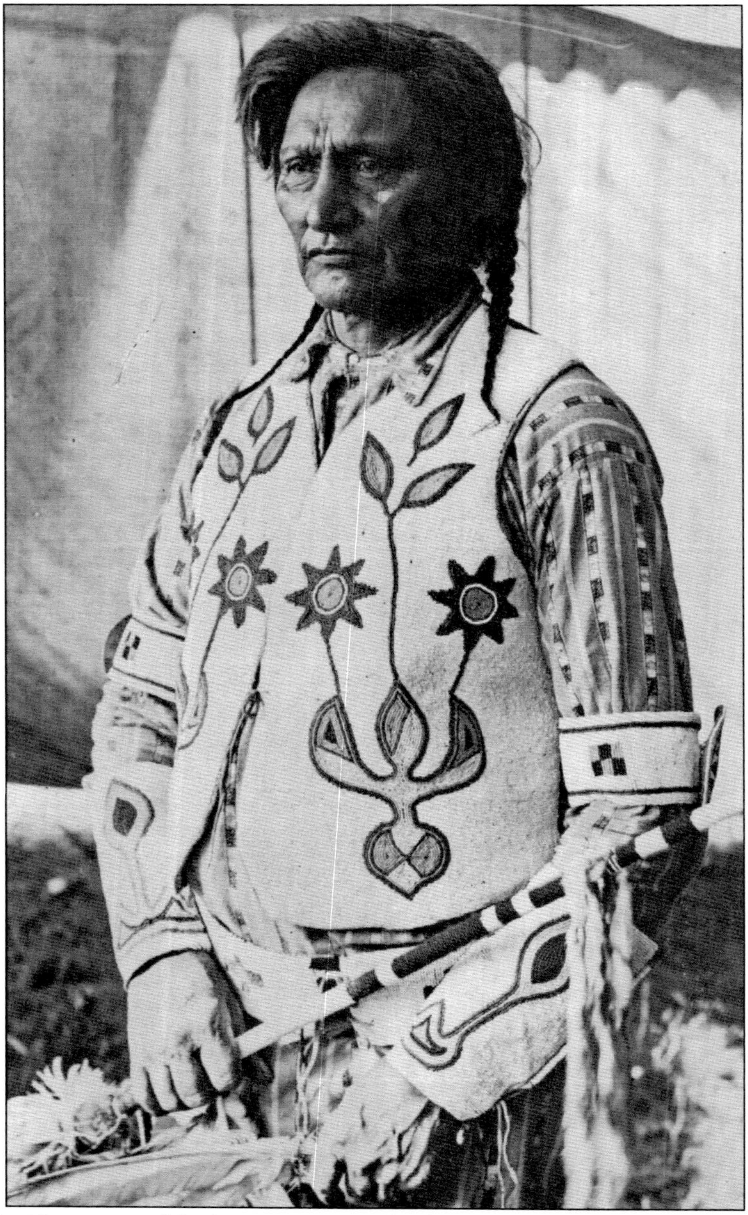

Chief Paul David was one of the longest-serving chiefs on record. Born in 1852, he succeeded his father around 1893 and remained chief until his death in about 1948. In 1887, Chief David, father of Paul David, was negotiating the boundaries of the Tobacco Plains Reservation with Canadian officials. "You come and ask me to pick out some of my own lands for me to live on. What will you do with the rest? Is it not mine also? . . . If you came to me [and said] 'We need land,' I would give you plenty of my land and treat you well. But now you come to me like a crying baby to an elder brother. Well, I will pity you. I will choose land to please you." The chief proceeded to describe a reservation that would have included land from Windermere to Stryker—millions of acres in British Columbia and Montana. When it was all said and done, the Tobacco Plains band was allotted 10,000 acres for their reserve.

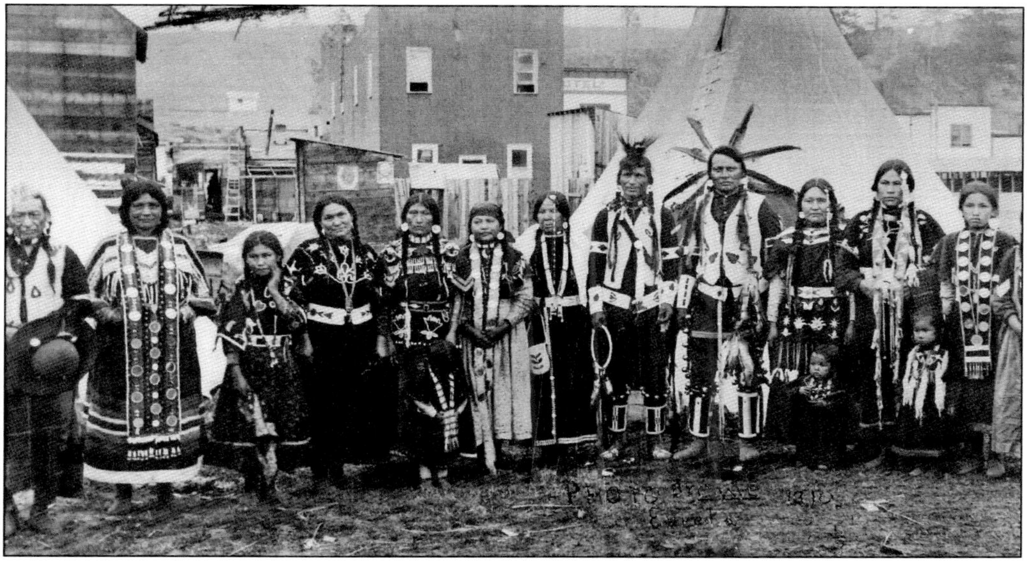

Members of the Native American band visited Eureka in the early days for various reasons. This shot was taken one block west of the National Hotel where they camped for the fair in 1910. From left to right are Joacham, Mary `akiyinik, Rosalie McCoy, Mary Ann David, Mary Shottanana, Lucy Phillipps, Mary Basil, Paul Luke, Joe David, Agnes Luke, Sophia (Louie) Phillip, and Annie Pierre. The child at the far right is Madeline Couture.

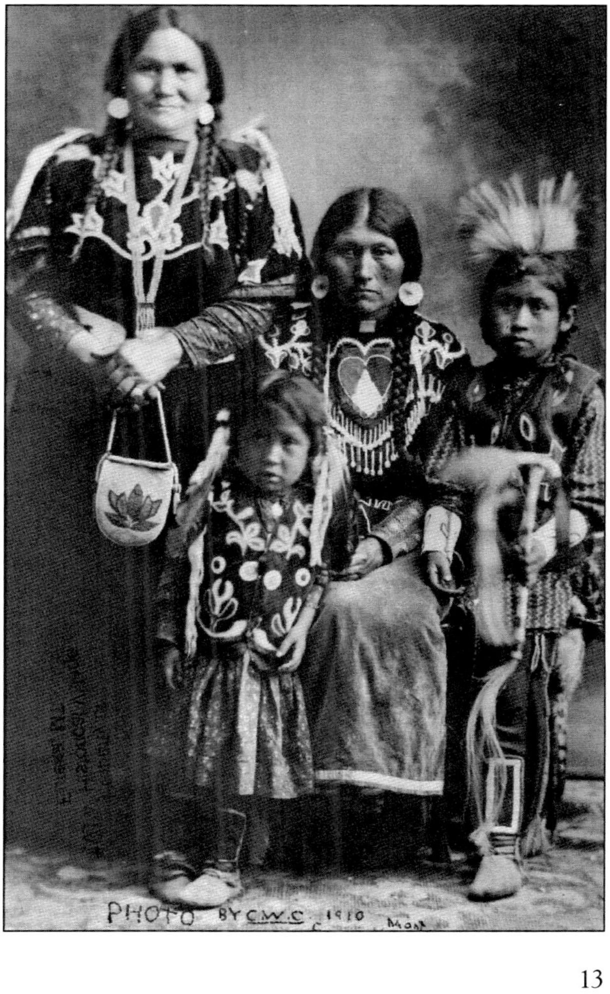

Kutenai women were noted for their fine beadwork and leatherwork. Pictured here are Mary Shottanana (seated) and Mary Ann David (standing).

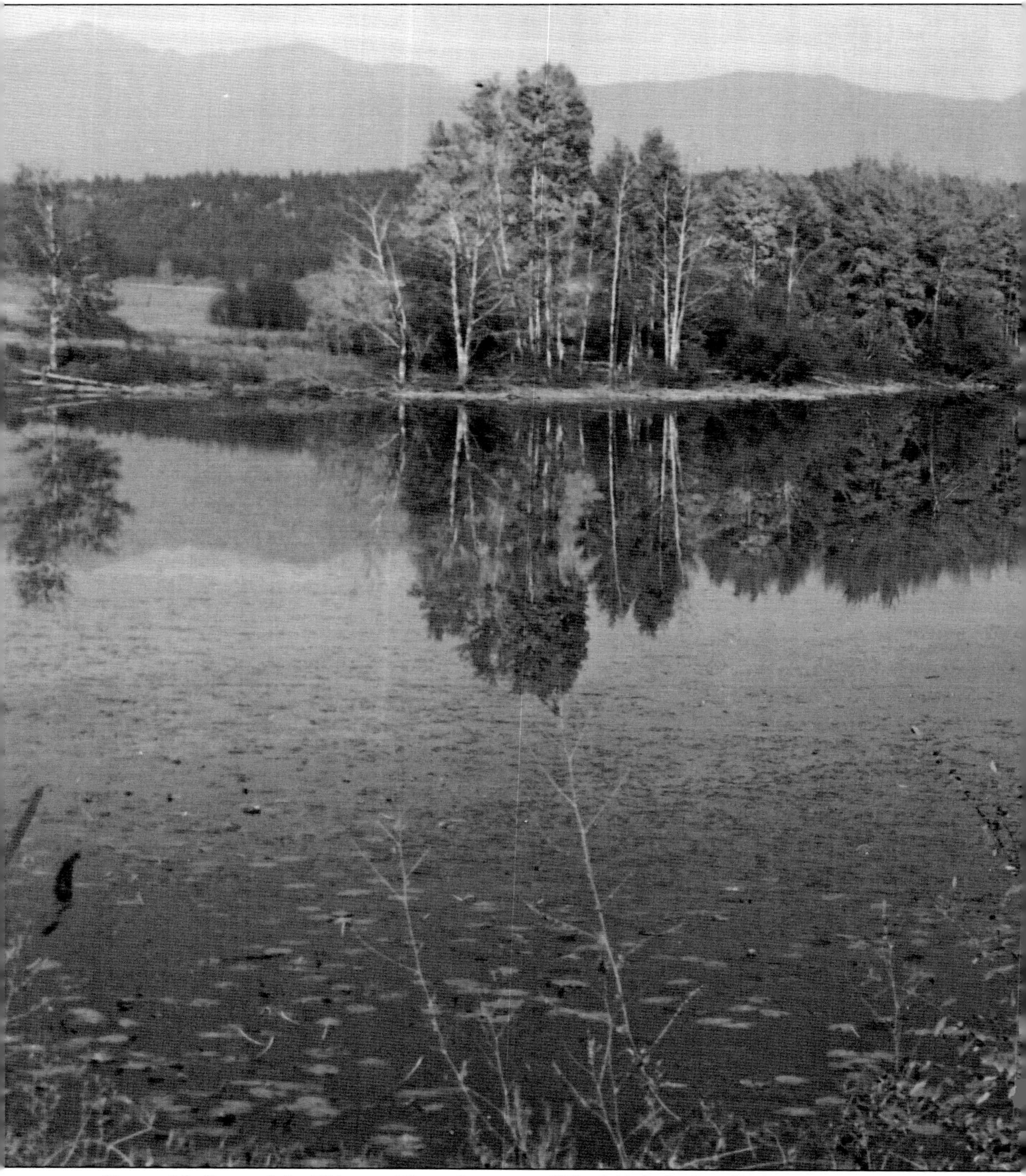

Kutenai Indians of the Tobacco Plains first met a "Black Robe" when Fr. Jean DeSmet visited one of their settlements on Flathead Lake in April 1842. Promising to visit them at Tobacco Plains sometime in the future, DeSmet arrived in August 1845. Father DeSmet learned that the Kutenai had carefully kept track of elapsed time with a rather unique calendar. It was comprised of a square stick on which they had notched 41 months and a few days since they had last seen him

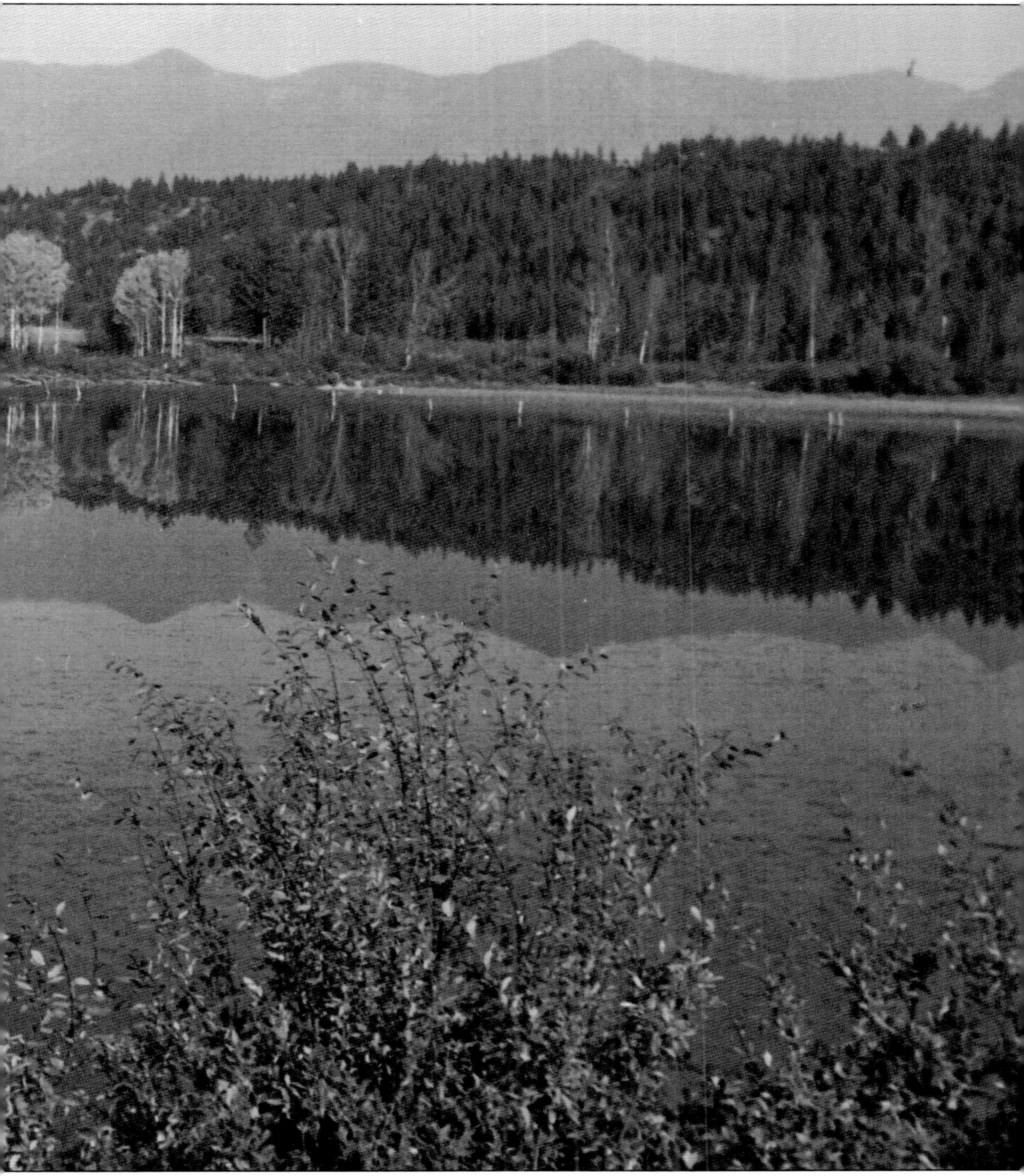

near Flathead Lake. By the time Dr. Augustus Thiebodo visited the valley in 1859, the Kutenai Indians had built a church on the shores of Lake Livermore (pictured above). "Services are held in the chapel morning and evening every week-day and three times on Sundays," he wrote. "When the bell rings the Indians drop everything at once and hurry to the chapel . . . I never saw people so quiet and apparently so contented as these." (Courtesy of Darris Flanagan.)

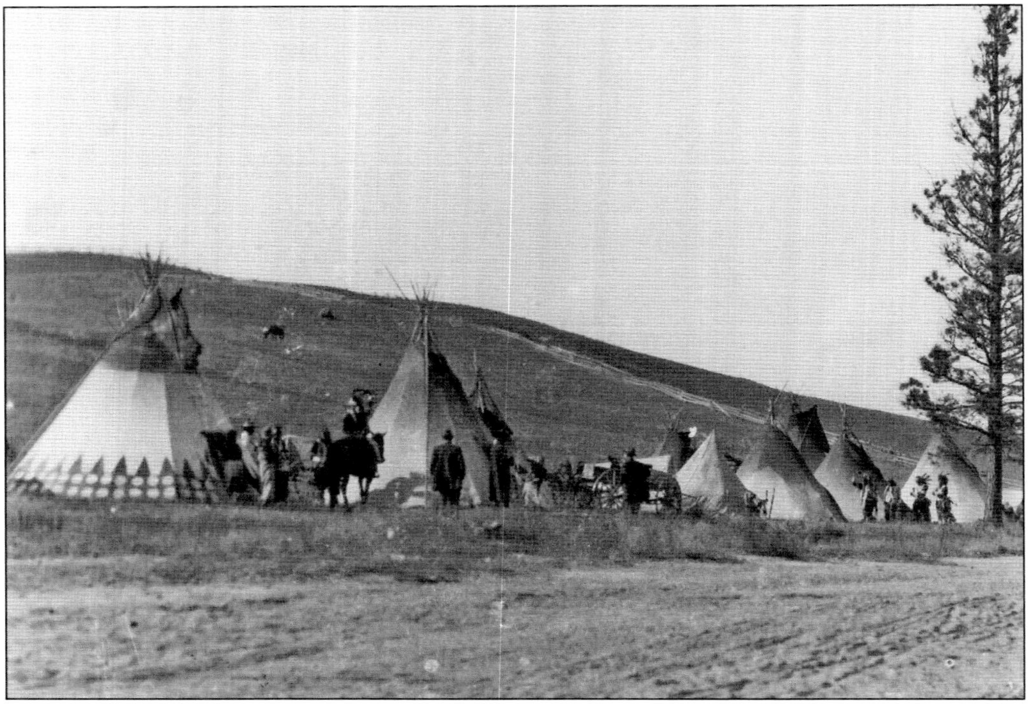

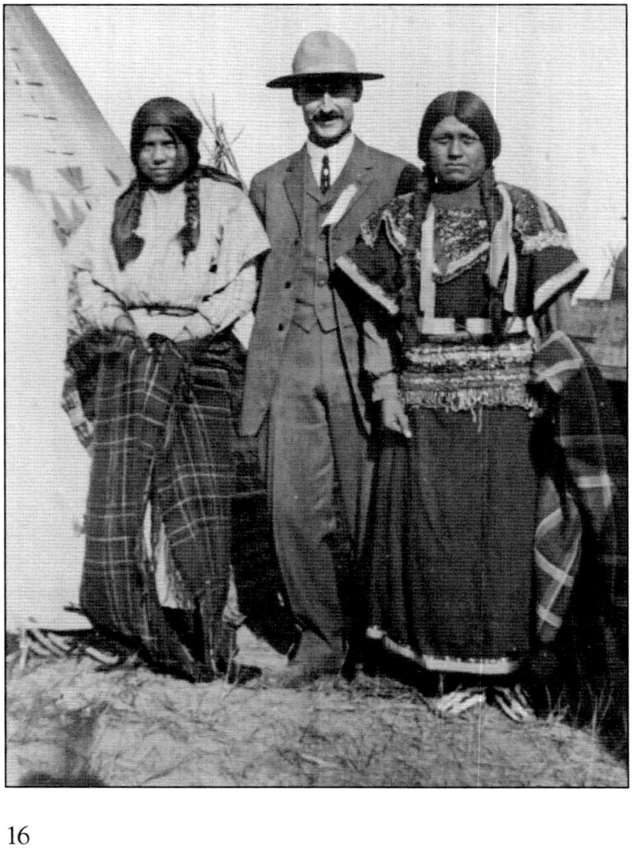

A favorite camping site, pictured here in 1913, when the Kutenai tribe visited was north of Eureka directly across from Ksanka Courts and below what is now known as L Hill. Assuredly, the Native American people had a different name for it. It was a time when they commonly came to town for the county fair, which was held in October.

It is likely that the growing white population maneuvered to pose in photographs with Kutenai people for the purpose of sending postcards to the folks back home. Here Sam Carpenter stands between two Kutenai women. While there were no major incidents with the natives of Tobacco Plains, there were times, particularly around the beginning of the 20th century, when relations were dubious at best.

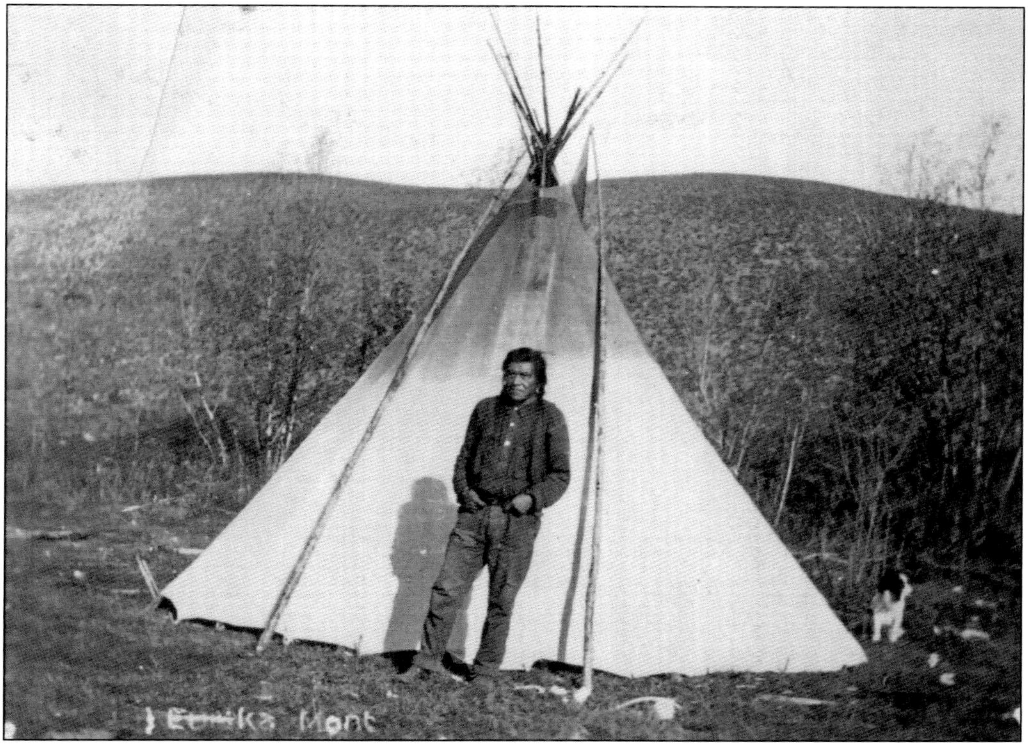

An unidentified Kutenai man (pictured above) and Louis Three Mountains were forced to adjust their lifestyles when they could no longer range freely south of the border. Although they supposedly had dual citizenship, that designation on the American side of the border meant less. Charles Sheldon, who homesteaded just above the site of the Native American mission and burial ground at Lake Livermore, told the story that when he first went out to plow the ground to which he had laid claim, a small group of Native Americans appeared and followed him, "making strange ceremonious motions over and over, and chanting in voices now like heavy waters going down, now like a lone little bird in the top of a balsam, now like a hungry wolf pack—an unfathomable farewell."

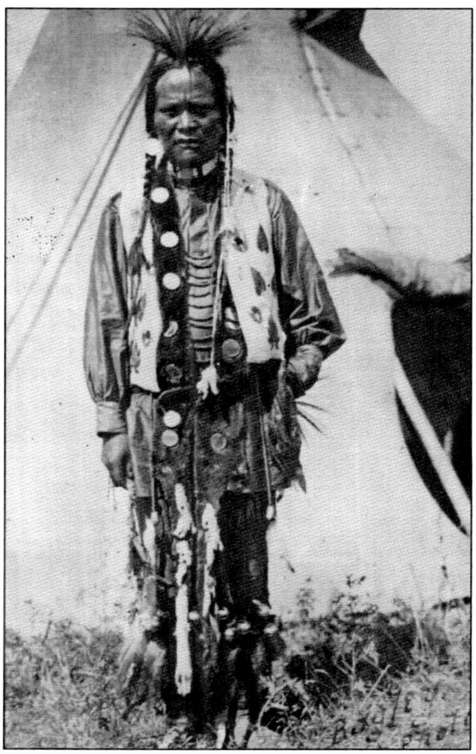

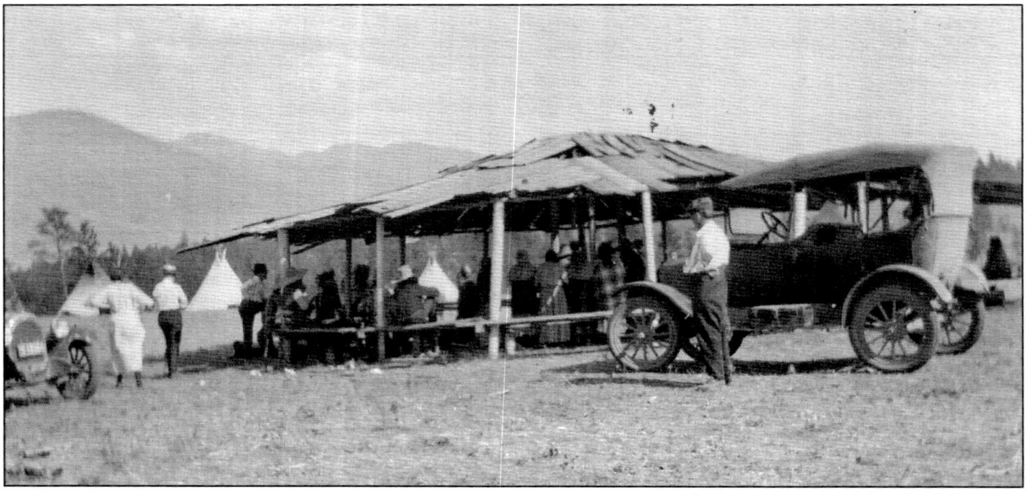

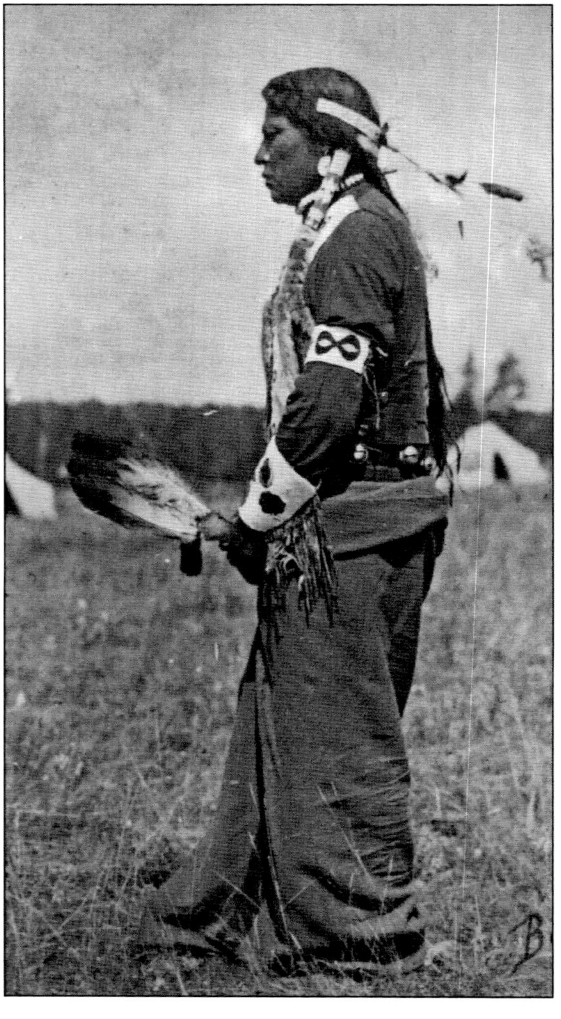

According to the *Tobacco Plains Journal* on July 13, 1916, "Edwards Lake . . . on the British Columbia side of the International Boundary, has proven quite a Mecca for Eureka auto parties . . . the attraction there being a big dance and other festivities participated in by about 100 members of the Kootenai and Stony Indian tribes. Hour after hour they reel off their primitive dances to methodical beat of the tom-tom . . . The deepest problems incumbent upon us of the civilized life doesn't even so much as trouble them with a passing thought."

Big Joe, brother to Chief Paul David, was not to be underestimated. An incident in about 1900, which was recounted in the *Story of the Tobacco Plains Country*, illustrates why. "Fred Herrig arrested some Indians for killing deer near Ant Flat . . . They were released but some of their horses were held as security. They returned with a large group of friends, some of whom were wearing war paint . . . The Indians refused to pay the fines and demanded the return of their horses . . . Fighting almost broke out when Bob Reid lost his temper and hit one of the braves with a neck yoke. When Big Joe tried to wrest Joe Peltier's rifle from his hands, only the intervention of Ovid Peltier and others prevented Big Joe's being shot."

Catherine Gravelle recalled a story in 1992 that her grandfather told her: "A woman had lost her husband in a battle with the Blackfeet. All she had left were her two boys . . . The mother sent the oldest boy to Sophie's Trading post for groceries. When he returned the younger boy was playing with a gun. The mother asked, 'Where is the flour?' When her son said he had forgotten it his younger brother threw the gun to his shoulder and laughingly said, 'For that I should shoot you,' and he pulled the trigger. The older boy toppled from his horse and fell, dead, at his mother's feet."

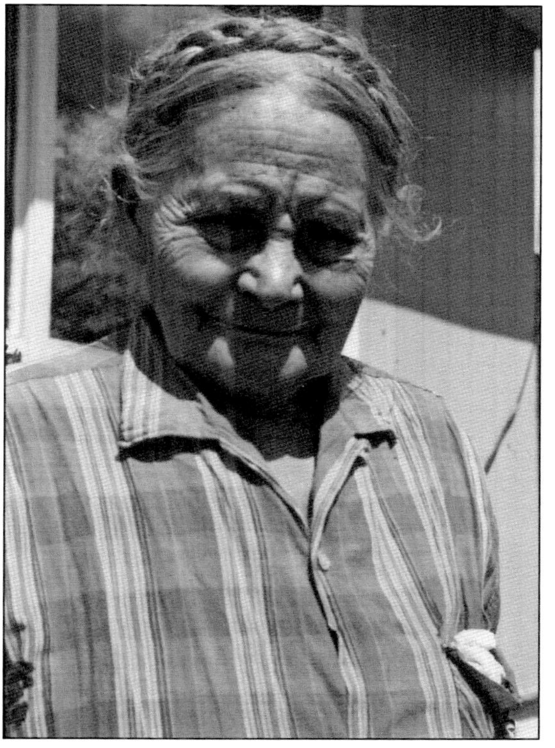

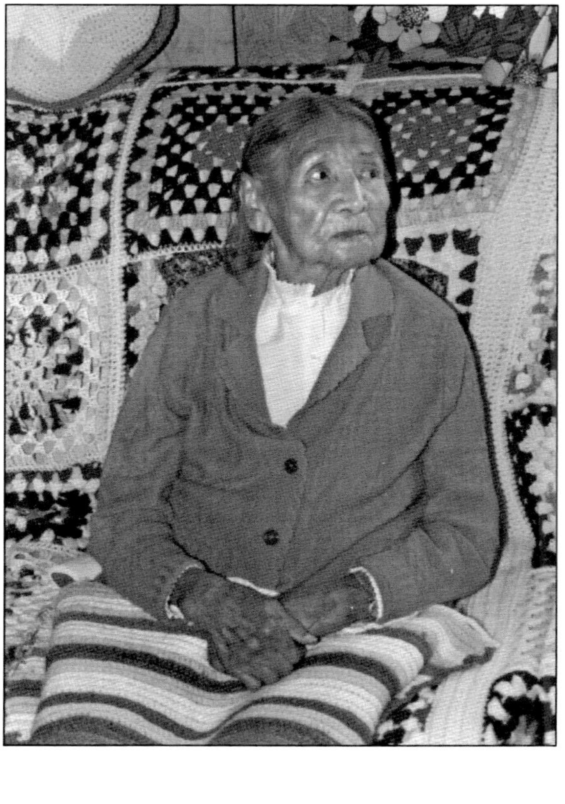

Madeline Morigeau, of the St. Mary's band near Cranbrook, British Columbia, traveled by horse and automobile numerous times to visit relatives at Tobacco Plains and on Flathead Lake. Born on a hunting trip in 1900, she recalled coming to Tobacco Plains as a young girl on whitetail deer hunts. "Our camp was right there where the immigration offices are standing (at Roosville). Whenever I go through it comes to my mind, 'This is where our teepees used to be, right on this spot.'" (Courtesy of the author.)

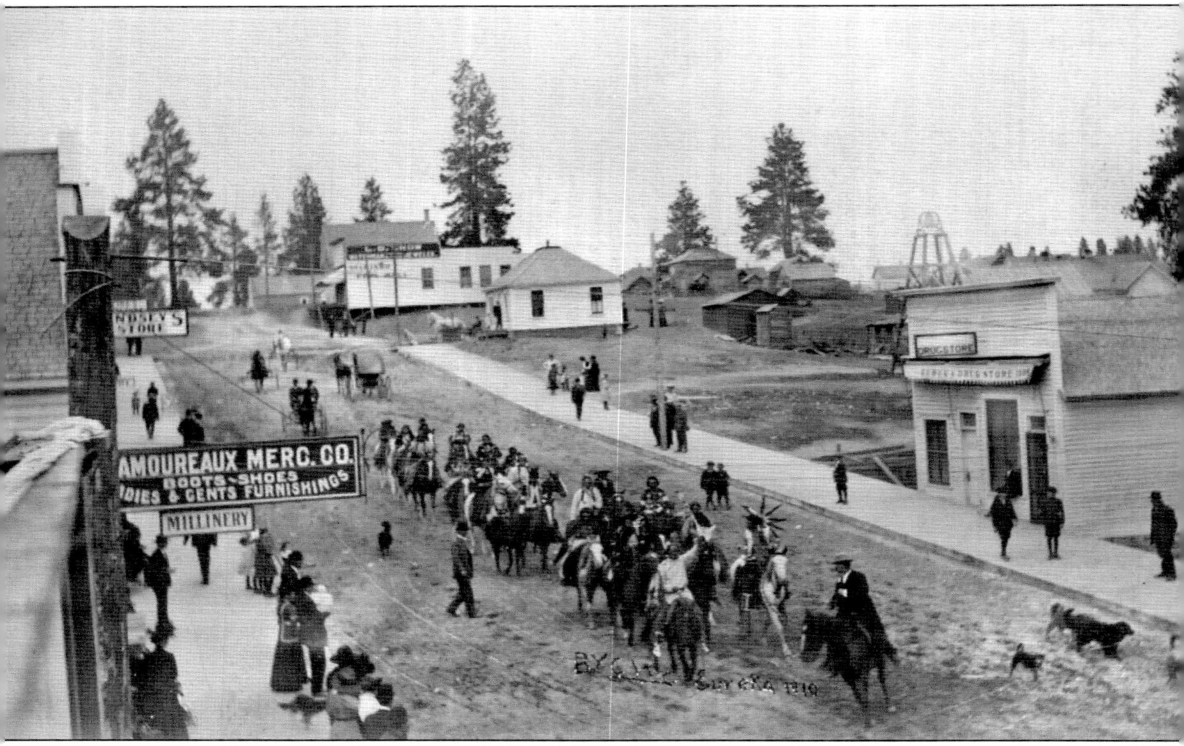

It must have caused quite a stir when the Native Americans rode through town. The *Tobacco Plains Journal* noted on September 23, 1910, that, "The Indians came down across the line in all their glory of festive dance costume and war paint and enjoyed the Fair equally as well as the pale faces. There were about 75 in attendance. They pitched their tepees on First Street west, where they held a dance the first evening. No one seemed to enjoy the occasion more, and in the way of diversion nothing contributed more to the festivities of the Fair." It is curious the way in which a rider seems to be turning in front of the column. The leader, possibly Chief Paul David, has his hand raised in what is likely a friendly greeting. The small house in the center distance was relocated to Pinkham Creek, and Glacier Bank now occupies that spot.

Two

OPEN RANGE BECKONS

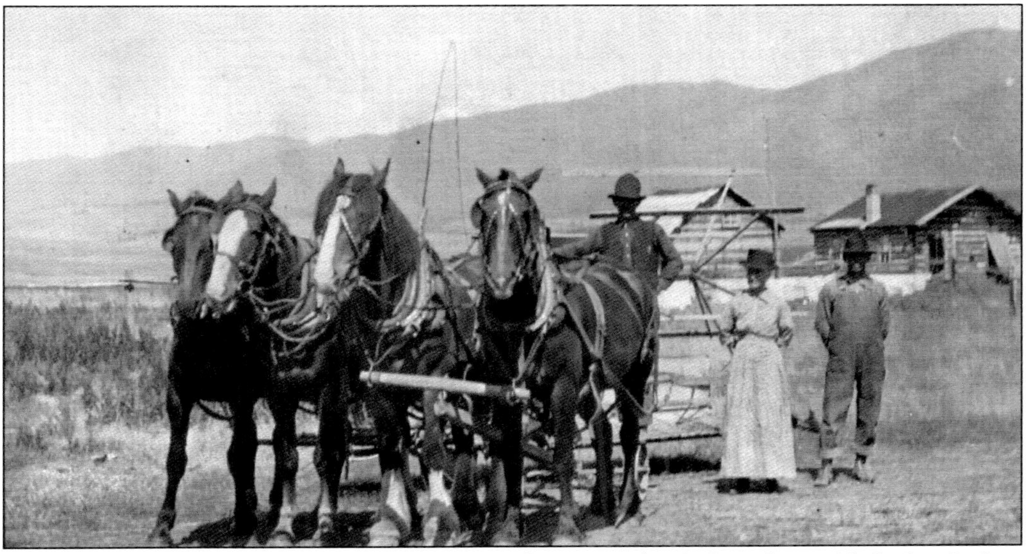

The first commercial cattle outfit on Tobacco Plains was the 69 Ranch, established at Indian Creek Flats in 1884. Before that it was a perennial Native American camping site. A succession of owners and renters, including Sophie Morigeau, worked the 69 Ranch through the years. A Mr. Downs, who is driving the team pictured above, and his wife lived there in 1915. Walter Sweet, a blacksmith, stands on the right. Where there was grain and hay, though, there will now be a golf course.

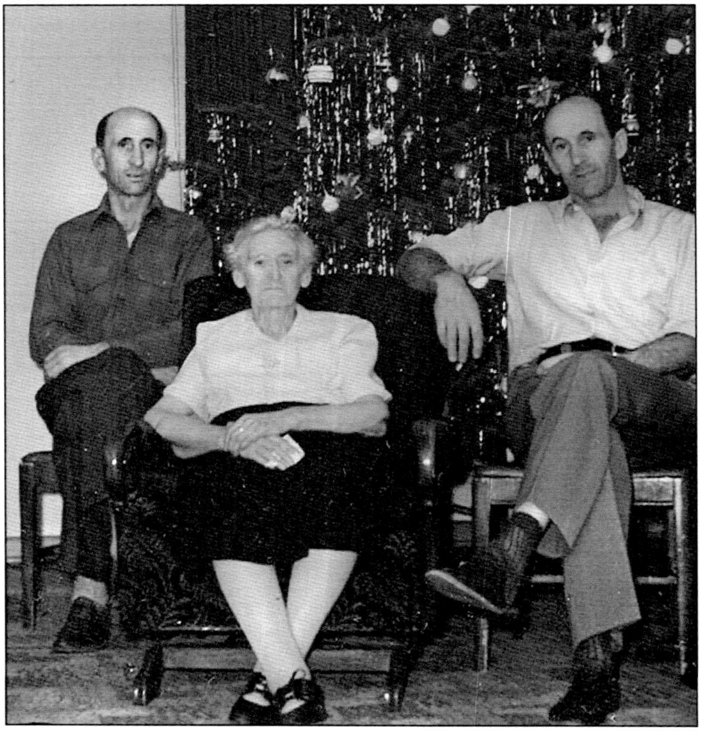

In 1886, Tom Quirk, an Irishman, filed homestead rights along Indian Creek, east of the 69 Ranch, and brought in some cattle. Tom never married, but his brother Maurice, who joined him on the 101 Ranch in 1900, did. Maurice and his wife, Mary, had four surviving children. Maurice died at the early age of 48, but Mary and two of her sons, Tom (left) and Emmet, remained on the 101 Ranch for the rest of their lives. (Courtesy of Faye Driggs.)

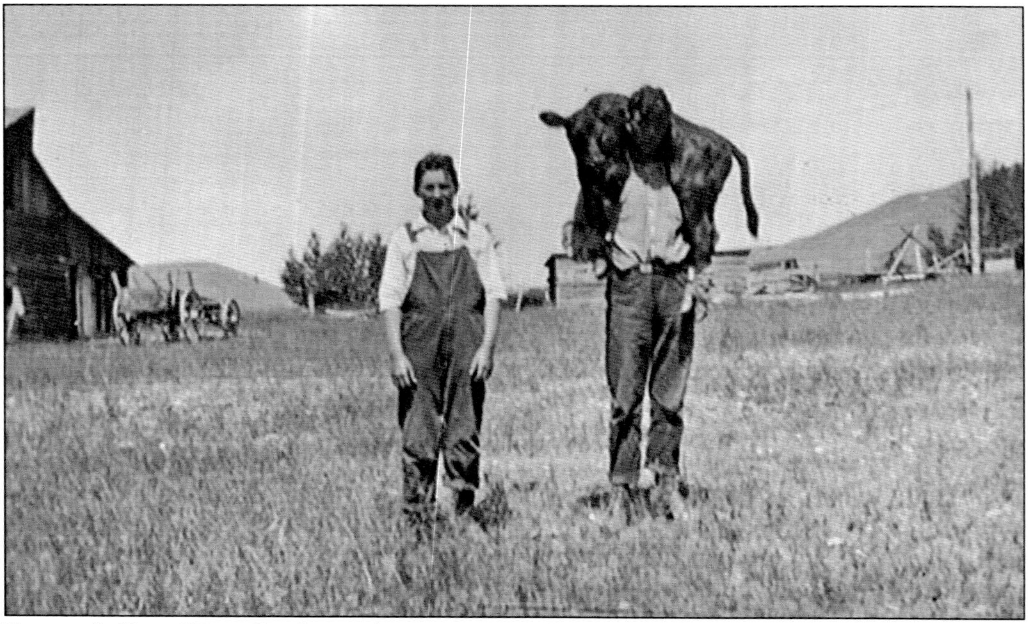

Emmet (left) and Tom Quirk were born in 1907 and 1904, respectively. Their uncle, Tom Quirk, who died in 1923, had a reputation for decisive action whether dealing with cattle rustlers, water rights, or threats from the native population. One of a handful of ranches maintaining its original boundaries, Faye and Leland Driggs, Emmet's daughter and son-in-law, work the ranch these days. (Courtesy of Faye Driggs.)

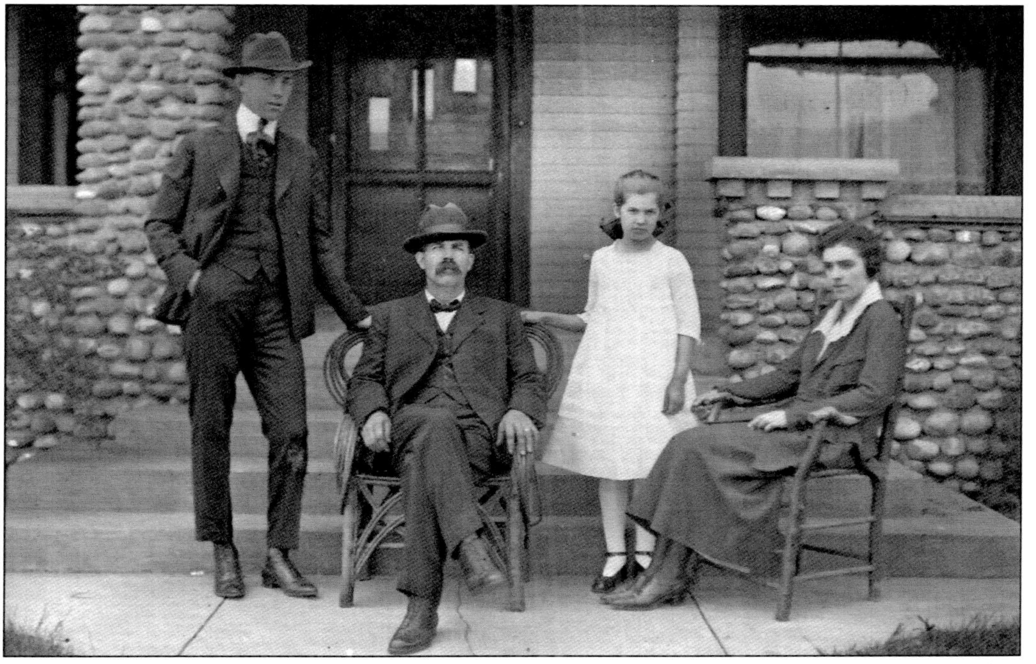

Three Frenchmen, Elzeor Demers, Ovide Peltier, and Frank Derosier, came to the valley with a herd of cattle in 1890. The Derosiers moved a short ways into British Columbia long ago. Peltier family members are peppered throughout the valley. Demers is represented here part time by one descendent. The Demers family is pictured here on a solemn day in 1917, the day of Amine Demers's funeral. Her husband, Elzeor (or Ed) is seated. Her son Albert is standing, while daughters Vera and Leila appear at right. (Courtesy of Maralyn Demers Turner.)

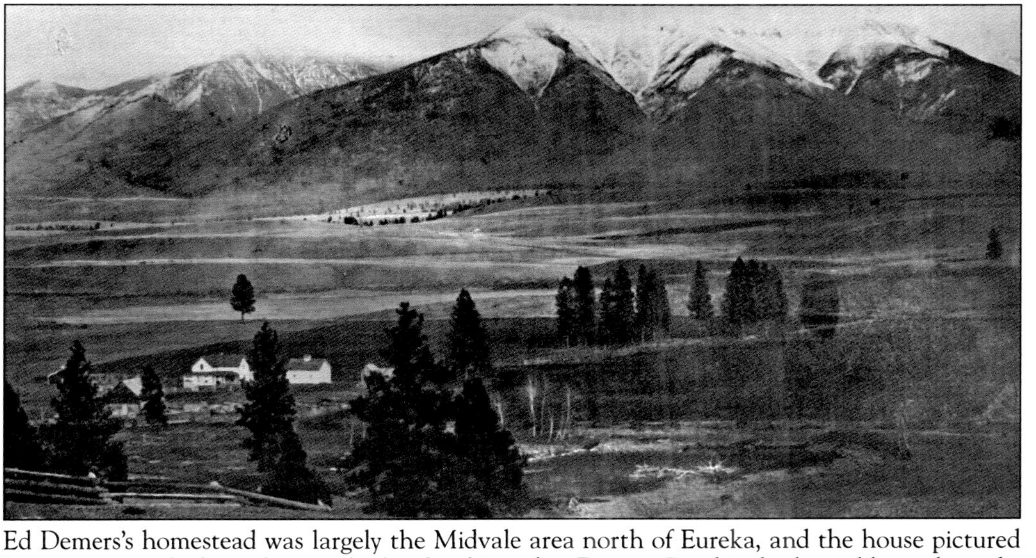

Ed Demers's homestead was largely the Midvale area north of Eureka, and the house pictured here once stood where the new high school is today. Demers Pond is dimly visible in the right foreground. At one time, townspeople cut their ice from the pond, but drainage patterns changed, and the pond dried up—almost. One drives through its remnants on First Avenue, east of the Ksanka Apartments, every time it rains or snow melts. (Courtesy of Maralyn Demers Turner.)

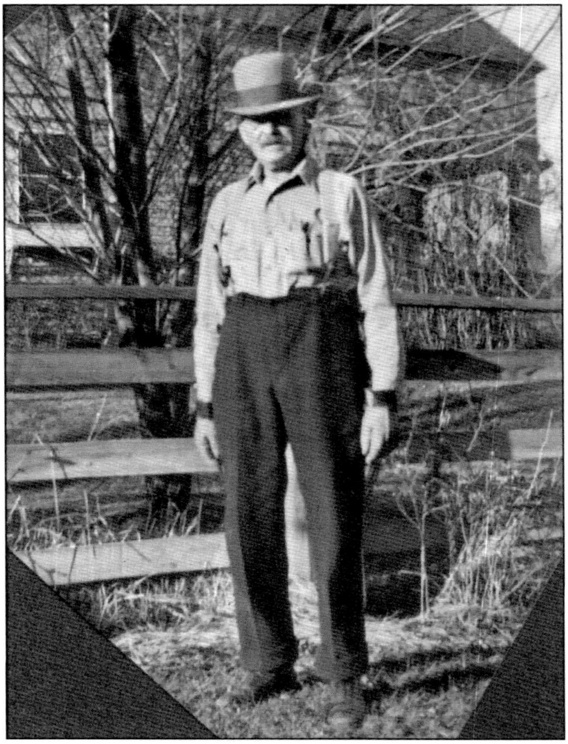

Joe Peltier followed his brother Ovide to Tobacco Valley in 1890, where he built the first structure on ground that would become Eureka in another 14 years. The cabin was originally located where the Farmers and Merchants Bank building stands today. It was moved and then moved again for the final time to the Historical Village, on land that once belonged to the Eureka Lumber Company. Nine other historical structures have also been preserved on the site. (Courtesy of Bobbie Johnson.)

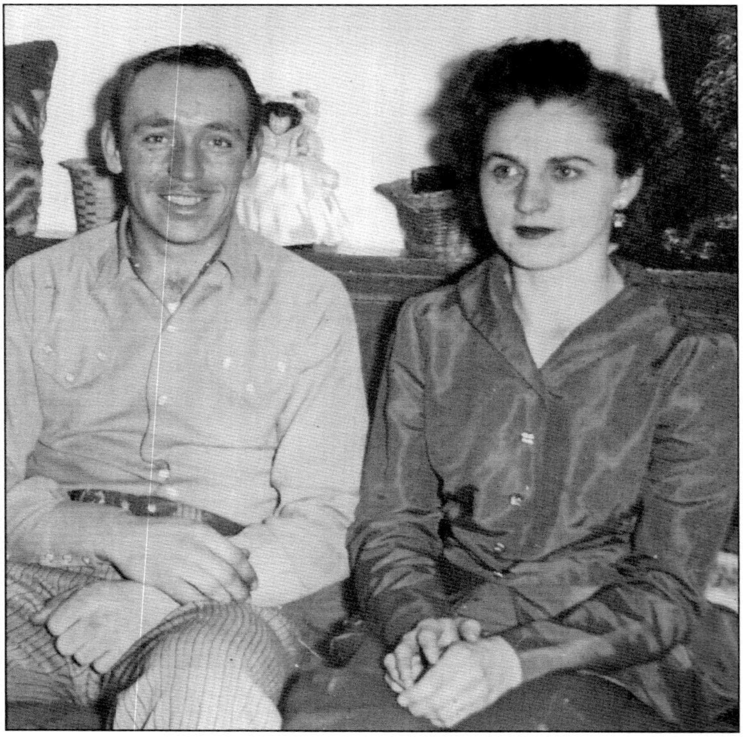

Dick Peltier and Dixie Brock grew up in Tobacco Valley, Dick in Eureka and Dixie on a West Kootenai homestead. Dixie graduated from Lincoln County High School, but Dick got sidetracked by World War II, where he served as a paratrooper. Later he became a smoke jumper and a pilot flying a spotter airplane. He packed for the U.S. Forest Service and was a sawyer on one end of a two-man chain saw. Dixie was a writer and an active member of the Friendly Neighbor Club. (Courtesy of Kathy Peltier.)

Clarence "Dickey" Rich rode into the Tobacco Valley as a boy with his parents, two siblings, and an uncle. All were mounted, leading a horse string that carried everything they owned. Dickey did a lot of trapping around a big beautiful lake just south of Murphy Lake and that is how Dickey Lake got its name. Not a healthy man, he worked close to home so he could always get in out of the weather. (Courtesy of Juanita Butts.)

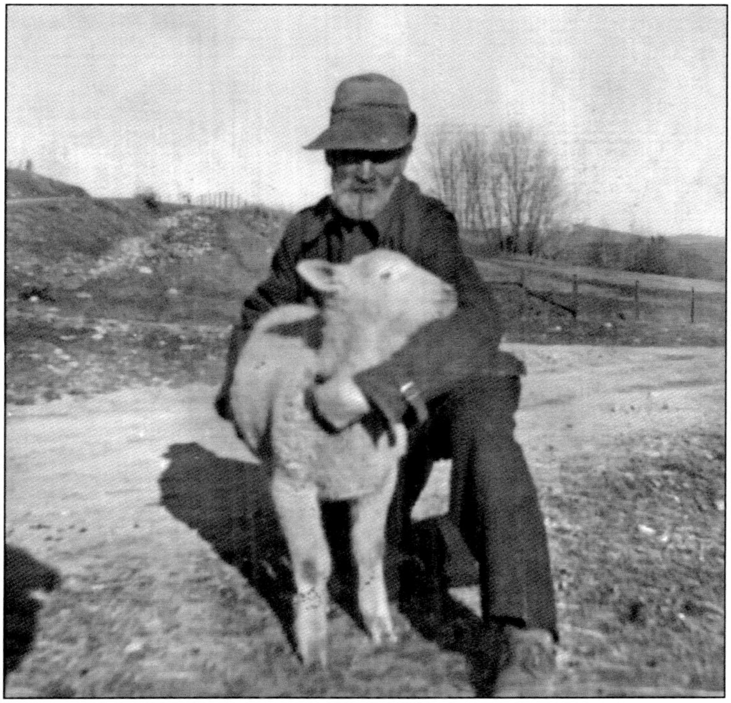

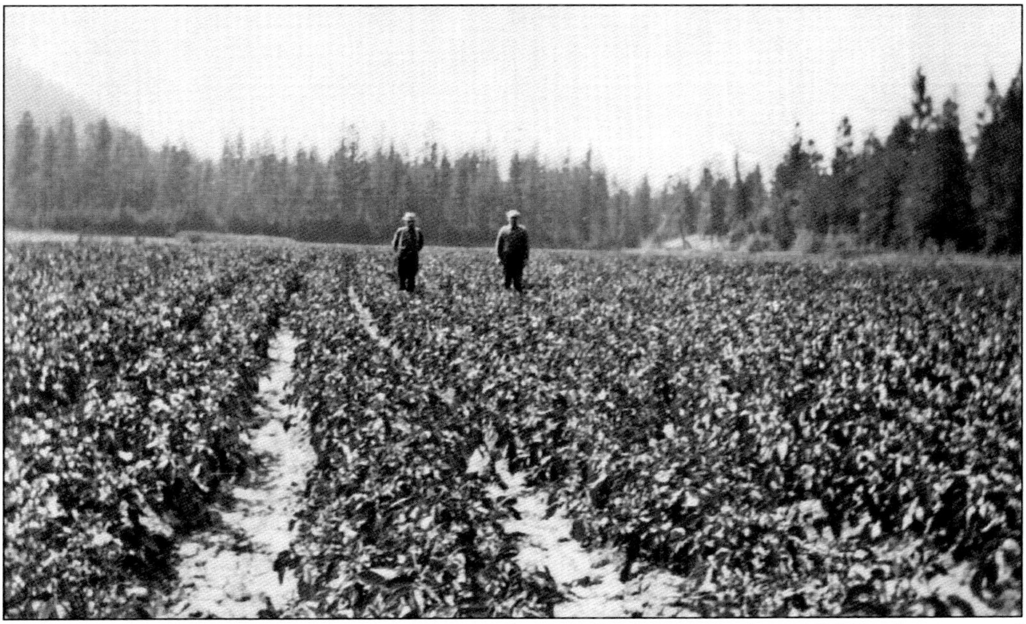

With adjoining homesteads on the valley's northeast side, George Rich and Ed Boyle partnered together in an attempt to grow merchantable tobacco. The September 30, 1905, *Tobacco Plains Journal* reported, "George Rich and Ed Boyle this week sent . . . home grown specimens of tobacco plants to the state fair at Helena." George Rich died in December 1910 after what was likely the first alcohol-related vehicle accident in the area. He had several drinks in town and, while returning to his ranch, took a corner too fast and wrecked his sleigh, resulting in brain trauma.

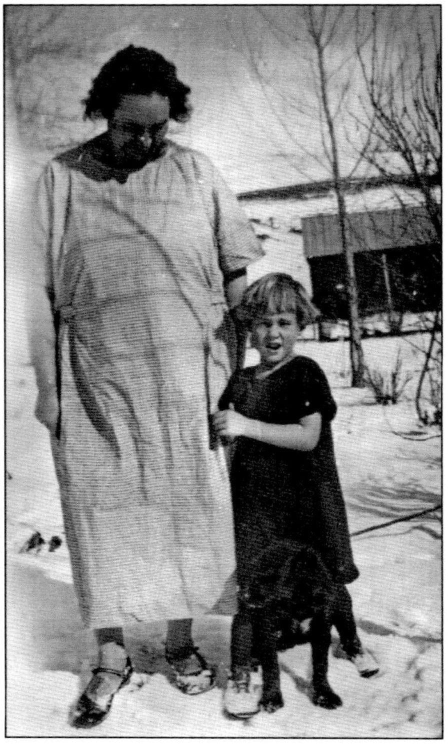

Barbara Rich, née Fox, pictured at left with daughter Juanita, came to the valley from Thompson Falls. There was work to be had in orchards that were being planted around the beginning of the 20th century. She met and married Clarence "Dickey" Rich and bore him three children. For many years, they ran a farm at the intersection of Mills Spring Loop and Indian Creek Road. She delivered butter, eggs, and butchered pork to local customers. (Courtesy of Juanita Butts.)

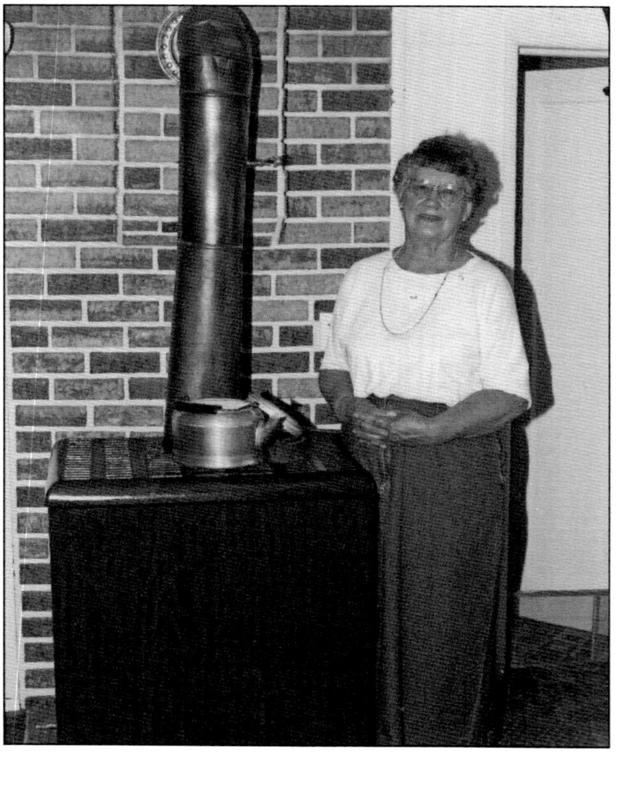

Juanita Butts, née Rich, fondly recalls days of yore: "There were a lot of hard times, but what I remember is coming in from the cold to the blessing of a hot crackling fire and a pot of coffee. I can still remember the smell of a crock of prunes . . . Mama always had a gallon crock of navy beans with bacon or a piece of ham on the back of the stove. We would cut off a big piece of homemade bread and pour the beans on it." (Courtesy of the author.)

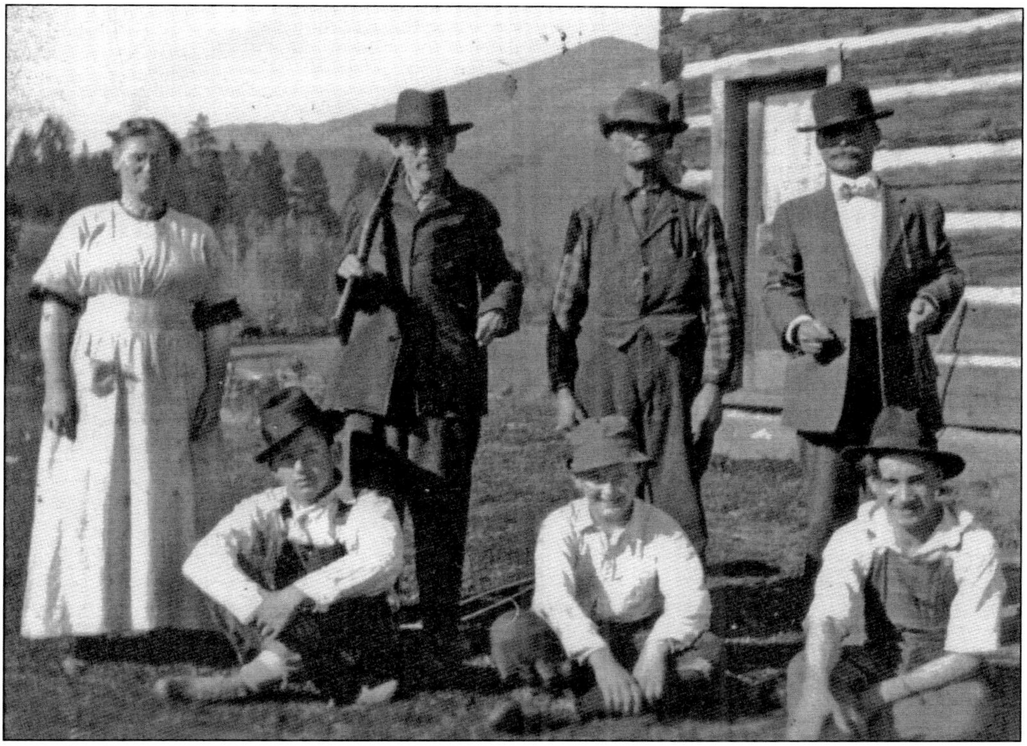

Patrick Shea came to the Tobacco Plains country in 1888 and homesteaded land on the northeast side of the valley, land that remains in possession of his great-grandchildren. Pictured above are, from left to right (sitting) John Quirk, Emmet Quirk, and John Cuffe; (standing) Mary Shea, Patrick Shea, John Crawford, and Daniel Shea. Both Mary and Daniel, Patrick's children, took up adjoining homesteads.

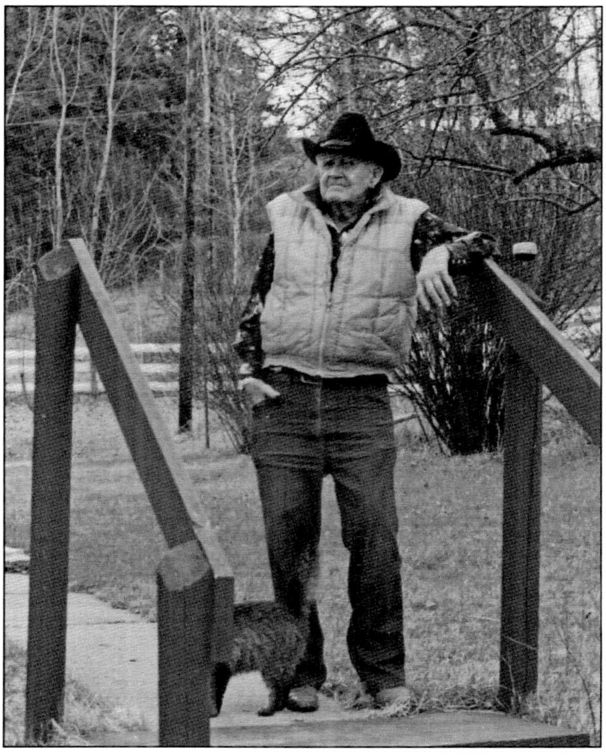

Born in 1913, George Shea was the third generation of his family to ranch in the Tobacco Valley. He recalls driving to the Flathead Valey in a Ford Model T and stopping at the Point of Rocks for lunch. There was no restaurant then. They stopped by a small creek where a rock outcropping crowded the road close to the Stillwater River. "Took pretty damn near all day to get down there," Shea recalled in 1995.

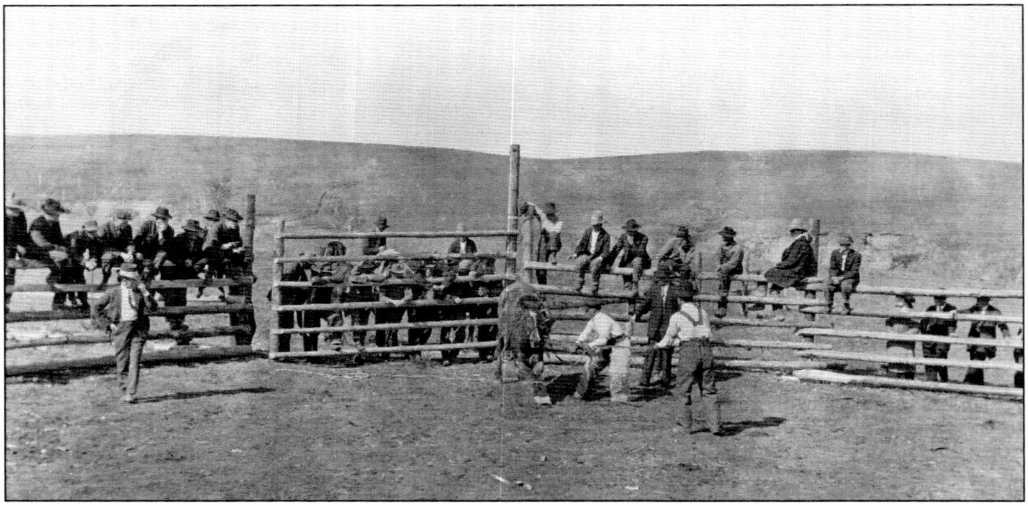

The early ranchers built corrals near Sophie Lake for use in working cattle and horses. Billy Baker, believed to be the one wearing chaps and a nontraditional cowboy hat, prepares to mount a hobbled horse. Moments later, when the hobbles were slipped, Baker would have had his hands full. Brokers sometimes came to buy rodeo stock. (Courtesy of Mike Gwynn.)

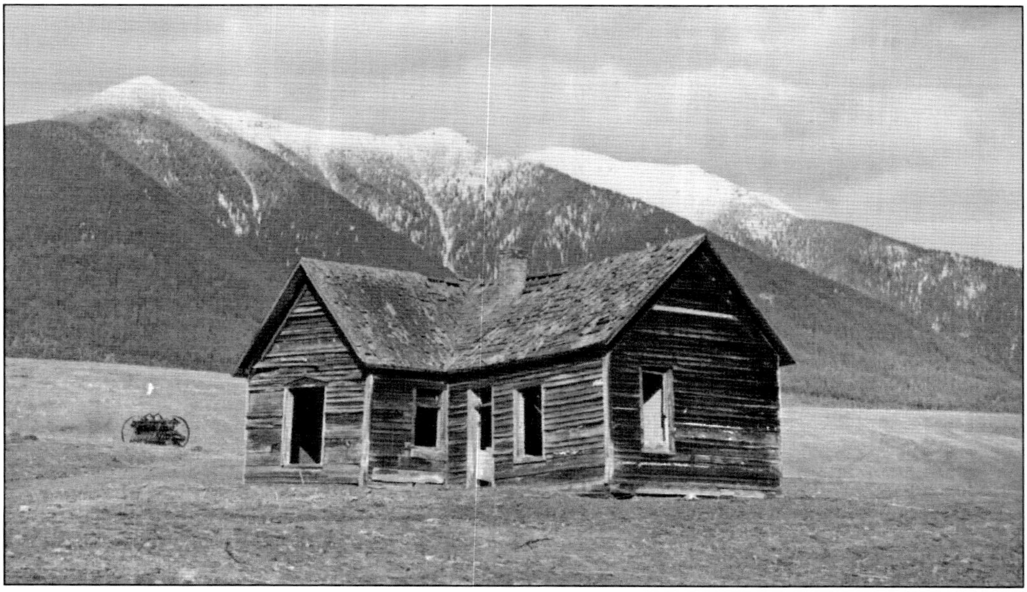

Antoine Therriault homesteaded land that is now part of the Shea Ranch. There, in 1895, he built a house out of locally milled lumber, the first in the valley not made of logs. A young man with a wife and a little girl, he died early one morning after having attended an Election Day dance the night before. They said it was septicemia of the throat, or lye taken as medicine, that killed him. Marie Shea in *Early Flathead and Tobacco Plains* tells the story of how his remains were transported down the Kootenai River by rowboat and then to Kalispell for burial. (Courtesy of the author.)

Three

Riverboats and Railroads

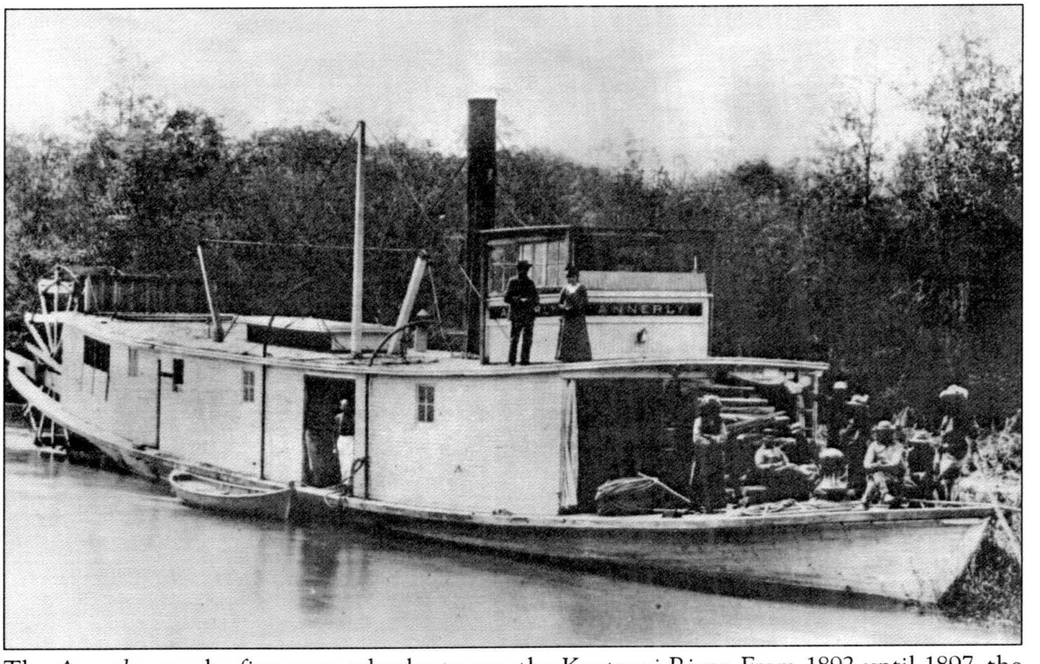

The *Annerly* was the first stern-wheeler to run the Kootenai River. From 1892 until 1897, the 90-foot boat hauled freight and passengers to Tobacco Plains and Fort Steele, then returned to Jennings with a load of gold ore. Running the river was no pleasure cruise as the current was unpredictable and rocks were many; some stretches were downright treacherous. Still, it was the easiest way to reach the country.

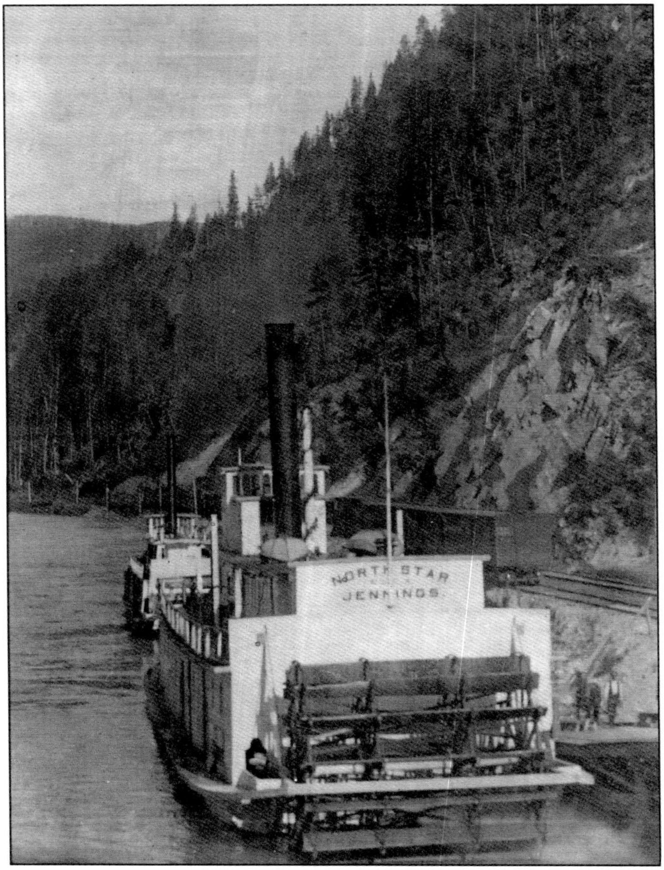

The steamboat era on the Kootenai River ended in 1901 when the Great Northern Railroad extended its tracks from Jennings to Rexford and then to Fernie. The *J. D. Farrell* was dismantled. The *Gwendolyn* was hauled away on a flatcar only to tumble off into a canyon of the river. Capt. Frank Armstrong of the *North Star* chose to steam her upriver to the deteriorating locks at Canal Flats, where he managed to squeeze her through into Columbia Lake.

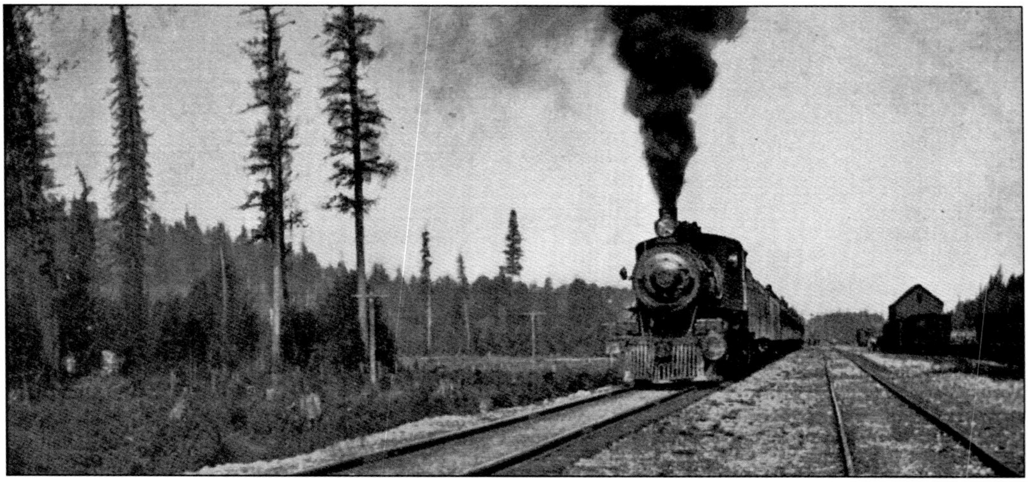

When the Great Northern Railroad was rerouted through Tobacco Valley in 1904 things changed in a hurry. What was once a two- or three-day journey by horse along the Tobacco Plains Trail or up the Kootenai River on a stern-wheeler became a trip that lasted only a few hours. Here the *Oriental Limited* pulls out of Columbia Falls. Aboard are all manner of optimists searching for opportunity.

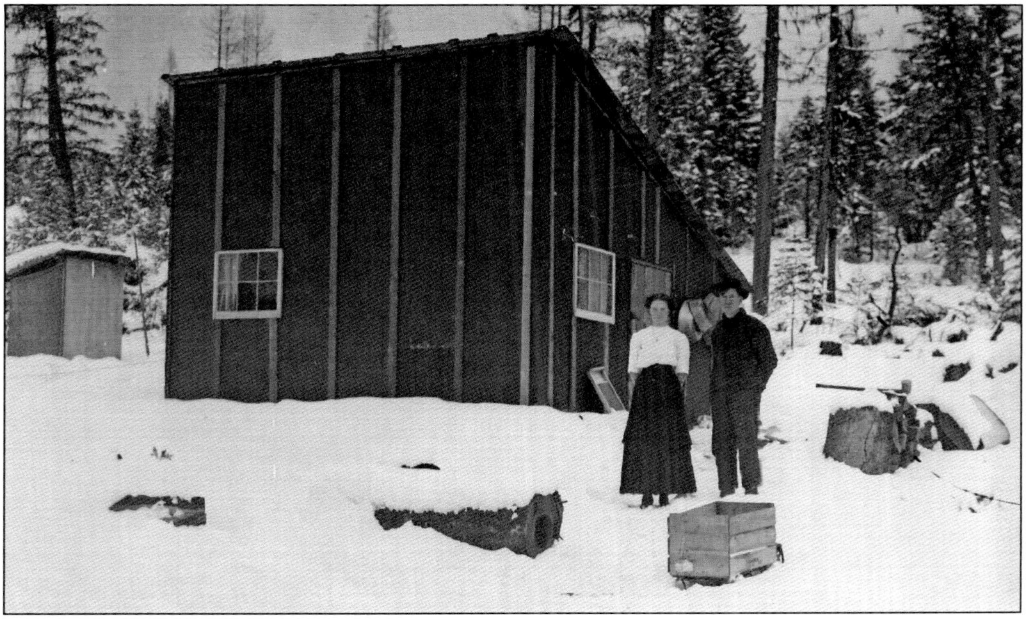

Some opportunities came in the form of railroad jobs. The unidentified couple pictured above lived in a tar paper shack near Rexford. There was always plenty of work, whether it was routine maintenance or repairing the aftermath of an engine taking a dive into the Kootenai or Tobacco River (shown below). Charles "Hoot" Franklin worked for the Great Northern Railroad in 1925 at Fortine. His wife, Mabel, recalled in 2002 that Franklin made 28¢ an hour working a 10-hour day. "Once in a while a train would hit a cow and break her leg or something and we'd get the meat. I canned that."

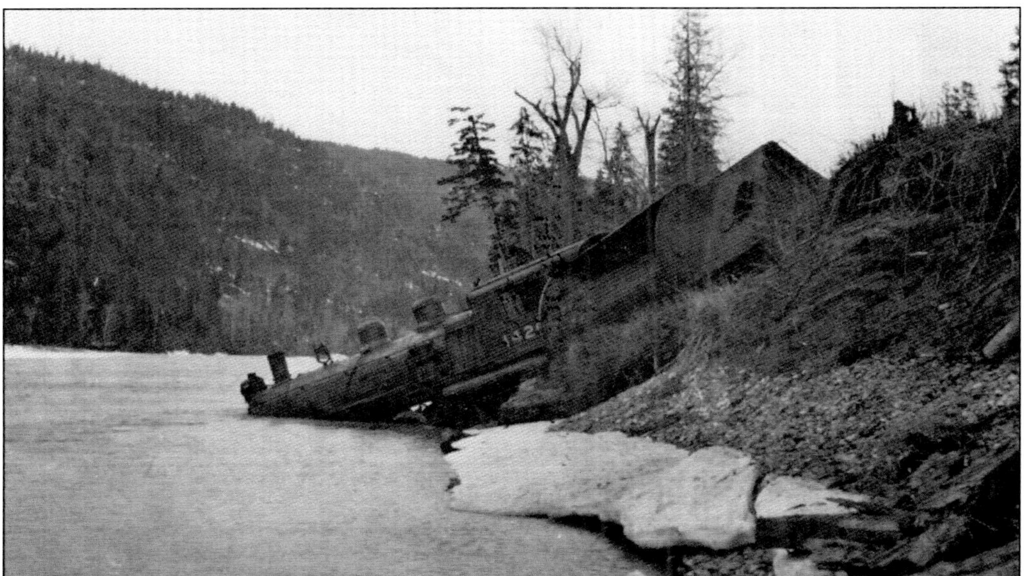

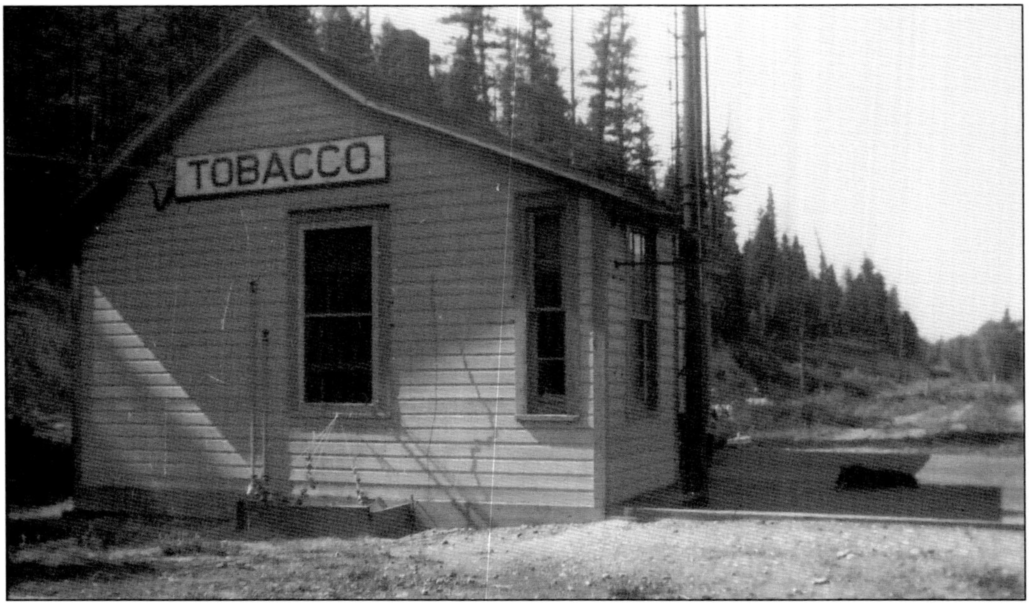

The depot at Tobacco Siding never amounted to much. The *Tobacco Plains Journal* of October 8, 1904, reported one woman's experience: "Rev. Blackburn's wife had a trying experience on her arrival here . . . Mrs. Blackburn wished to go to Dewey, and on being informed that there is no such station . . . not knowing that Dewey had been changed to Eureka, asked for a ticket to Tobacco. Tobacco is known by the railroad employees to be Siding No. 10 . . . and it was here the unfortunate lady was told by the conductor to be her destination. The scenery at this particular place is very beautiful. However, the welcome extended by the gentle kine [archaic for cow] and the distant hills did not fill the bill. Fortunately, Mrs. Blackburn was discovered and heroically rescued by Rev. Craven, and again was placed in communication with the civilized world." A young couple (shown below) is doing what they are not supposed to do—play on the tracks!

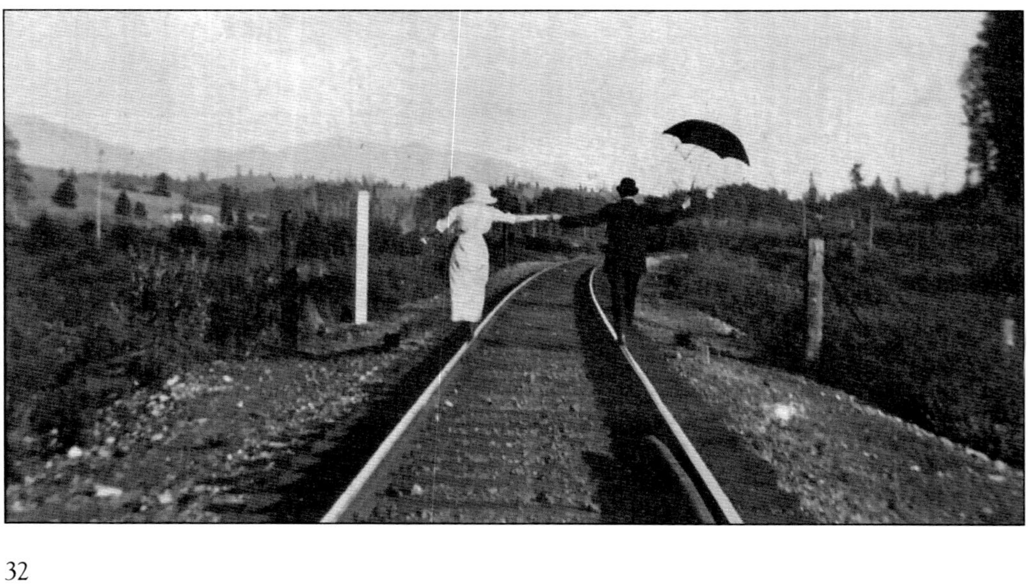

Four

Towns Begin Popping Up

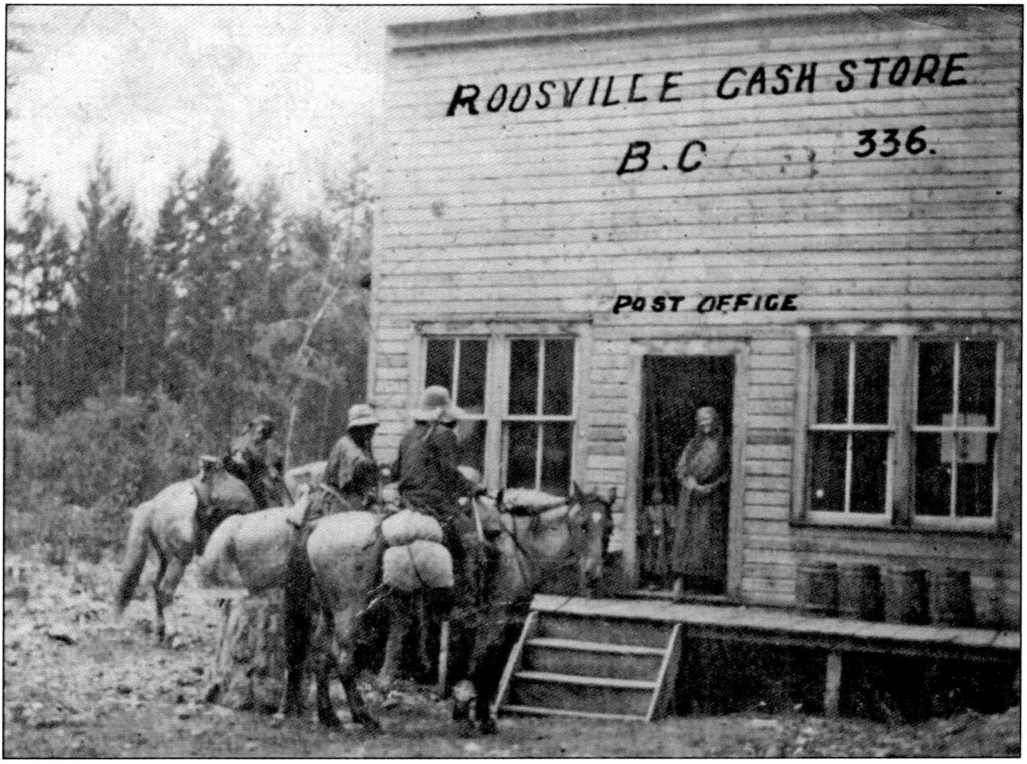

The first center of commerce on Tobacco Plains was founded by Sophie Morigeau at Indian Creek Flats in 1880. Later the site transitioned into the 69 Ranch and the diminutive town of Tobacco. The woman in the doorway may be Morigeau as someone has written "Sophie" on the back. As for the Roosville Cash Store, it was founded by Fred Roo, a larger-than-life Canadian entrepreneur, a short distance north of the International Boundary. Sophie would surely have been there at one time or another. (Courtesy of Darris Flanigan.)

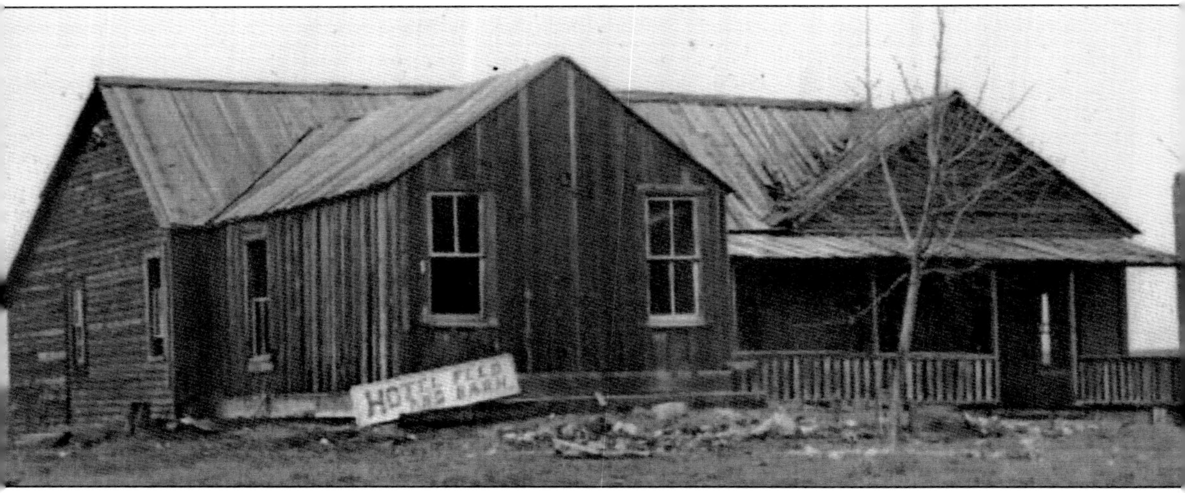

Ralph and Billy Ramsdell bought out Sophie's trading post around 1884. As settlers came in, it was natural that activity would grow around the enterprise if for no other reason than mail sent from Kalispell, by a variety of means, was dropped there. Around 1892, the Ramsdells sold out to Frank, John, and Will Leonard, who then built a new store and established a post office named Tobacco. In 1895, a mere quarter of a mile south of Tobacco, William and Theora Mills built the area's first hotel while A. Y. Lindsay and John Smith constructed a store. The tiny settlement became known as Mills Spring. Though outsiders considered them as one, the two settlements of Tobacco and Mills Spring considered themselves rivals. A school went up at Mills Spring, and a church went up at Tobacco. Their rivalry became pointless when the railroad came through in 1904, and the impetus was shifted to an upstart town about 2 miles to the south by the name of Dewey, later Eureka.

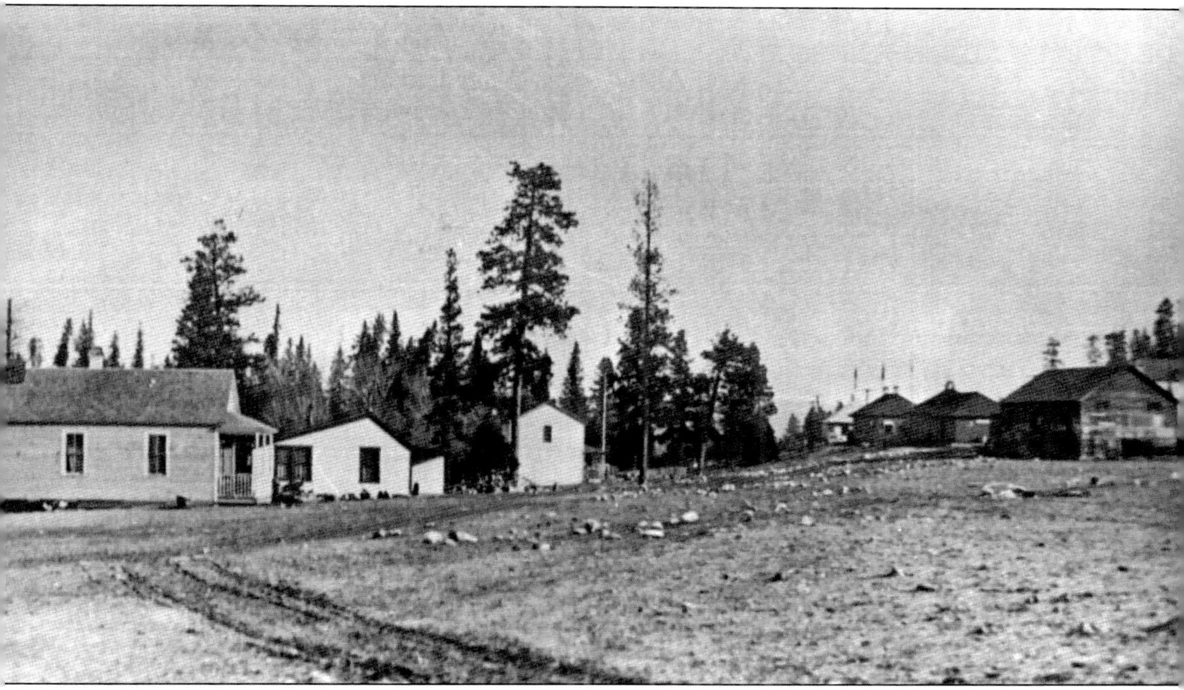

The Great Northern built up the Kootenai Valley from Jennings to Fernie, British Columbia, in 1901. Entrepreneurs from all manner of persuasion sensed that the area where the tracks crossed into Canada might be a good place to build a town. The part in Canada was called Newgate. South of the border it was called Gateway. Gateway was tough in its formative years. When the 1920s rolled around, it did not improve much as bootleg liquor flowed through on the trains because it was impossible to check all the coal cars. Addie Scott Irwin, née Brock, grew up there. "There was a big place where they had a dance hall and, of course, a beer parlor, I guess. And my uncle had a store there, the depot, and probably a dozen families, but that's about all. . . . We had dances in this big hall and every year this big mulligan. The grown-ups would . . . peel vegetables, take them all day. Maybe my brothers would go out and get a deer, and we'd put it all in this mulligan [stew]. Everybody that came had to bring their cup and spoon."

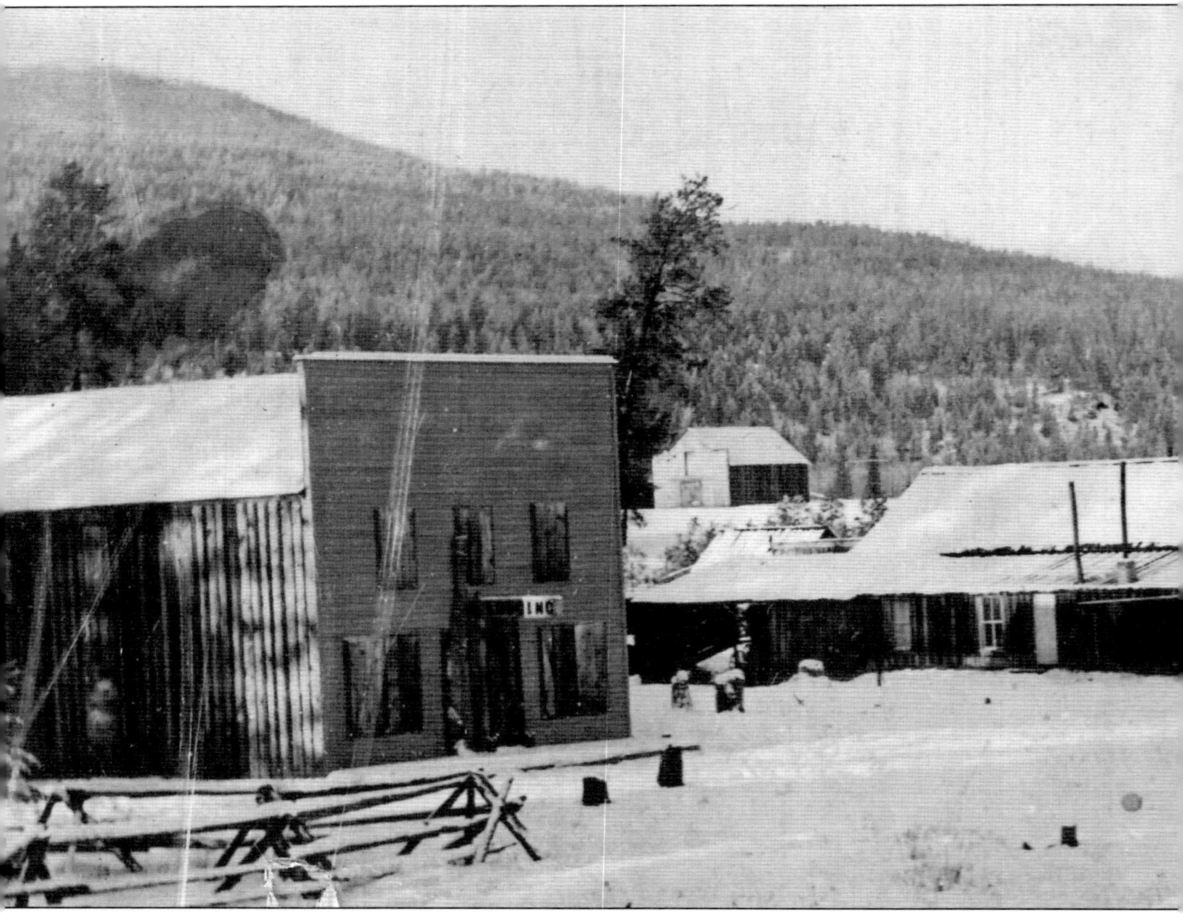

The town of Rexford was established along the east shore of the Kootenai River in 1901 when it was learned that the Great Northern Railroad was extending a spur line from Jennings to Fernie. But then, in 1904, when the tracks were rerouted through Eureka and into the Kootenai Valley to connect with the spur line, the Great Northern built an extensive yard facility about 2 miles north of the original Rexford. Given Rexford's inherent impermanency, it was only a minor

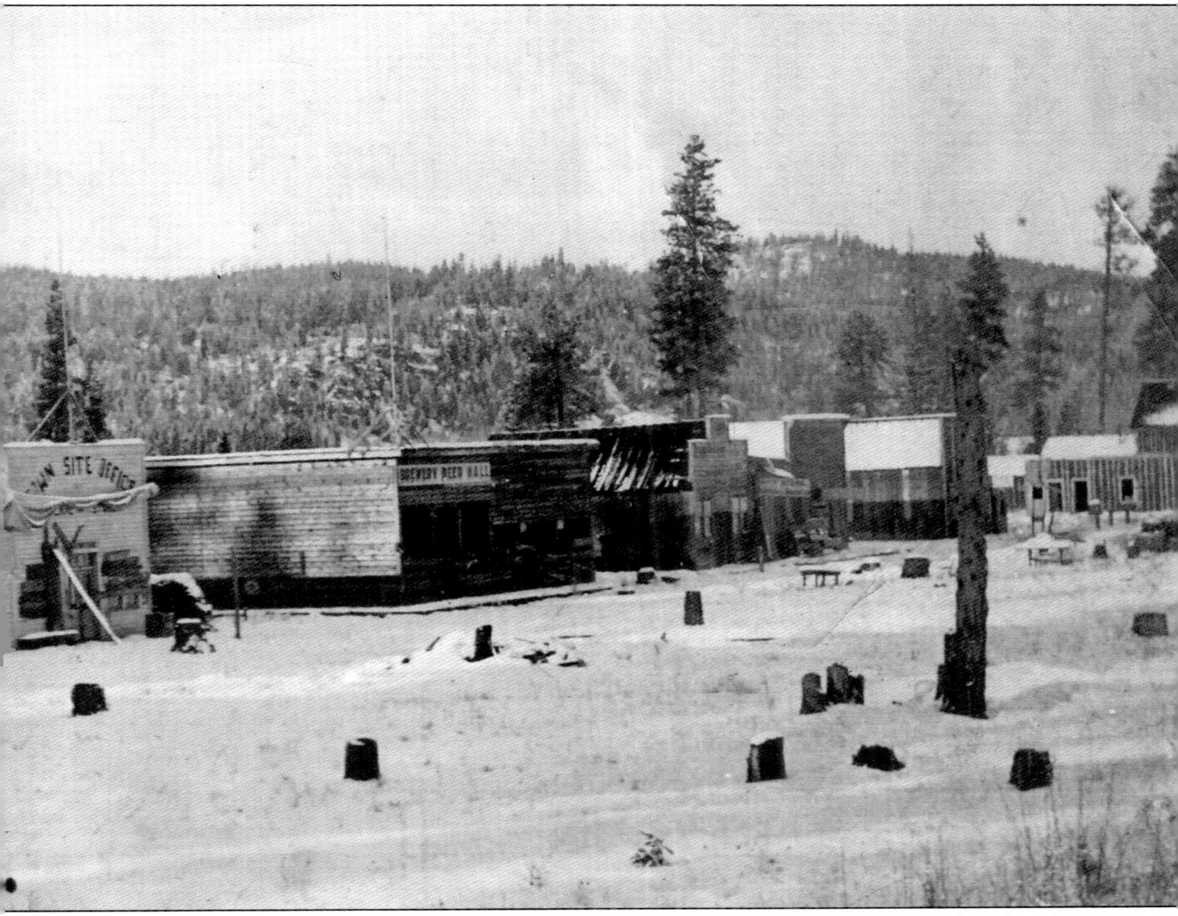

inconvenience to move it. Rexford now sat at the nexus of an east/west mainline railroad with a spur line coming out of Canada that connected with the Canadian transcontinental line. It is no surprise that the town soon gained a well-earned reputation as being wild and bawdy. By 1970, Libby Dam forced yet one more move, and the present Rexford has outlived its rowdy past.

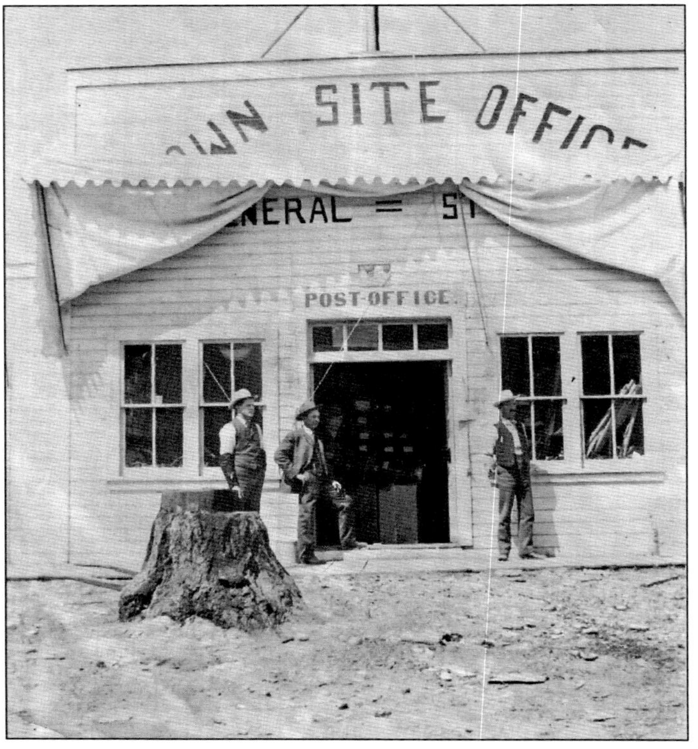

Harrisburg sprang up anticipating the arrival of the Great Northern Railroad. Several stores and quite a number of saloons were built. One of the mercantile enterprises was the Brown and Fewkes Store. Jack Harris laid out a town site and must have promoted it through the store, but Harris got his town on the wrong side of the creek, and as a result, Fortine was born. Pictured here from left to right are D. F. Fewkes, Fred Carder, unidentified, and Fred McMurray. (Courtesy of Darris Flanagan.)

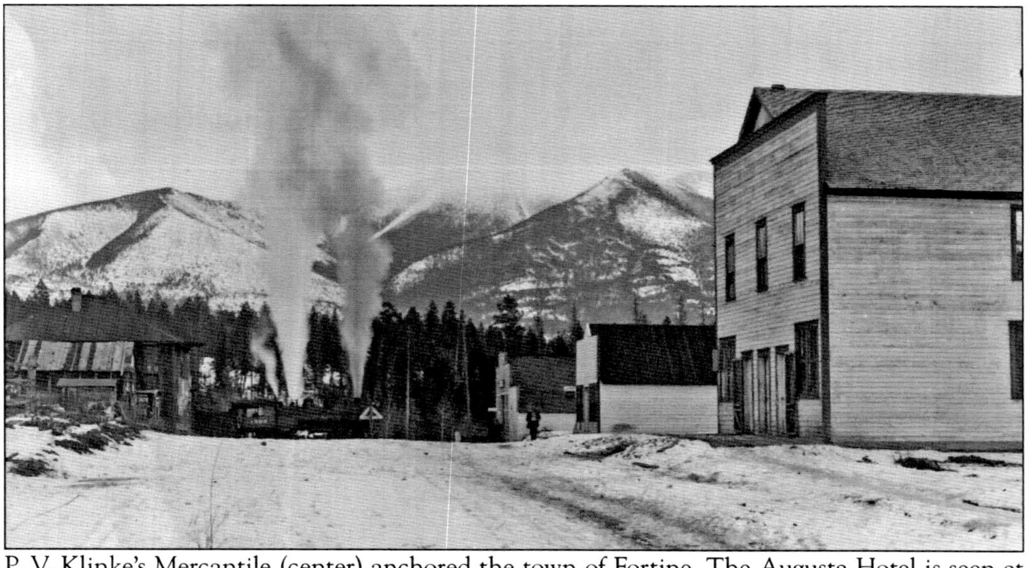

P. V. Klinke's Mercantile (center) anchored the town of Fortine. The Augusta Hotel is seen at far right. In 1913, Klinke and several prominent men built an amusement hall and invited folks from Eureka to attend the gala opening. As reported in the *Eureka Journal*, "The visitors were entertained at the fine new hall of the Fortine Amusement Company with a free dance . . . Shortly after midnight the visitors were bidden to the Augusta to partake of a sumptuous feast . . . The Augusta is an elegant two story, 14-room structure, and would be a credit to a town several times the size of Fortine." (Courtesy of Darris Flanagan.)

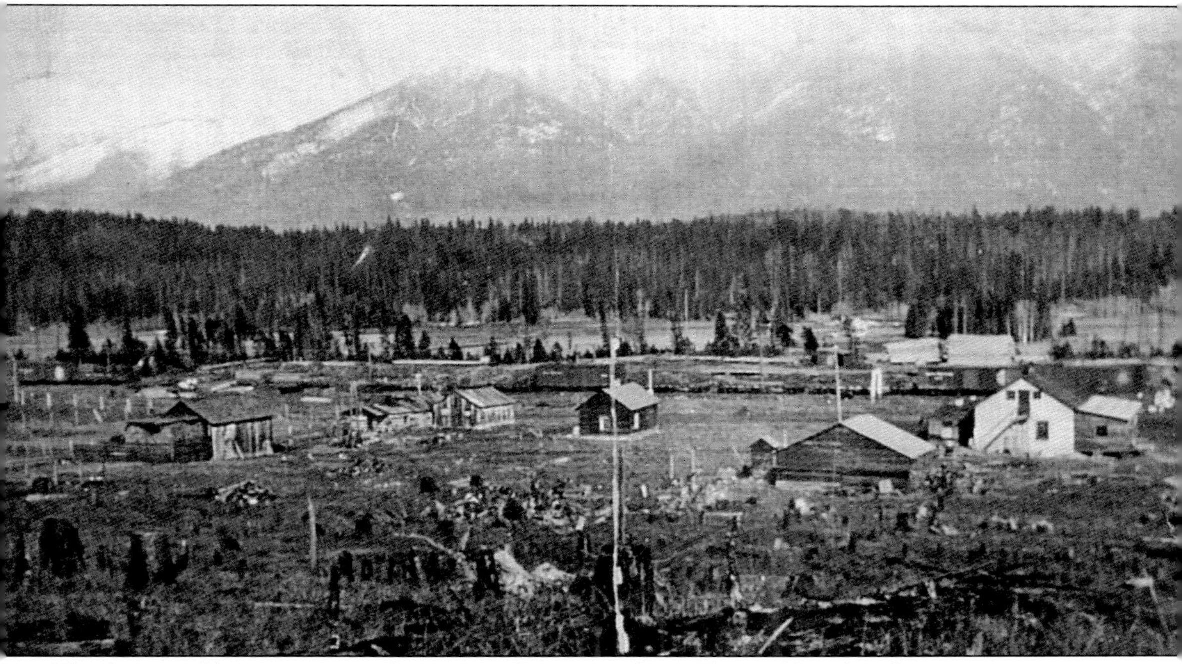

The first notable presence in what is now Trego was Oscar Fortin. His white house, sitting in the middle of the meadow as one drives into Trego, was once a stopping place on the Fort Steele Trail. It seems the railroad should have named Trego after him. Actually they did, and Fortine was named Trego. But on the railroad timetable their names got reversed, and since the railroad named the towns to begin with, it was far cheaper to switch the names than reprint tens of thousands of timetables. Trego was chosen by one of the construction engineers to honor his wife's maiden name. The Trego Store, far right, is still in business. Stryker was the next railroad stop south of Trego, but it came into being when Frank Stryker built a stopping place on the Fort Steele Trail. It has maintained a post office, but that is about all. Stryker has always been pretty much what it is today.

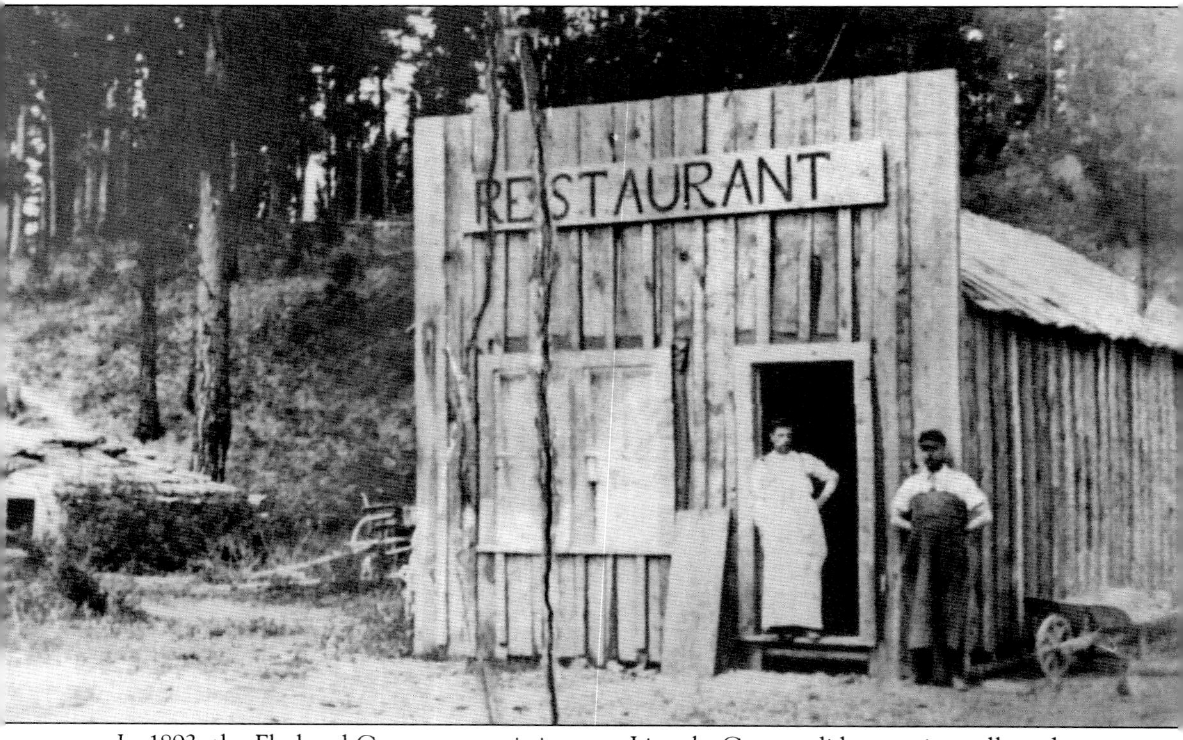

In 1893, the Flathead County commissioners—Lincoln County did not exist—allotted money to improve the old Indian trail leading to Tobacco Plains into a wagon road. That was how Cy and Nellie Marston found their way to a site just north of Grave Creek and founded the town of Marston, establishing a way station and post office by 1895. Brothers Howard and William joined in, and soon a general store, stable, inn, saloon, laundry, and even the Marston Band were in existence. Marston flourished but died when the Great Northern passed by several miles to the west. Cy and Nellie moved to Edmonton, then Denver, and finally to Leavenworth, Kansas, where he worked in the prison and later died in a soldier's home at 63. Howard and William remained, but Howard was a confirmed bachelor, and Bill divorced without having any children. Both the family and the town are but a dim memory in Tobacco Valley history. Pictured above are Frank Laderoot (left) and an unidentified man. (Courtesy of Darris Flanagan.)

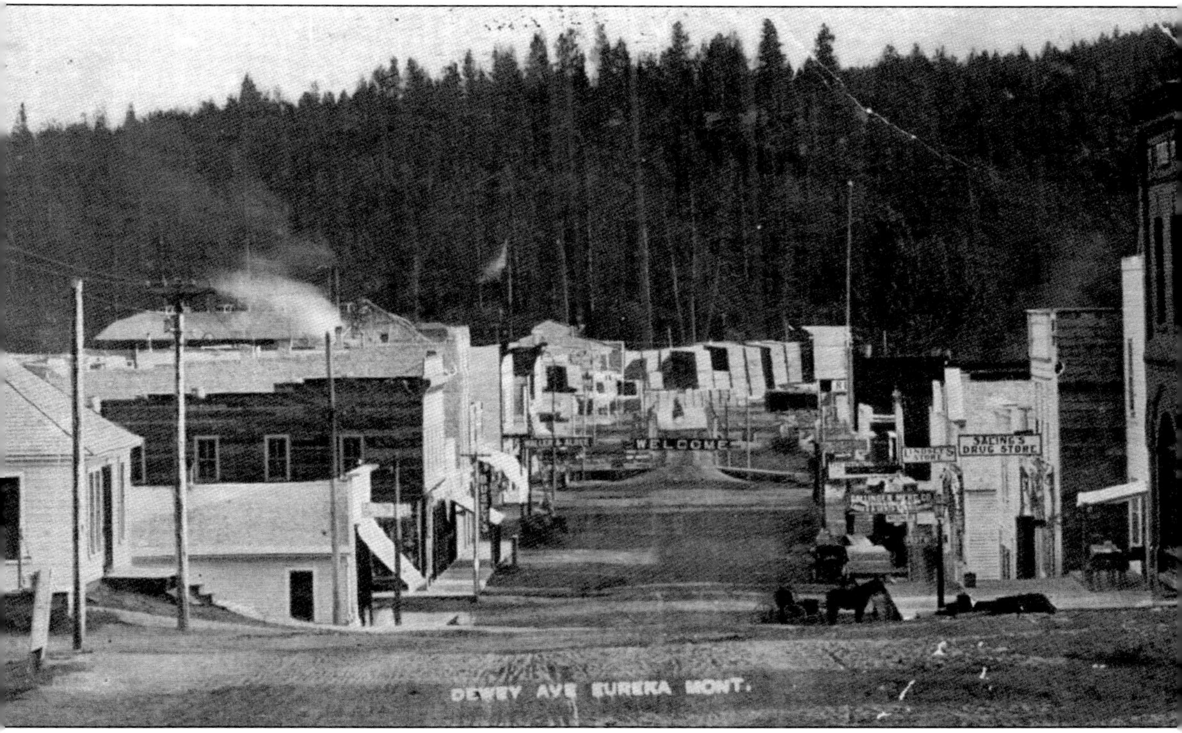

The Eureka Post Office opened its doors in April 1904. It was then that G. E. Shawler, who founded the *Tobacco Plains Journal* in August 1903, changed the masthead on the newspaper from Dewey to Eureka. Eureka was never called Deweyville, but the town site company did organize under that name. The center of commerce quickly moved from Tobacco and Mills Spring 2 miles south to the spot where the Great Northern chose to erect a depot and train yards. With Shawler providing optimistic narratives, merchants, homesteaders, and prospective workers poured in to exploit resources that, until the railroad came through, had remained inaccessible. Shawler envisioned orchards and grain fields, a copper refinery in the eastern foothills, and limitless timber resources. When veins of quartz were found on Water Tank hill, he even envisioned a gold stamp mill with "a thousand miners going and coming between shifts." Here is Dewey Avenue as it appeared in 1915.

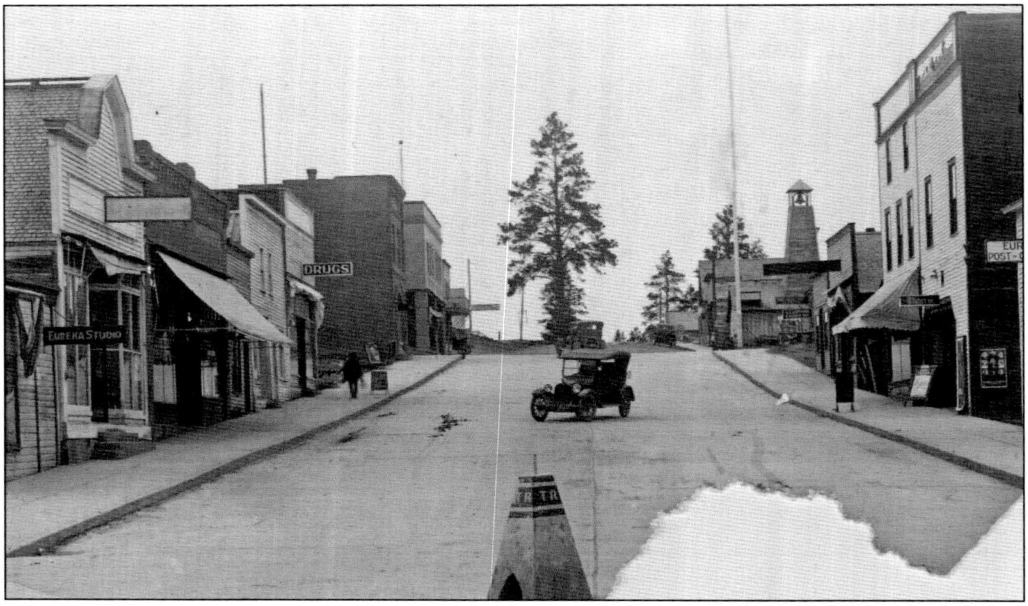

By 1918, there were paved streets and sidewalks in Eureka. Cars replaced buggies as the most popular means of travel. One of the town's most notable assets was the Douglas fir tree that stood in the middle of Dewey Avenue near where the library is today. Addie Scott Irwin, née Brock, recalled that her first husband, Merlin Scott, worked for the electric company, and he "harnessed" the tree each year with colored lights. Even as late as the 1990s old-timers were still grousing about the highway department removing the tree in the 1930s.

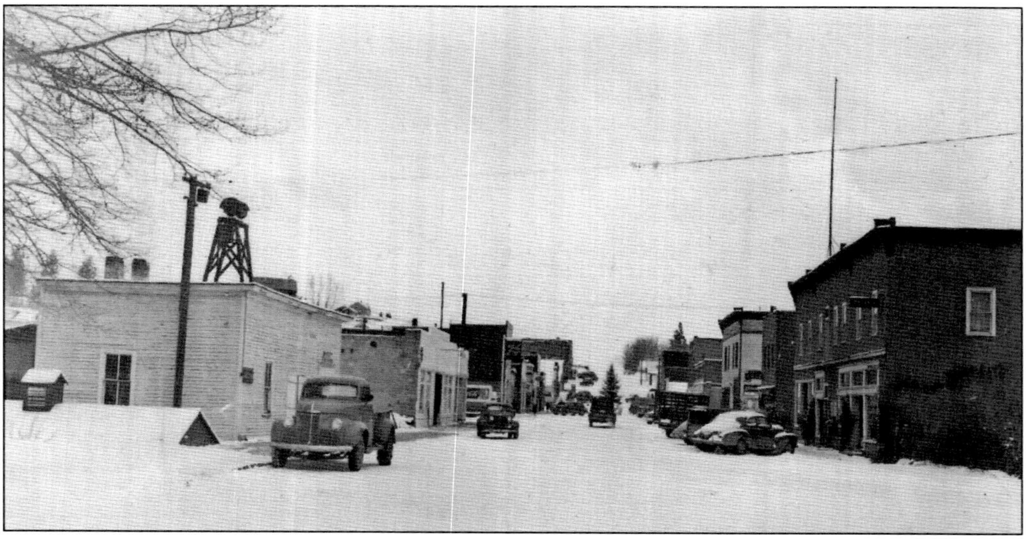

The year 1944 found Eureka emerging from the Great Depression. Employment was high, mainly because so many of the young men were doing Uncle Sam's work in Europe and Japan. Many young women and some married couples were working on the West Coast building ships and airplanes. Not giving up on the Christmas tree, the townspeople simply erected one in the middle of Dewey Avenue.

Five

Getting Down to Business

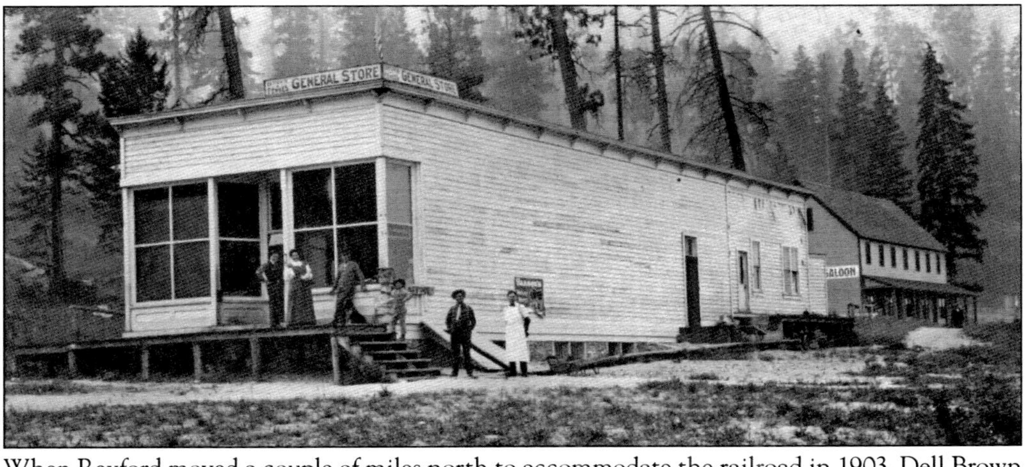

When Rexford moved a couple of miles north to accommodate the railroad in 1903, Dell Brown and William Fewkes Sr. built a mercantile store, and the McCafferys erected a hotel behind it. Bill Fewkes Jr. took over from his father in 1942, operating it until the inundation of Rexford forced it to close in 1971, Sherman Butts being the store's last customer. The building was moved to the Historical Village, where it makes a fine museum today.

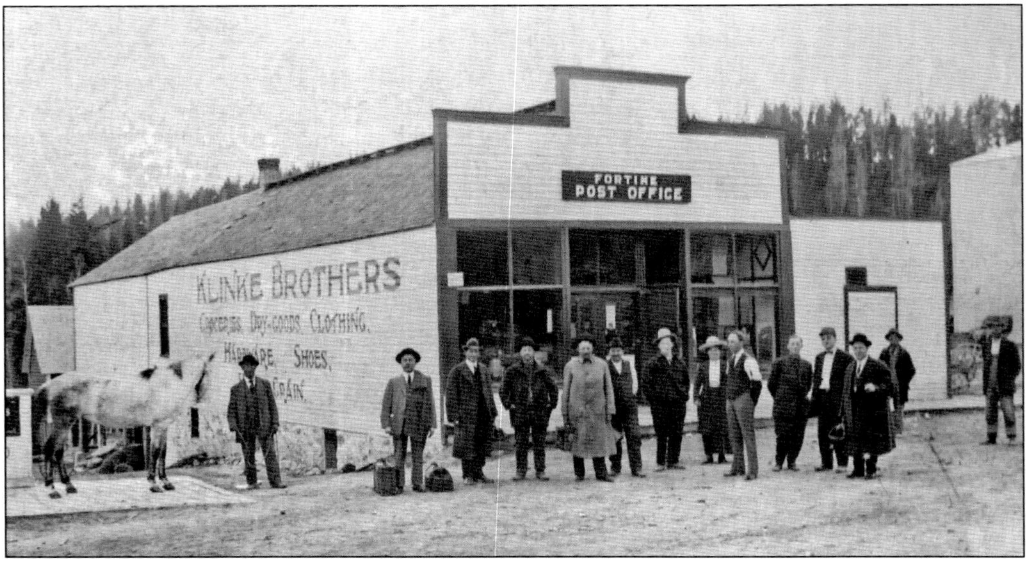

C. C. Bradley moved his mercantile store from Harrisburg to the budding Fortine in 1903. In 1907, he branched into Eureka, building the town's first brick structure, which is still in use. P. V. and Louis Klinke bought Bradley's Fortine store in 1909. Pictured here *c.* 1910 are some traveling men and several locals. From left to right are five unidentified men, Abe Johnson, Alvin Curtiss, an unidentified woman, Louis Klinke, and five unidentified men. (Courtesy of Pete Klinke.)

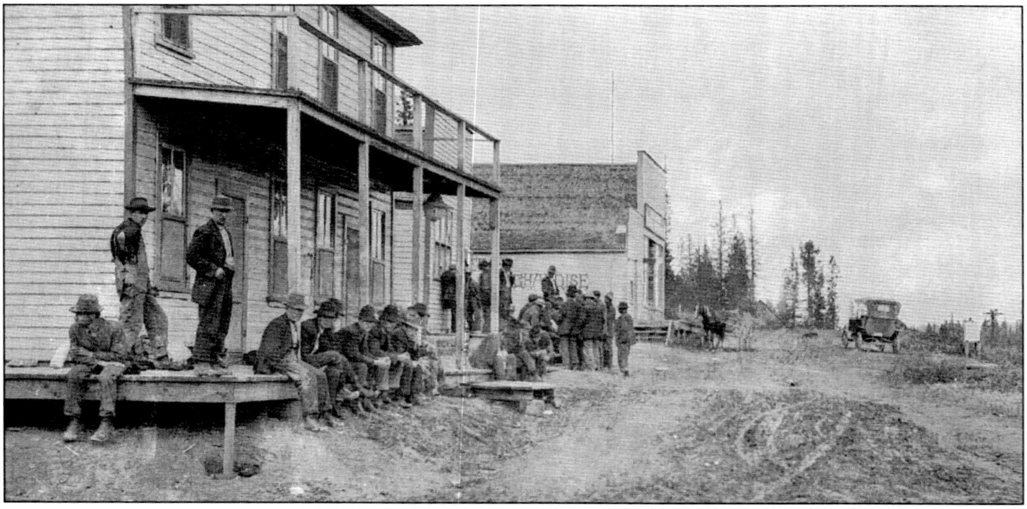

Quite a few workmen, likely employed in some aspect of logging, are shown here sitting and standing outside Fortine's Sherry Hotel around 1915. Many such men were members of the International Workers of the World (IWW). In 1917, National Guardsmen were called in during a strike and arrested local IWW leader Fred Hegge, saying that "he tore down the Stars and Stripes and stamped them under his feet and made uncomplimentary remarks about the flag."

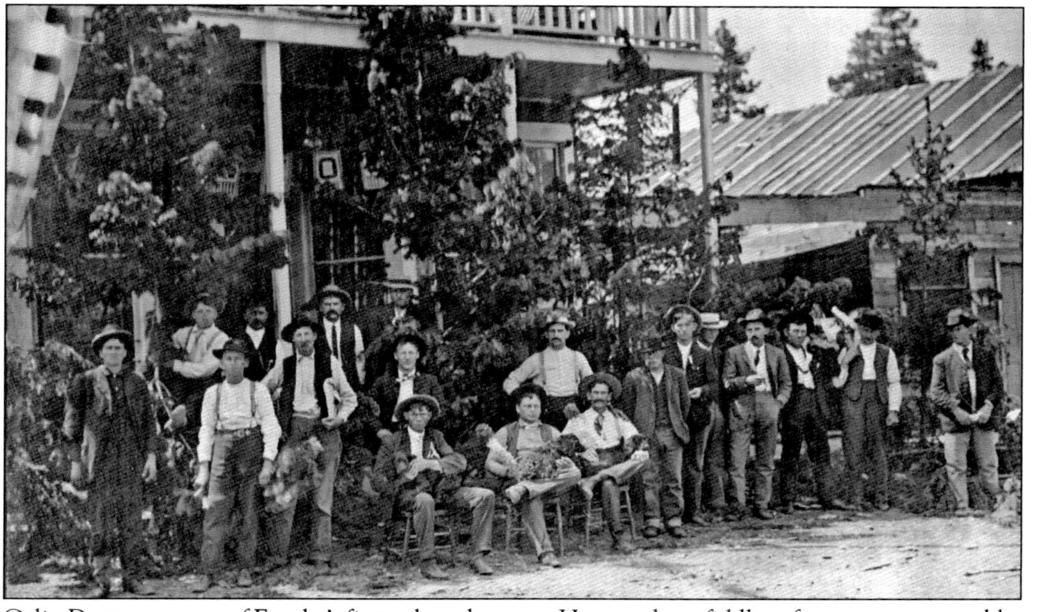

Calix Dugas was one of Eureka's first saloon keepers. He was also a fiddler of renown, a constable, the chief of police, and the town's first taxi driver. His saloon sat across Dewey Avenue a short way up the street from the National Hotel. Dugas is pictured here sitting in the middle chair. Deb Harvey is second from the left. Jimmy Forsyth is standing beside the man in the chair to the right of Dugas. (Courtesy of Mildred Berner.)

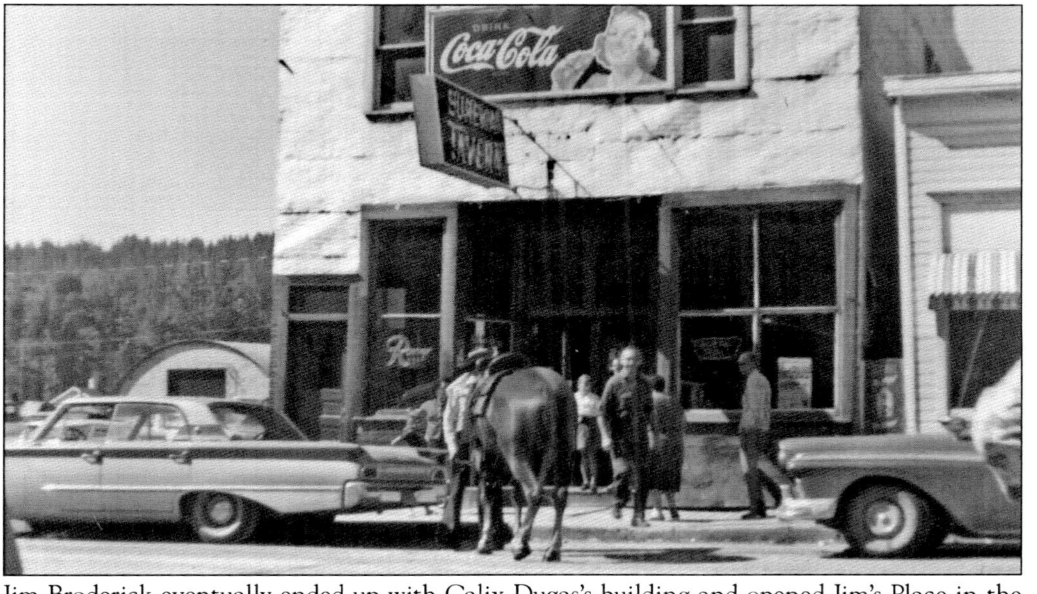

Jim Broderick eventually ended up with Calix Dugas's building and opened Jim's Place in the early 1930s during a time in Eureka when money was tight. At Jim's Place men could drink or play cards, and boys, entering through the back door, could play pool and buy a hamburger or a bowl of soup if they had two-bits in their pocket. The derelict building was razed in the 1960s, and the lot remained vacant until the completion of the Whitefish Credit Union building in May 2009. (Courtesy of Mildred Berner.)

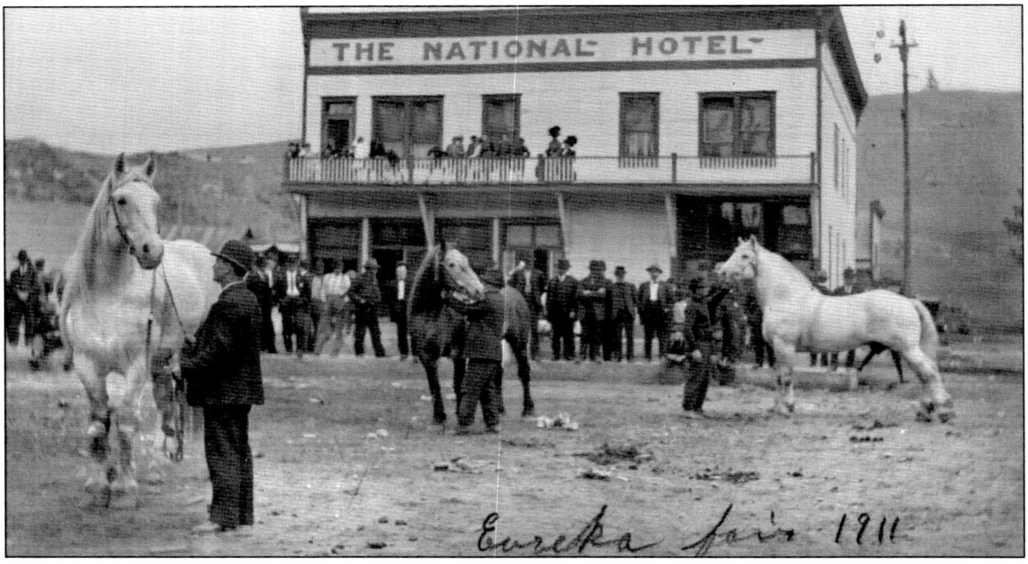

Pat Cunningham and Peter Doxie first built the National Hotel in 1905. It burned to the ground in September 1906, along with a number of other downtown businesses. Within seven months, they rebuilt the hotel, and thanks to a recent renovation, it has now endured for more than a century. It was last occupied on a nightly basis during the construction of Libby Dam. Pictured here is the draft horse competition, which took place on the street out front at the 1911 fair.

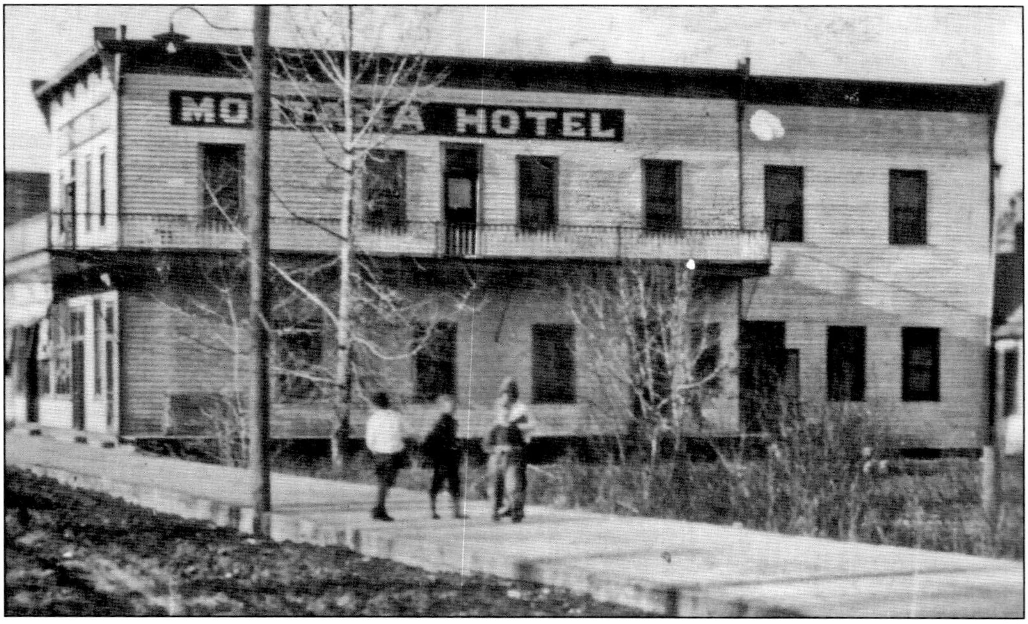

The Montana Hotel went up a few years after the National and stands where the Town Pump gas station and store is today. It came to a terrible end one cold February night in 1950. At the time, it housed the post office, a bar, five apartments, and 25 sleeping rooms. The Browning basketball team, having defeated the Lincoln County High School team 49-48, was asleep there. Around 3:00 a.m. the heater exploded, quickly engulfing the old structure in flames. Five perished, including two of the young basketball players.

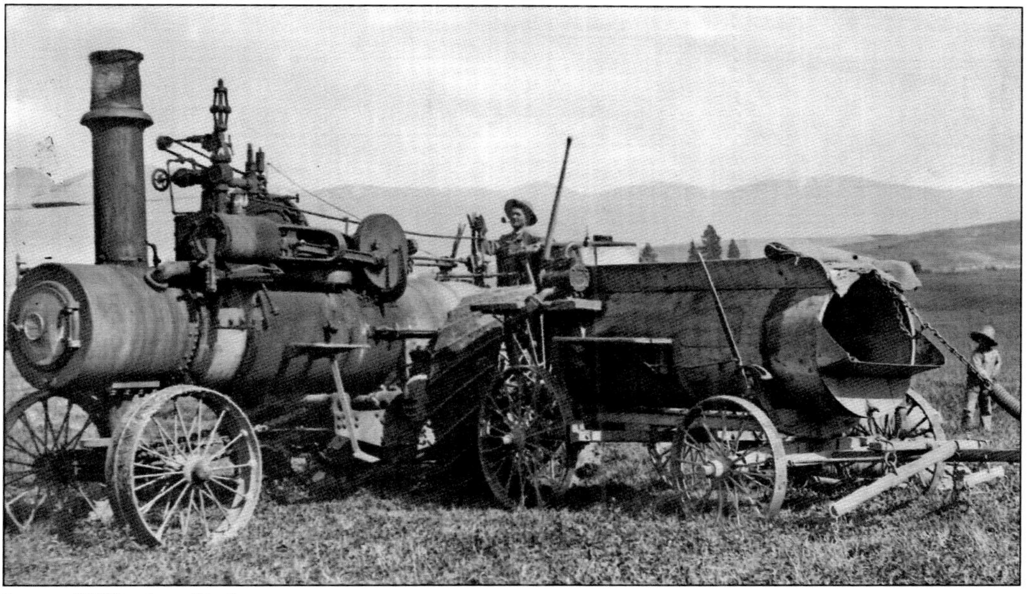

It was 1903 when Eralsey Costich brought a threshing machine into the valley to process the wheat and barley that was being planted at the time. "Ralsey" was the oldest son of Frank and Sarah Costich. They moved into the valley with their eight children in 1897 and homesteaded on the east side near a lake, which bears their name today. The threshing machine was destroyed in a fire scant months later.

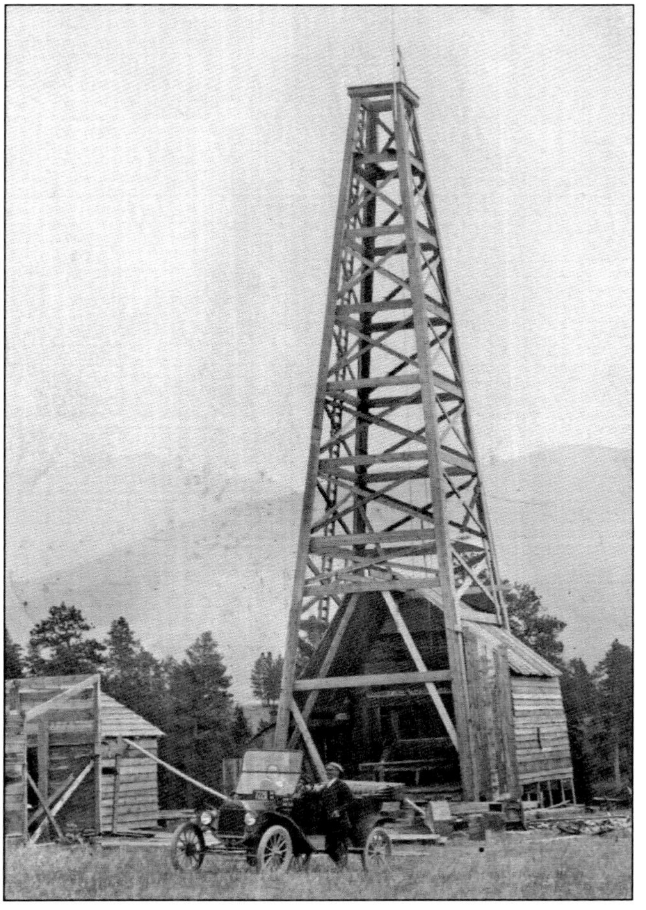

The Montana International Oil Company, with Will Leonard as its prime mover, organized in July 1914. Within one year, Leonard purchased drilling equipment and erected a derrick north of Eureka. Unfortunately for the company (but fortunate for those who would take a dim view of having an oil refinery in the valley), they encountered a dry hole. Leonard ended up back in Pennsylvania, and the drilling rig went to Greybull, Wyoming, where oil had been found.

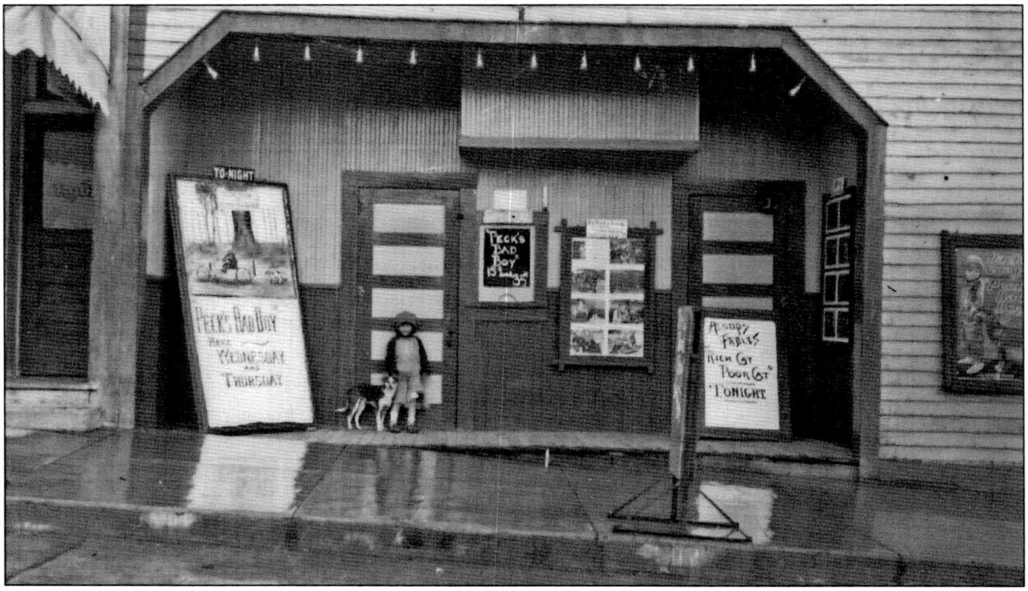

The Alhambra Theatre, date of origin unknown, was remodeled and opened as the Majestic Theatre in 1913. It went through three owners in the early years until Frank Sabin bought it in 1920. Sabin's daughter Donna is pictured above in 1922; *Rich Cat, Poor Cat* is playing at the theater, and *Peck's Bad Boy* is coming soon. Sabin built a new theater across the street around 1935 (shown below). Carl and Eedee Pershall bought the theater in the late 1960s and operate it as of 2009, having owned it longer than anyone else. The Majestic Theatre is Eureka's oldest continually operating business at 96 years. Only one other Tobacco Valley entity is older—the Quirk Cattle Company.

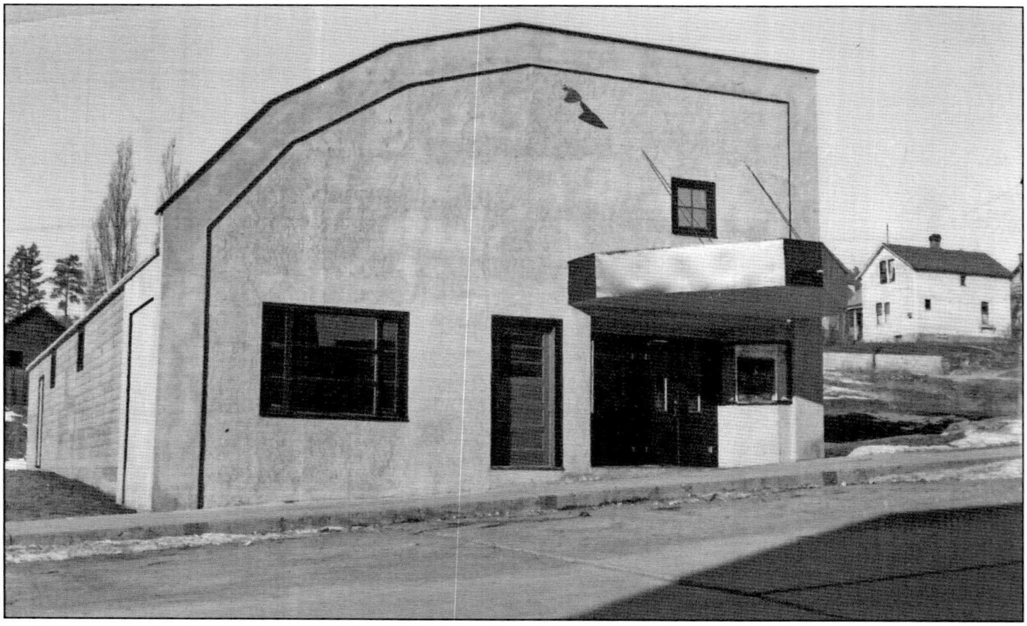

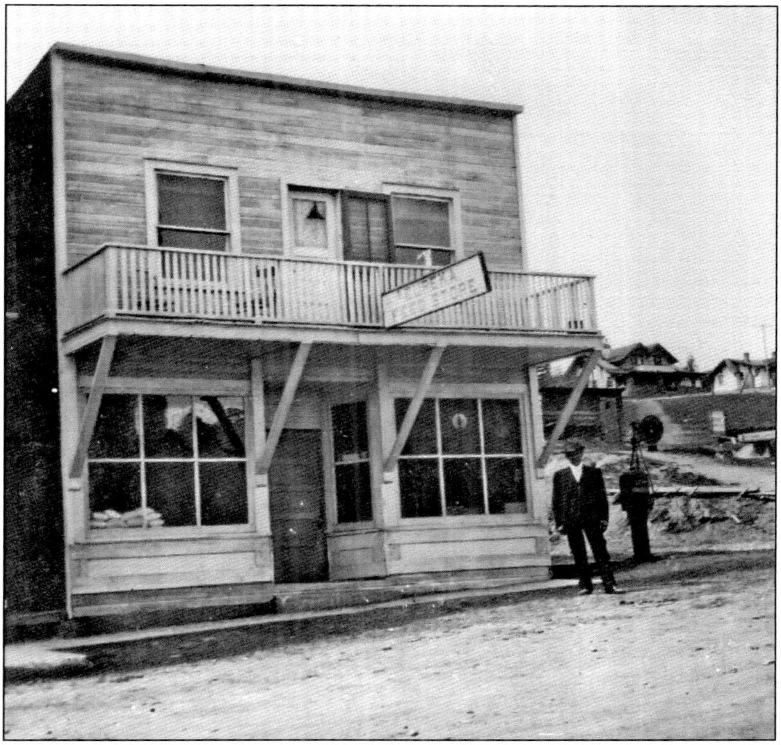

Frank Cael opened his feed store about 1920 and pronounced in regular weekly advertisements in the *Eureka Journal* that he was the proprietor. Cael was innovative, quickly adding gasoline and tires to his line of goods. He died in the early 1930s, leaving a wife, Marie, and three children. She then married "Irish" Tom Quirk, who was a nephew to "Old" Tom Quirk.

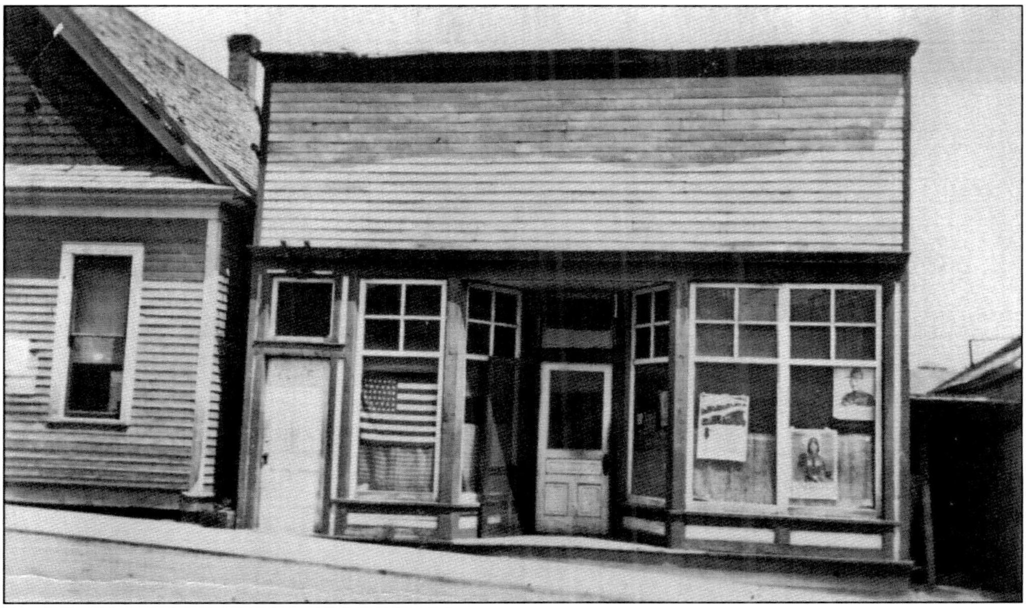

G. E. Shawler founded the *Tobacco Plains Journal* in August 1903, announcing that it would have a Republican slant. The original office burned in the fire of 1906. Shawler moved up Dewey Avenue, south of where Glacier Bank is today, and rebuilt. Perly Bernard bought the newspaper in 1910 and changed the name to the *Eureka Journal*. In 1911, Oscar Wolf took over and ran it until April 25, 1929. In the grip of the Great Depression, he suspended publication.

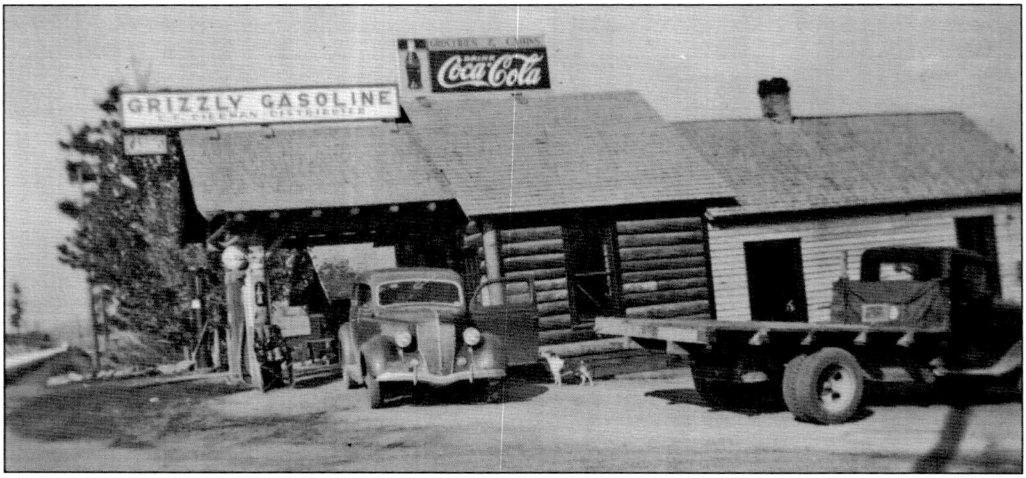

Dierman's Service was built in the 1920s to take advantage of tourists that were coming through in growing numbers. Many tourists camped free at the tourist park downtown where Riverside Park is today. Those with a little money in their pockets stayed at the tourist cabins that Clarence Dierman built behind the service station. Located on the north side of Sixth Street where one turns to go to the school, both the occupied cabins and the abandoned service station were razed in 1992 to make way for new construction.

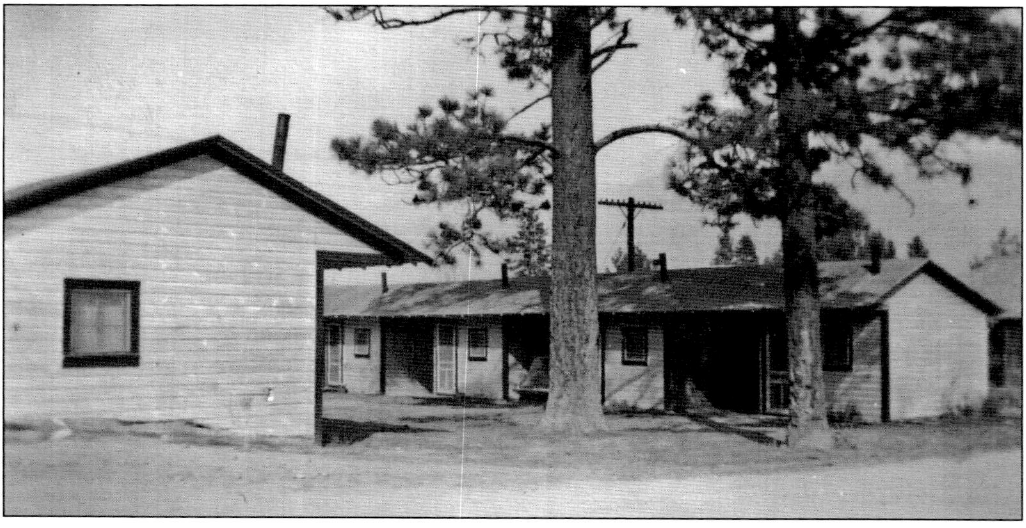

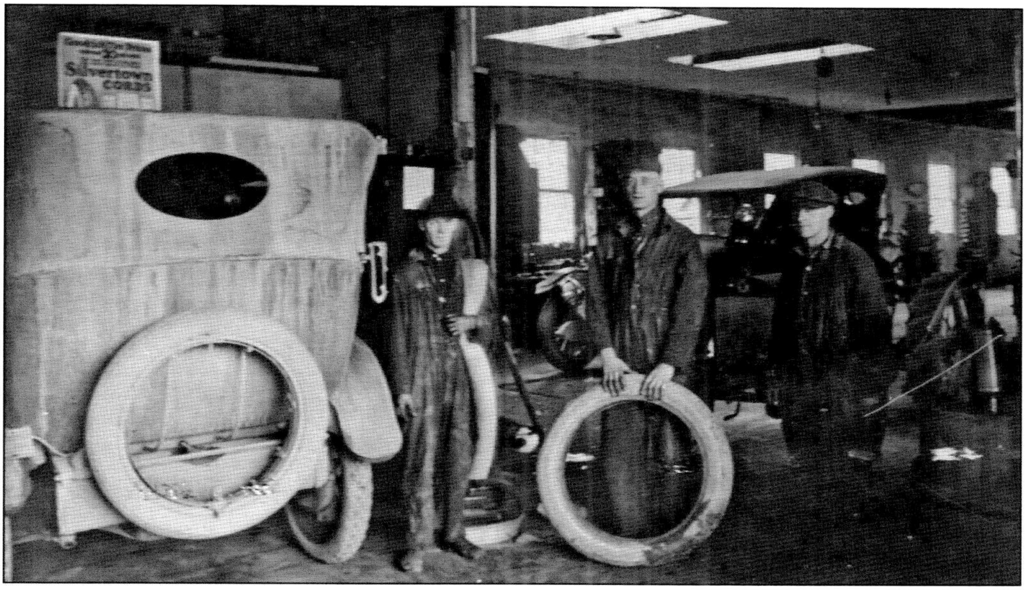

By 1920, car sales were hot, and Jim Garey got into the business as the town's first Ford dealer. Inside the Eureka Garage (pictured above) are, from left to right, unidentified, Jim Garey, and Guy Brock. After World War I, federal funds became available to improve roads between towns, which throughout much of the West spanned long distances. When it became known that the Teddy Roosevelt Highway would be built from Columbia Falls to Libby, Kalispell and Eureka squared off to have it routed through their respective towns. Eureka won that round, and it was not long before tourists began showing up. When the stretch along the Kootenai River between Jennings and Warland was completed, the *Eureka Journal* exclaimed, "There is nothing like it anywhere else in Lincoln county. Wide enough for two cars to pass anywhere, with a grade such that a Ford can go the entire distance on high." The location of the T R Garage (shown below) is not known but is believed to have been near Rexford.

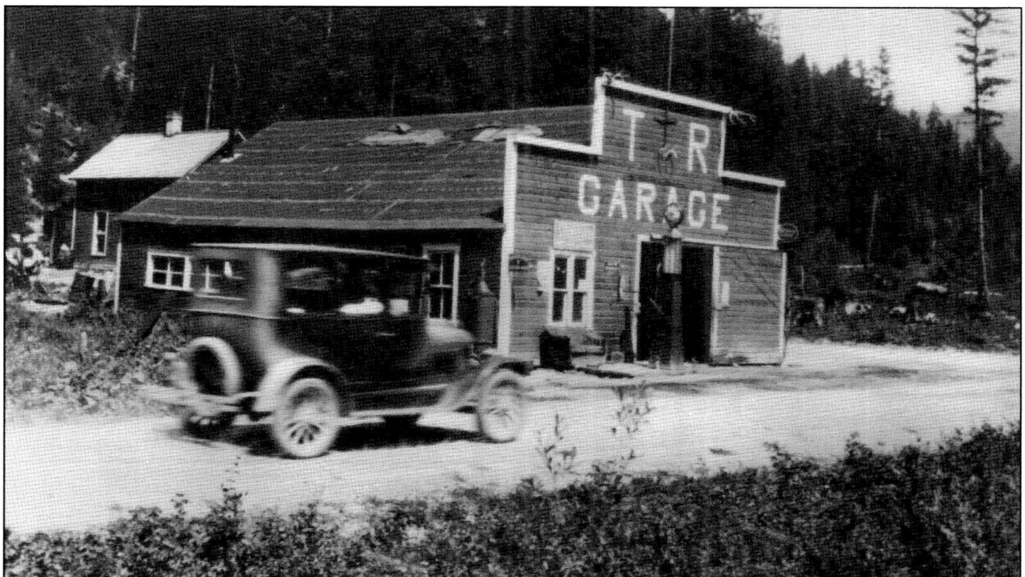

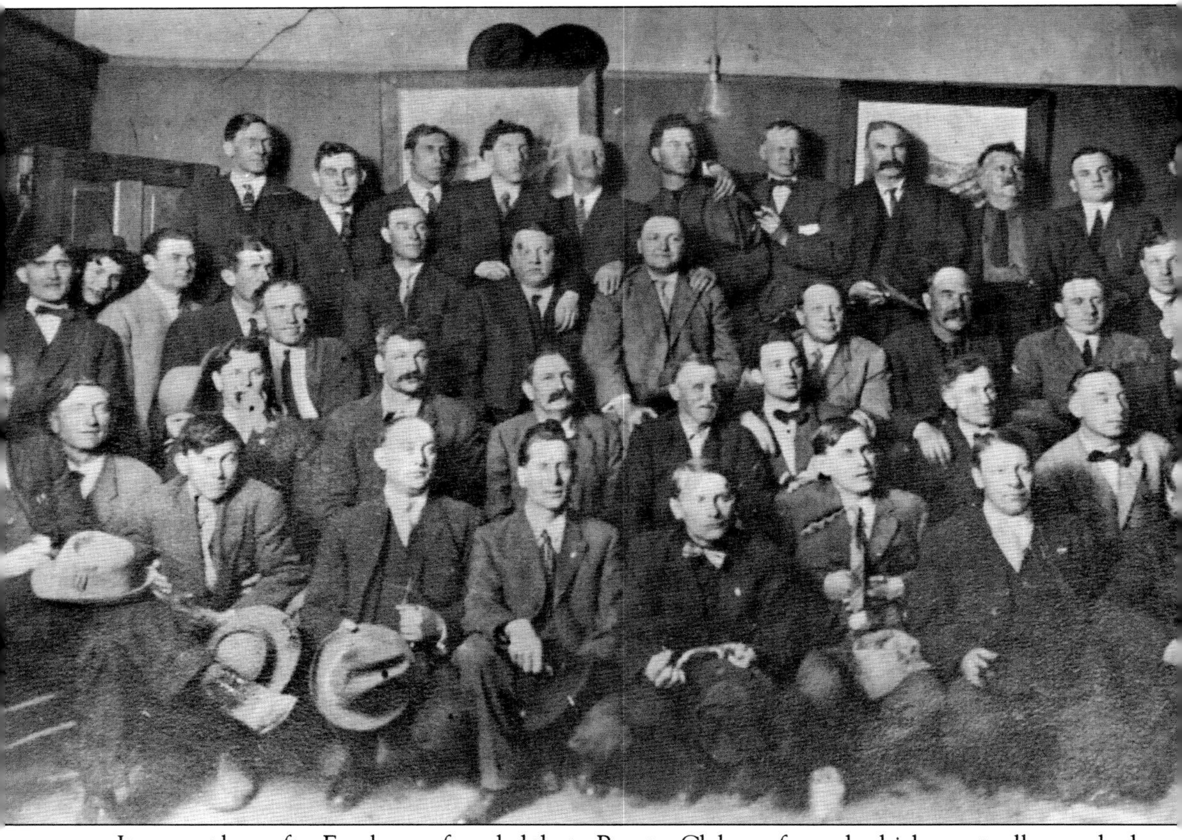

It was not long after Eureka was founded that a Booster Club was formed, which eventually morphed into the Commercial Club, seen here at a 1917 meeting. Among those pictured are druggist Jay Saling (third row, seventh from left, with one hand on his shoulder) along with (from left to right, beginning on Saling's right) movie theater owner Val Kordus (two hands on his shoulders), bank president Charles Hamman, and town founder Elzeor "Ed" Demers. Pictured in the fourth row are real estate agent C. E. Davis, newspaper publisher Oscar Wolf, George Guy, confectionary store owner Bill McCalder, contractor John Dahlberg, Sheriff Frank Baney, Dr. Fred Bogardus, Eureka Lumber Company manager C. A. Weil, and U.S. Forest Service ranger Fred Herrig. All others are unidentified.

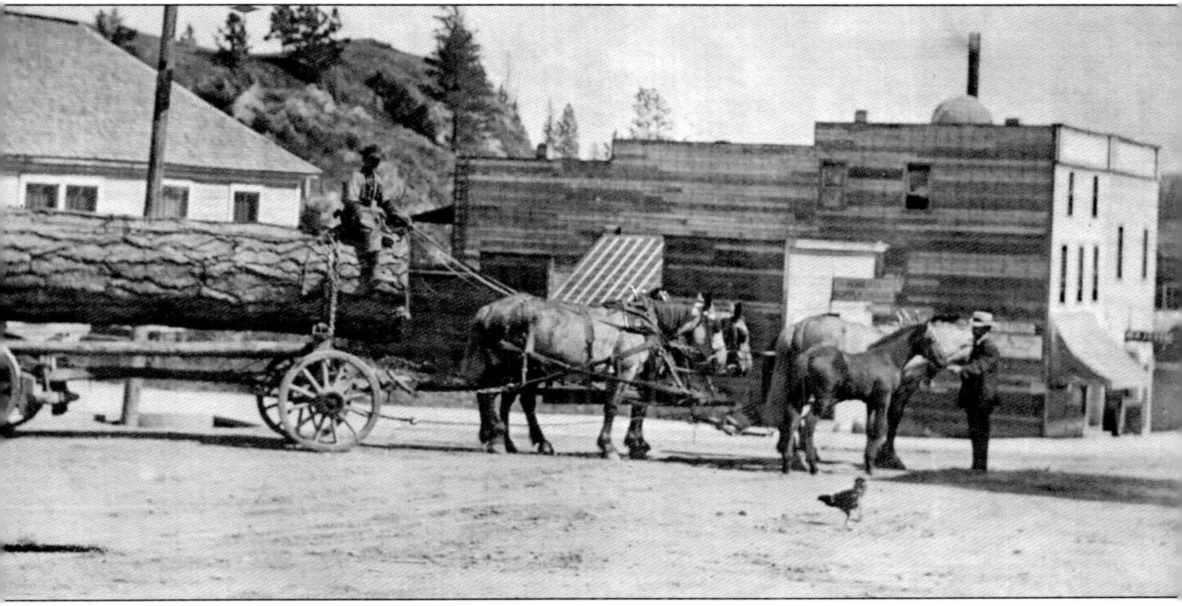

The first sawmills in the valley were small operations that supplied a growing demand for lumber as new arrivals began putting up all manner of buildings. The surrounding foothills and mountains were thick with virgin timber. Some of the largest trees, like this one being hauled down Dewey Avenue, were ponderosa pines that grew over parts of the Tobacco Plains. Falling, bucking, and transporting logs like the one shown here was a serious undertaking.

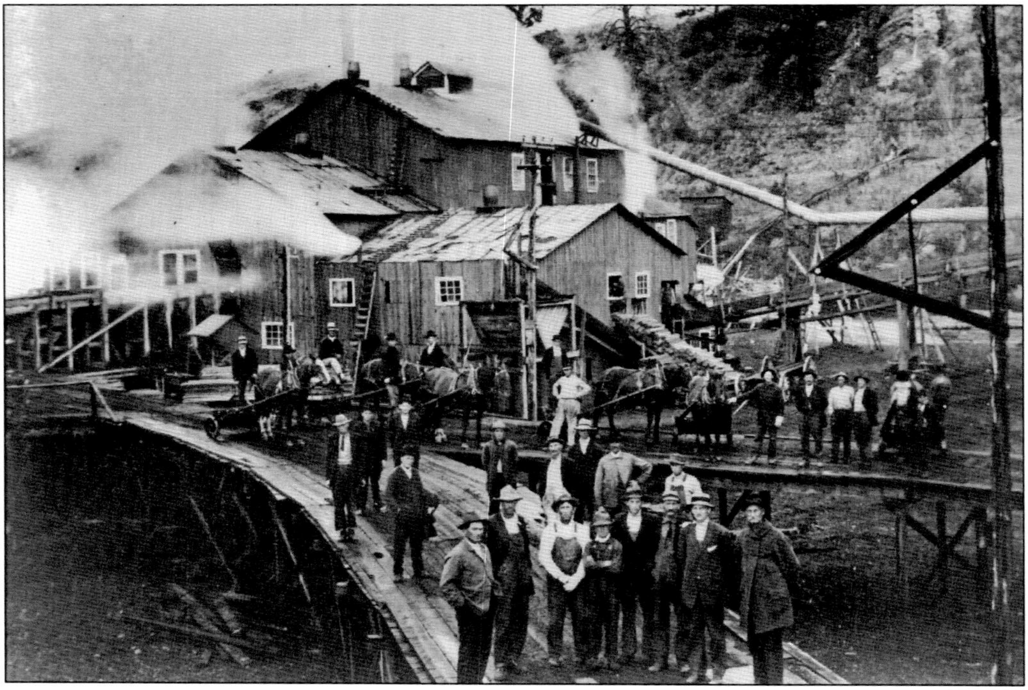

In 1905, E. W. Bader and S. B. Bottum set about building a large lumber mill (pictured above) on the site occupied today by the Interbel warehouse, the Historical Village, and the River Walk. Within two years, Bader and Bottum sold out separately to investors who had gotten their start in grain elevators. C. A. "Big Daddy" Weil, with P. L. Howe assisting, took over management of the mill. Upstream logging camps were built, and the involved task of harvesting and transporting logs to the mill was begun. The town got into a rhythm. Log in the winter, transport in the spring, then run the mill until there were no more logs in the yard. When things were running smoothly, the planer crew in 1914 (shown below) shared a $10,000-a-month payroll with other mill workers.

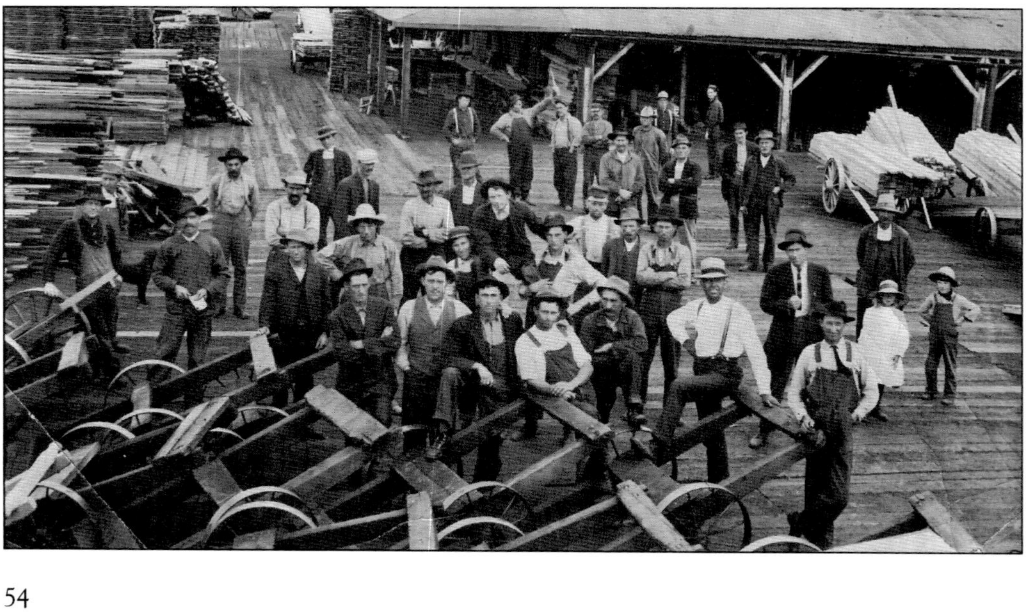

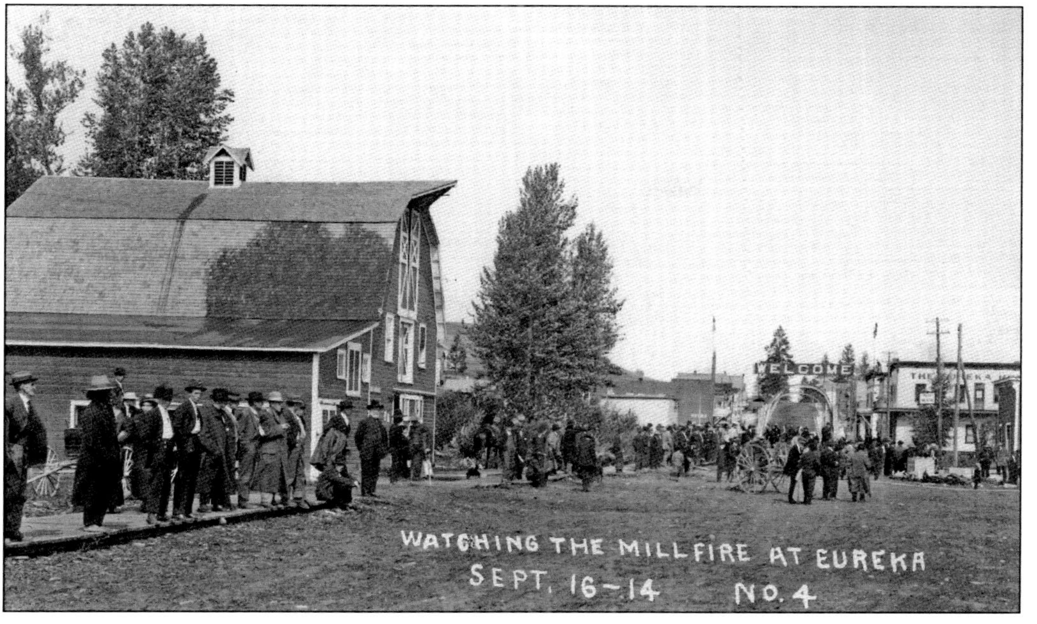

The whole town watched anxiously on September 16, 1914, as fire destroyed the mill (pictured above). The *Eureka Journal* chronicled the event: "A pall of gloom, such as has not been equaled since the fire catastrophe a little over eight years ago . . . settled over the town of Eureka, when the alarm from the mill whistles and the clanging of the fire bell announced that the big sawmill of the Eureka Lumber Company was on fire." Pres. C. A. Weil announced immediately that the company would install a larger and better mill to be in operation by the following March. Weil kept his word. The March 18, 1915, *Eureka Journal* exclaimed that the "mammoth new sawmill of the Eureka Lumber Company" (shown below) would be up and running in early April.

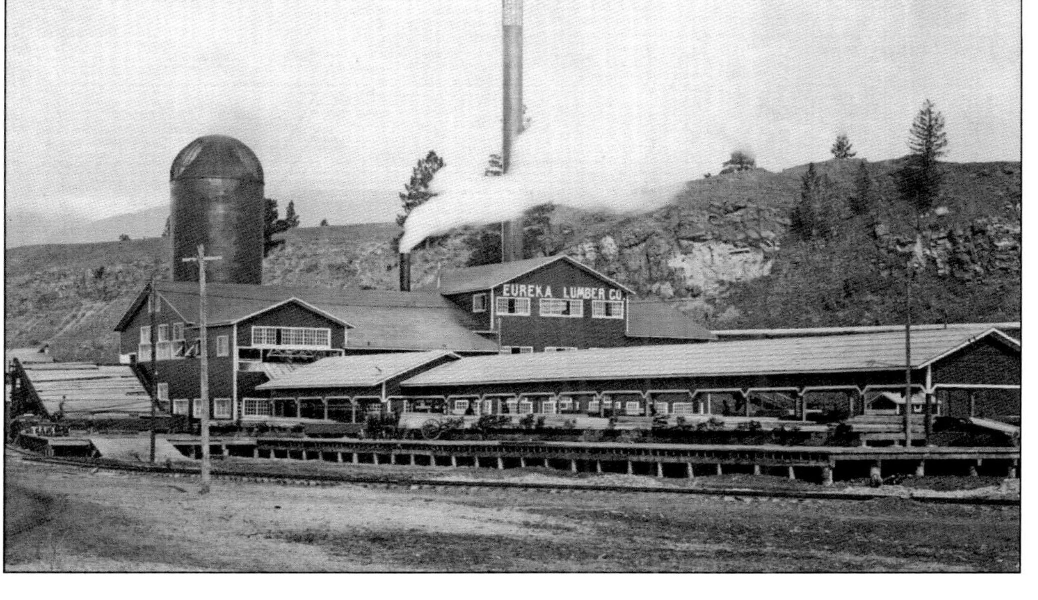

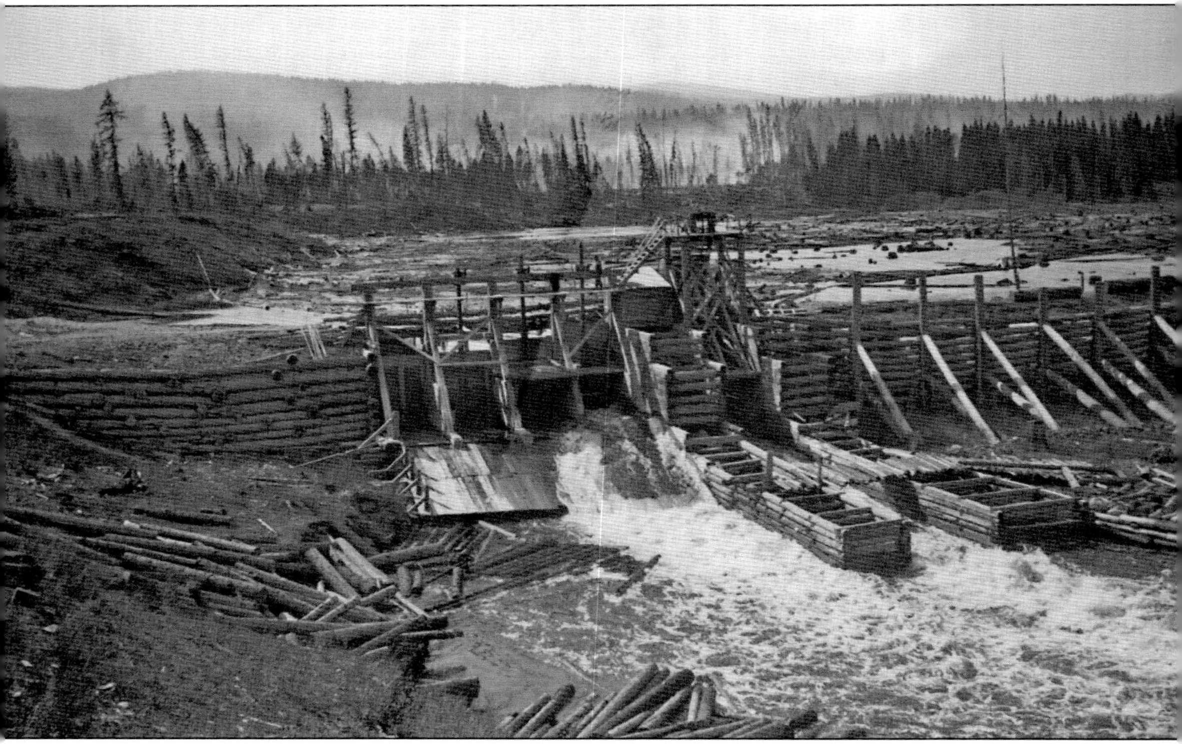

Without splash dams, it was impossible to float logs to Eureka. They tried it for several years, but it did not take long to blow out the banks of the river, creating a bed so wide that water only trickled over it. By 1910, there were four dams on the Tobacco River, including the first one to create a millpond and power-generation capability. The function of the other three was to store up enough water to float logs downstream. This did not happen in one fell swoop, so the gates were closed to store up water for successive floods. Splash dams were not particularly simple structures, even if they did go up in a hurry. Such institutions as environmental impact studies were far into the future. This splash dam near Trego was wider than a football field and 24 feet high.

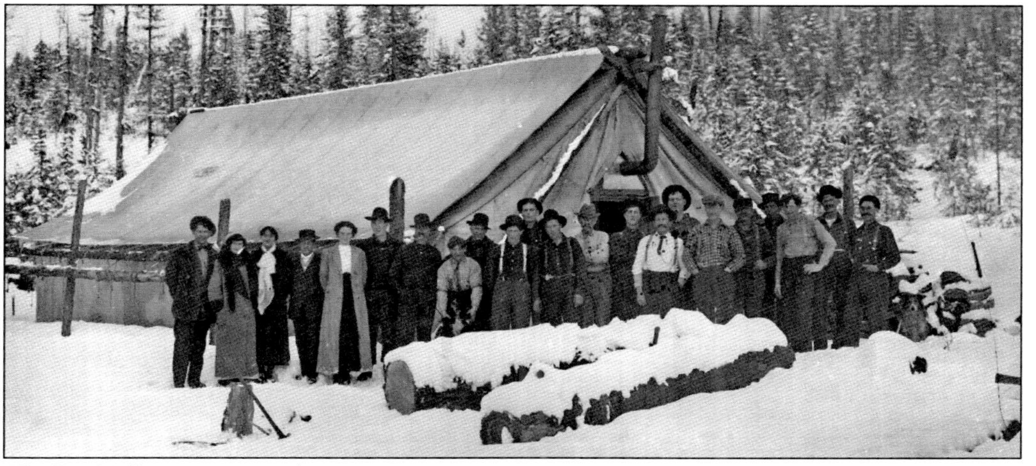

The Big Mill, as it came to be called, required a steady stream of logs, and the only way to provide that stream was with the Tobacco River and its two main tributaries, Grave Creek and Fortine Creek. Logging camps were put in place upstream such as the one pictured near Trego (above). They were often haphazard affairs, particularly early on when they were concerned only with harvesting timber in the close proximity of the river. Age, education, gender, and ethnicity were no barriers to working at a logging camp kitchen (shown at right).

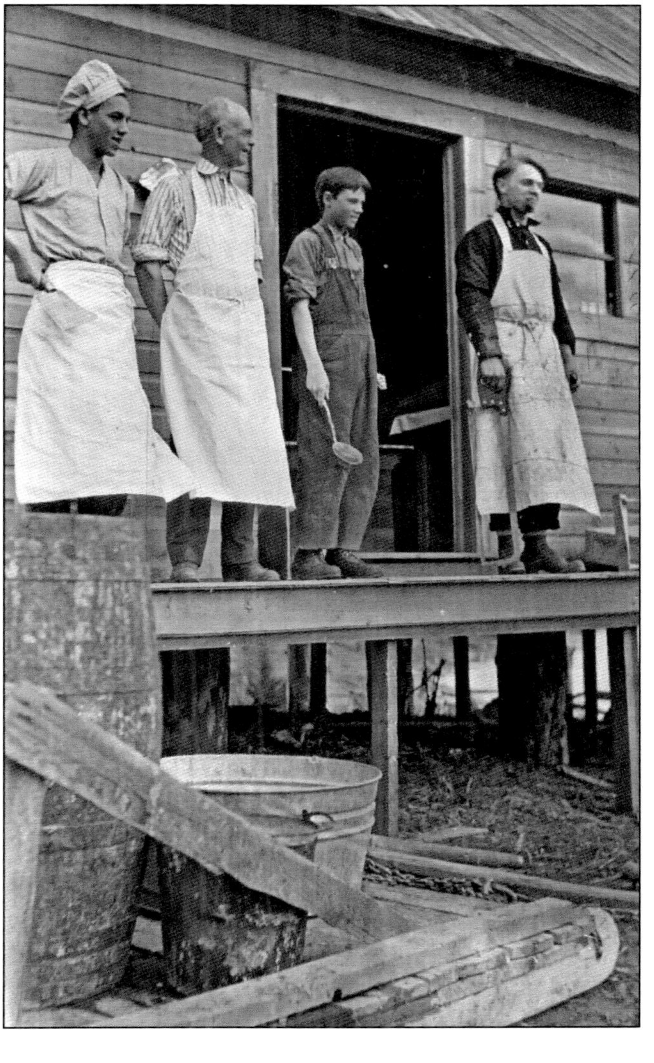

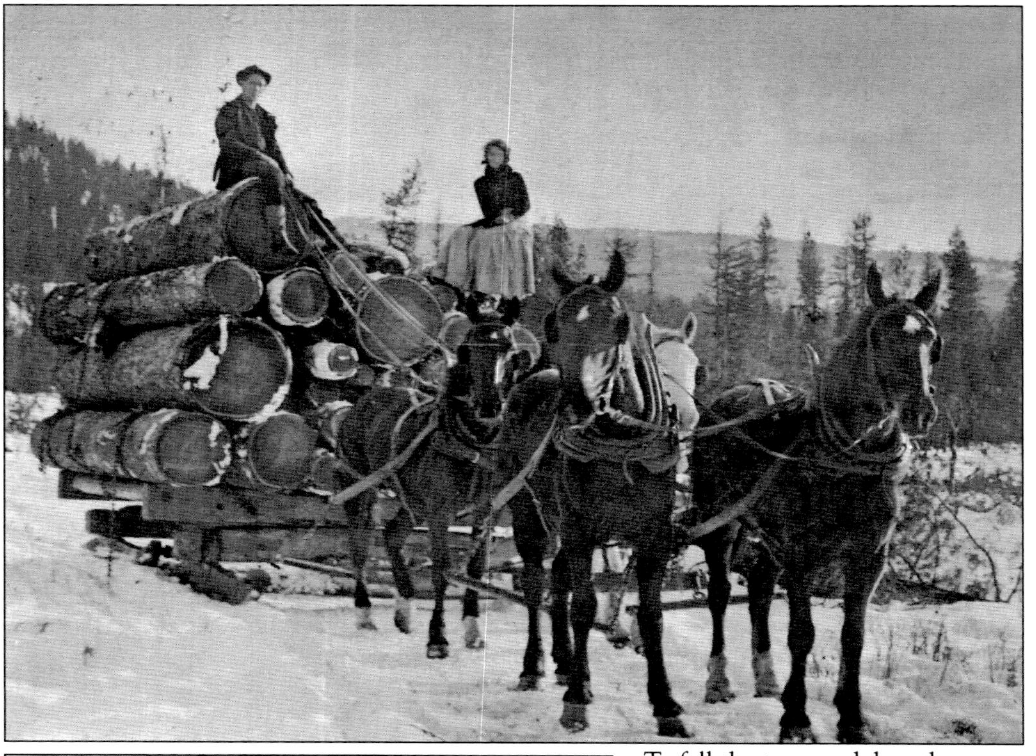

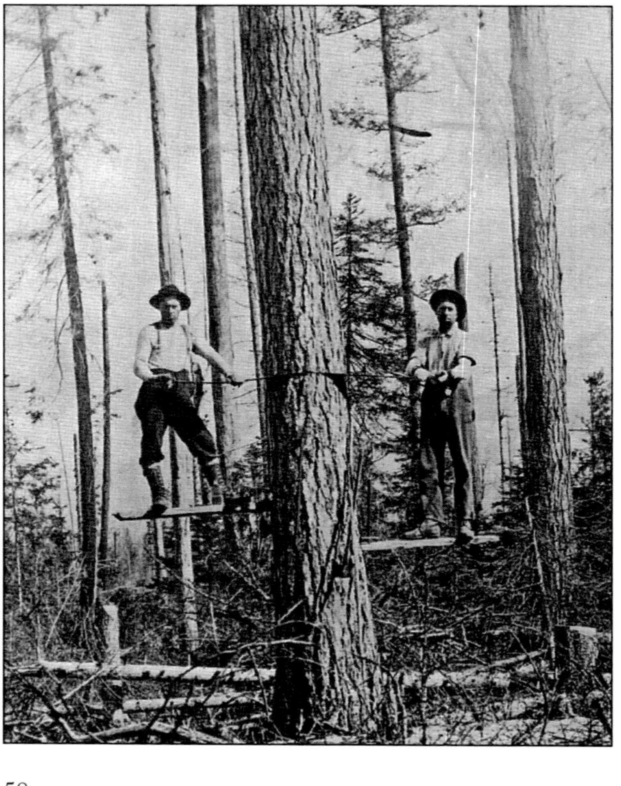

To fall the trees and drag them to the riverbank required fallers and horse skidders. The distance from the stream bank determined whether they would build a load on a sleigh (pictured above) or simply pull them there with horses. Either way, winter was the favored time to log for the simple reason that it reduced drag. Sand was sometimes used on slopes to increase drag. At such times, the conscientious teamster would advise a rider that they would be better off walking. Fallers (shown at left) may have had trouble getting to a tree in deep snow, but once there they placed their springboard, they went to work about 6 feet up the trunk where it narrowed up several inches. The bell or butt was left in the woods because it would have only caused trouble down the line—from skidding it, floating it down the river, or running it through the mill.

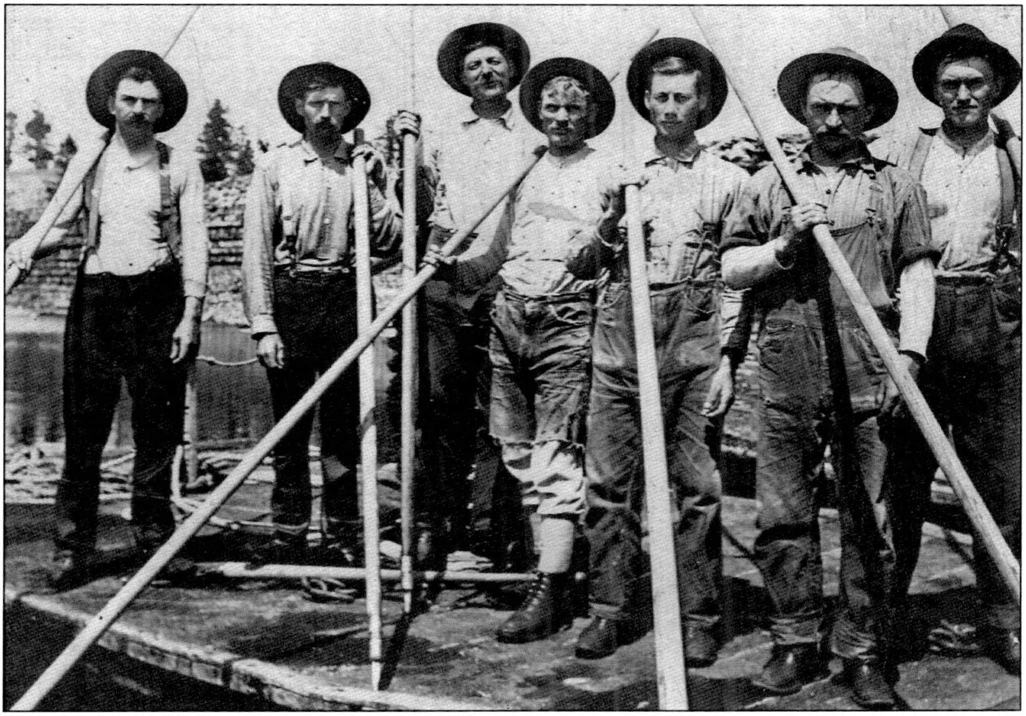

River rats (pictured above) were necessarily daring men. Some locals worked the log drive each spring, but more often, they were men who drifted between Minnesota, Montana, and the Pacific Northwest. They were used to crude living conditions, and when they had time on their hands commonly ended up in saloons going through their money. In the photograph above, Michael Smith is third from the left. Their tool of choice was the pike pole, used for pushing logs around. They also used Peaveys, a short thick lever with a hinged hook for rolling logs. It is easy to see how a man might become maimed if he fell in between the logs (shown below), especially if they were moving in a heavy stream. River rats wore caulked (spiked) boots. Jumping from log to log was an acquired skill, and heaven help the man who did not learn to stop at the same time his feet did.

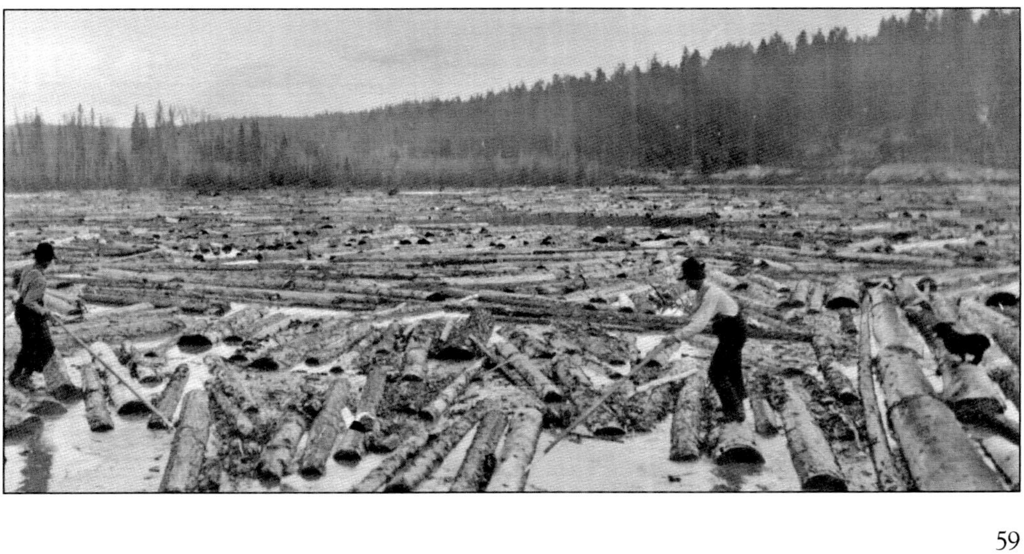

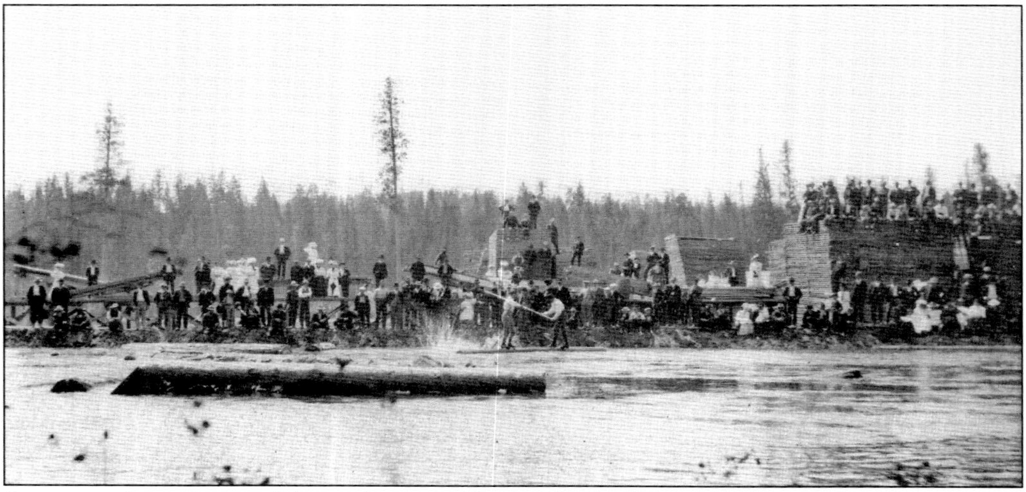

Sometimes logging was all fun and games. Above, a log-burling competition is being held on the Fourth of July in 1907 at the millpond of the brand new Eureka Lumber Company. While they are no doubt ignorant of the fact, the onlookers perched atop stacks of lumber are probably more imperiled than the men who are struggling to be the only one left standing on the spinning log.

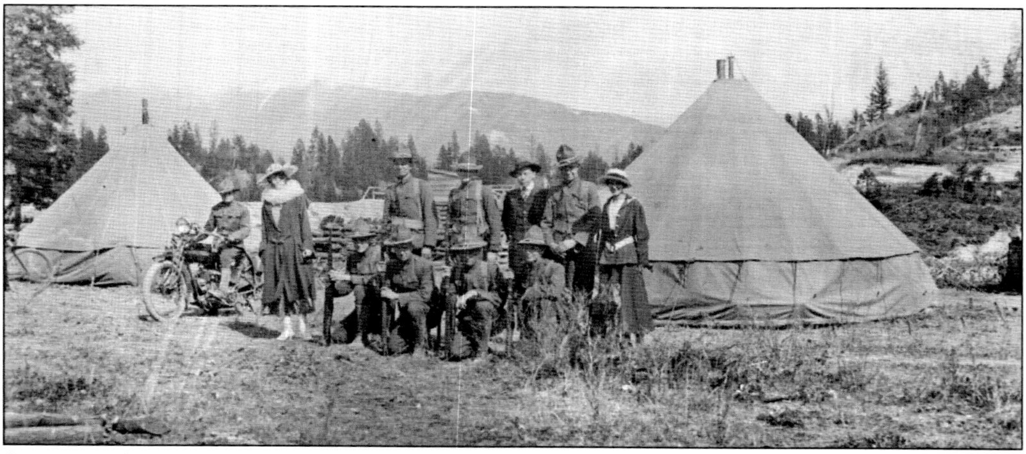

Sometimes logging was not all fun and games. In 1917, workers went on strike for better conditions, including free blankets, an eight-hour day, and $5 a day with board, better food, and sanitary conditions. Charles "Big Daddy" Weil wired the governor asking for troops to guard infrastructure, believing that IWW radicals might sabotage it. Washington National Guardsman were sent but were not in the area long—although long enough for the ladies to come and visit. At far right, LaEtta Whilt visits Lawrence Smith.

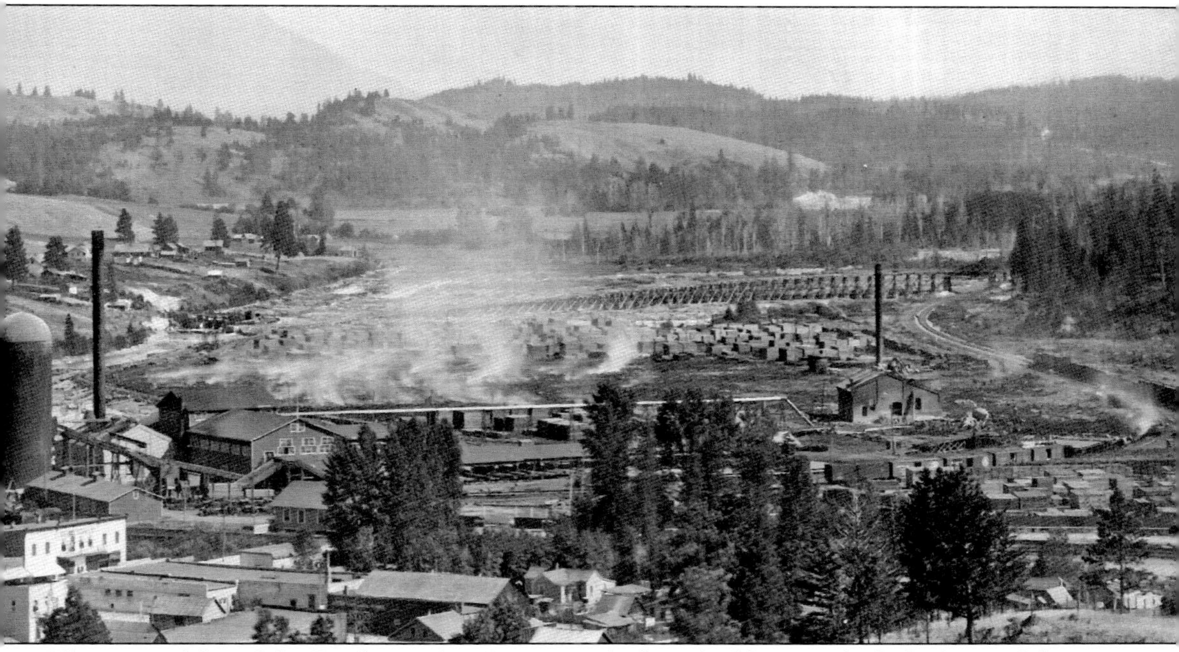

The main edifice of the Eureka Lumber Company, the large building in which the heart of the mill machinery was housed, stood where the Interbel warehouse is today. Pictured here in about 1922, the Big Mill had by this time reached its full potential. Logs that could be floated down the Tobacco River were exhausted, and the company was now under the management of P. L. Howe, Charles Weil having moved on to the oil patch that was developing near Shelby, Montana. Indeed, the name was changed to the P. L. Howe Lumber Company. Howe moved to harvest timber that was not accessible by the Tobacco River, building a logging railroad into Frank Lake. Pilings can still be seen on the lake's north side where the tracks ended abruptly. The trestle, which crossed the Great Northern mainline, can be seen in the middle distance.

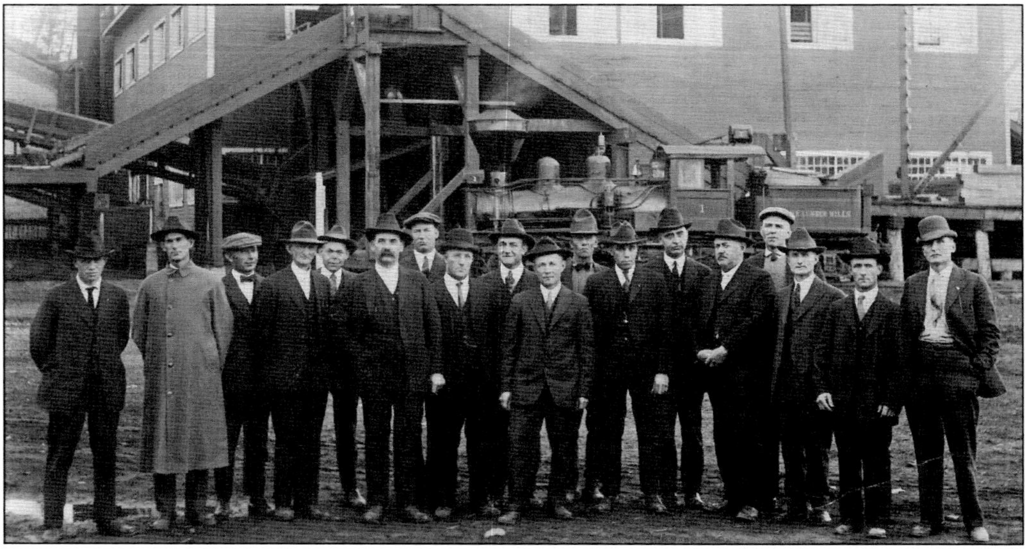

The occasion for the gathering above is obscure, as are the names of most of the men. Charles "Big Daddy" Weil is sixth from the left. P. L. Howe, who succeeded Weil when Weil was elected to the state House of Representatives in 1918, is believed to be 13th from the left. Although Howe had been associated with the operation from the beginning, he never really engaged the townspeople or the workforce as Weil had. Howe disdained organized labor and hated the IWW. This photograph postdates September 1919; that is when the Shay engine arrived from the factory and went to work moving logs to the mill from the area around Frank Lake. Walt Holder (shown below) was the engineer, and Clarence "Clancy" Dierman was the fireman. The 32-ton locomotive ran on standard-gauge tracks and was in service scarcely four years before it was sold to a lumber company working in the Half Moon area near Columbia Falls. Today this locomotive sits idle in a small park on the north edge of Columbia Falls.

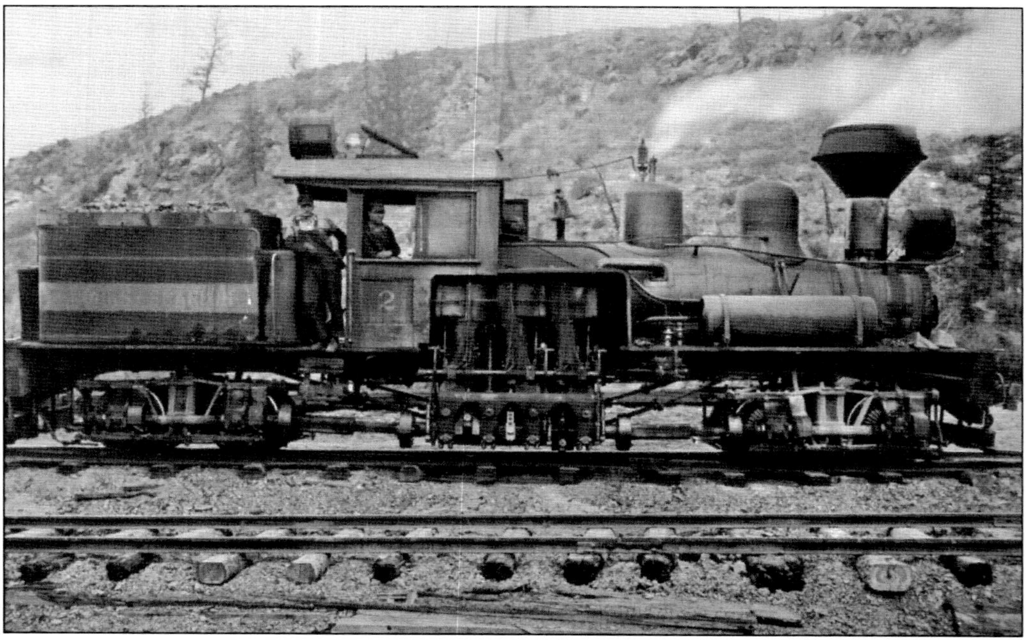

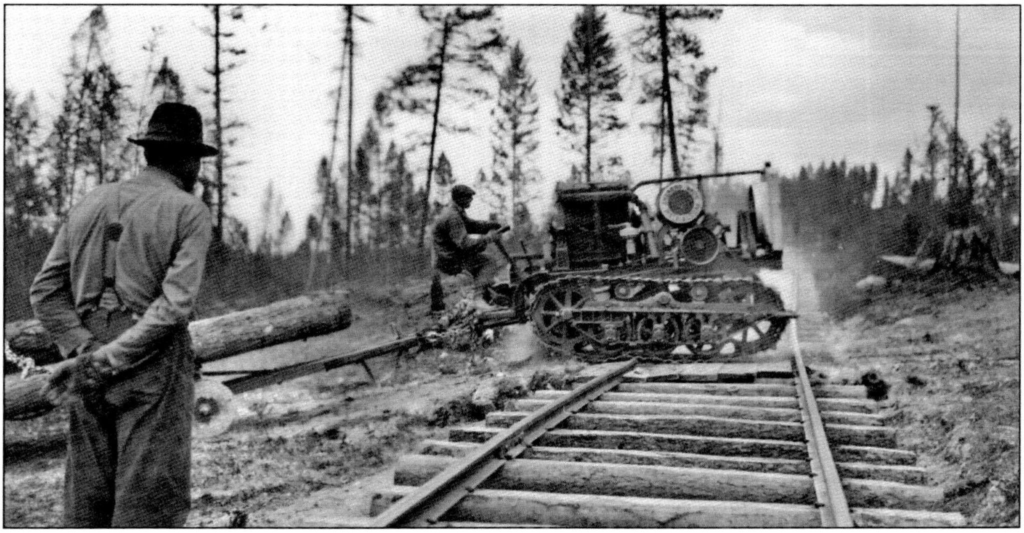

Logging with horses began to wane with the advent of tractor crawlers (pictured above). It took World War I to bring the technology to a point of usefulness. Although this photograph was obviously taken when P. L. Howe's railroad was still in operation, logging continued on a smaller scale after the mill shut down. For as crude as these machines were, they quickly caught on because they had many advantages over horses. That is, once they were successfully running. As with tractor crawlers, World War I also advanced truck technology (shown below). In 1920, there were about five truckloads per day coming through town, thus supplementing the river drive. Level ground remained a logger's best friend, but as the decades wore on, they were forced to access increasingly difficult terrain.

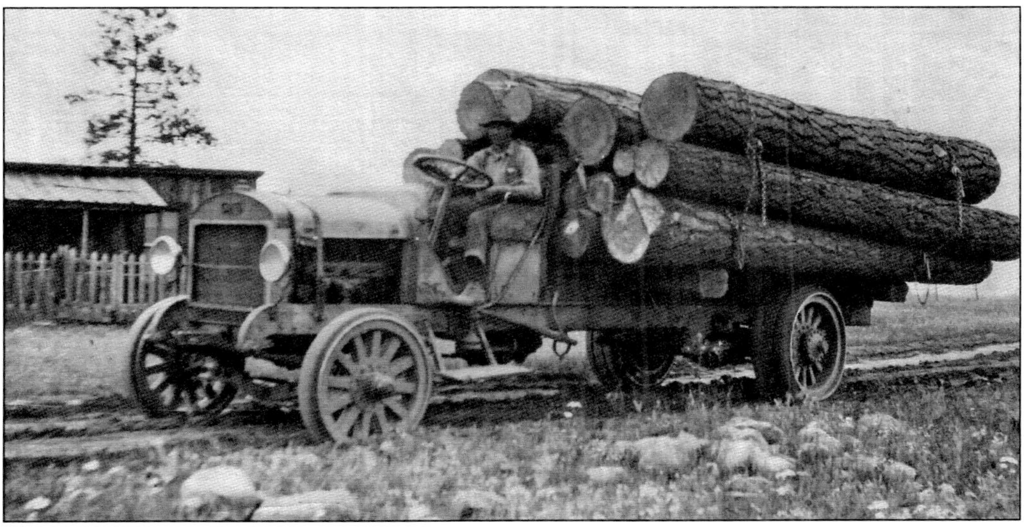

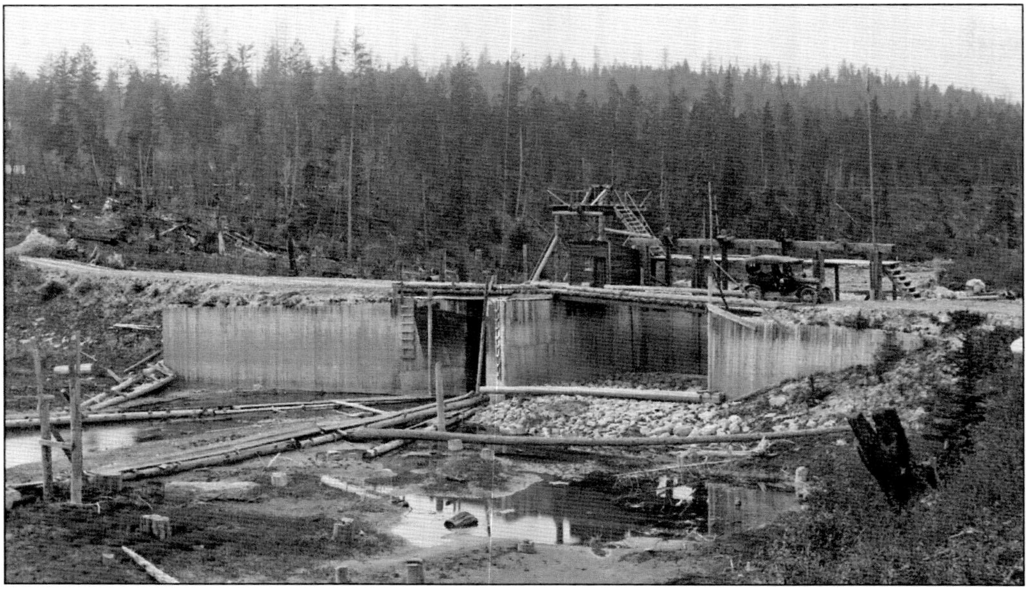

This is likely the last splash dam (pictured above) on the Tobacco River, possibly replacing one that washed out because this one is made of concrete and apparently functioned as a bridge too. In the process of filling the reservoir behind the dam, the river was reduced to a mere trickle. Logging camps (shown below) commonly had a kitchen and mess hall, bunkhouses, cabins for married men, an office, a barn or shop, and sometimes a school. This was Camp 4, located above Fortine. In later days, there were roads to the camps when cars came into common use to transport supplies. A note in the May 17, 1928, *Eureka Journal* told the story of George Bowen, a teamster in a camp near Trego. Following lunch, he went out to the shop/garage like the one pictured below, and to his detriment laid down for a nap. Bert Svenrud arrived at the camp in his car and drove into the garage, with fatal results to Bowen.

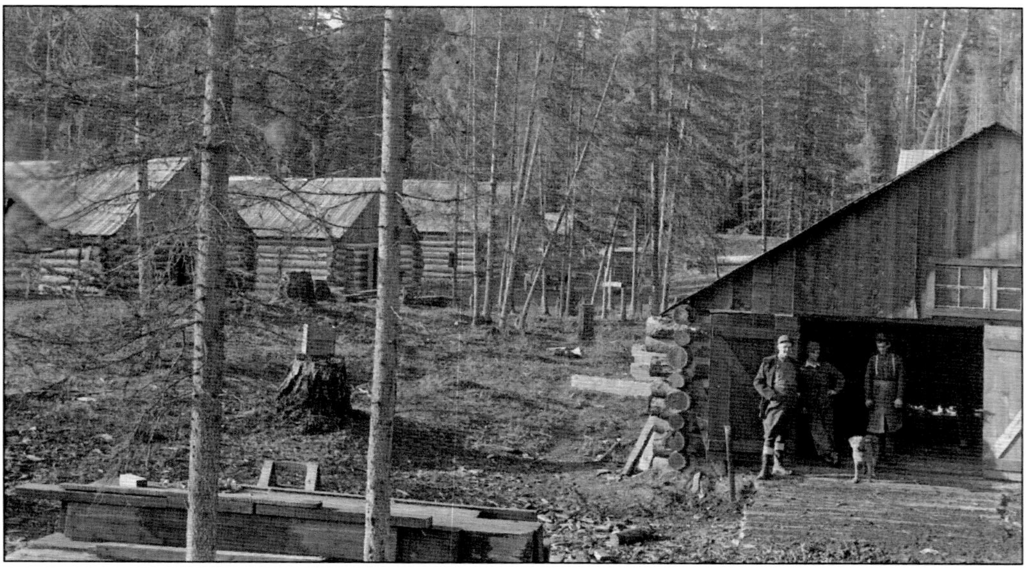

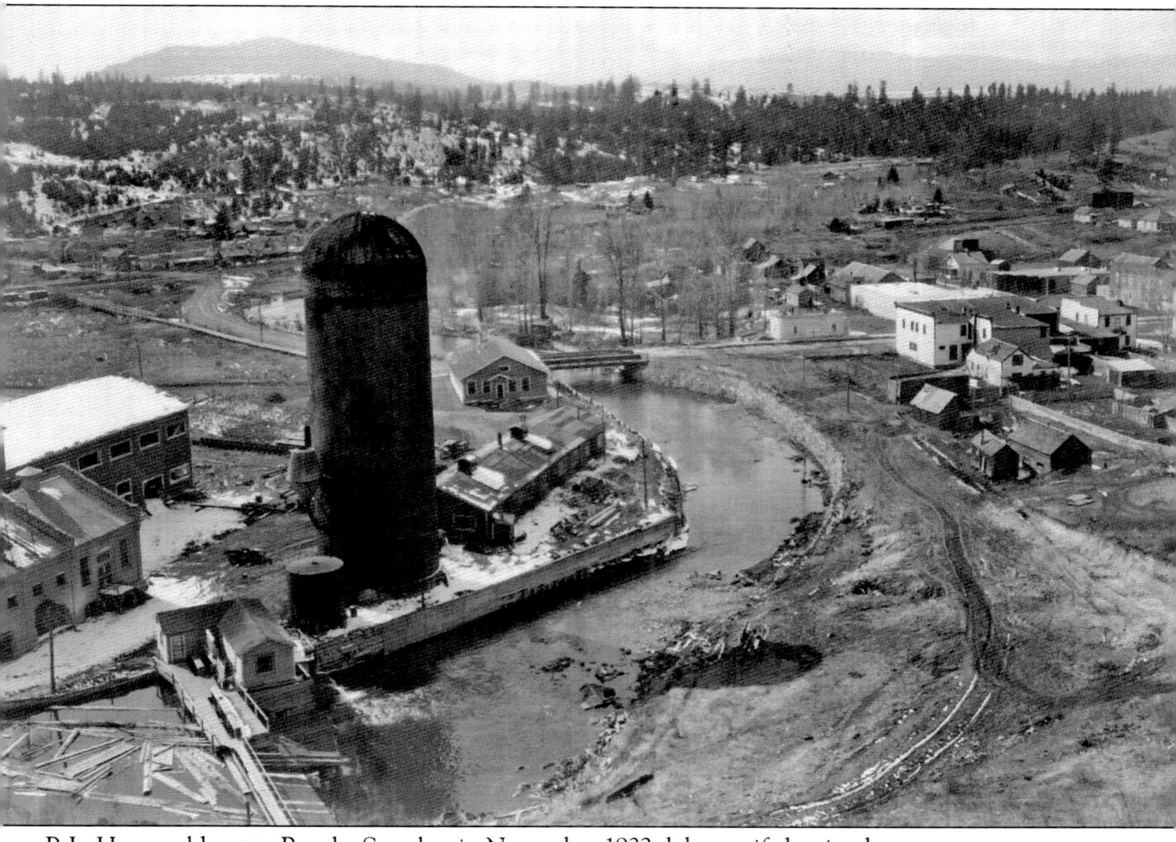

P. L. Howe sold out to Brooks-Scanlon in November 1922, labor strife having become a constant headache. In April 1923, there was yet another strike, and regardless of whether Brooks-Scanlon was willing to negotiate or not, at least one of the demands was impossible to satisfy. Along with more attainable demands, strikers called for "the release of all class-war prisoners." The management wired Mayor Oscar Wolf, who was visiting in Minneapolis, complaining that with continued labor problems, they would have to follow through with their original plan when they bought the mill from Howe, which was to dismantle it and move it to Washington. A planer fire in August 1923 sealed the deal. Little was done at the mill after that, and by October 1924, the Big Mill was gone. All that remained of it was the electrical generating plant that Homer McCullough purchased for the Tobacco River Power Company. The turbine and power plant were located at lower left. Errant boards floating near the spillway bear silent testimony to what once was.

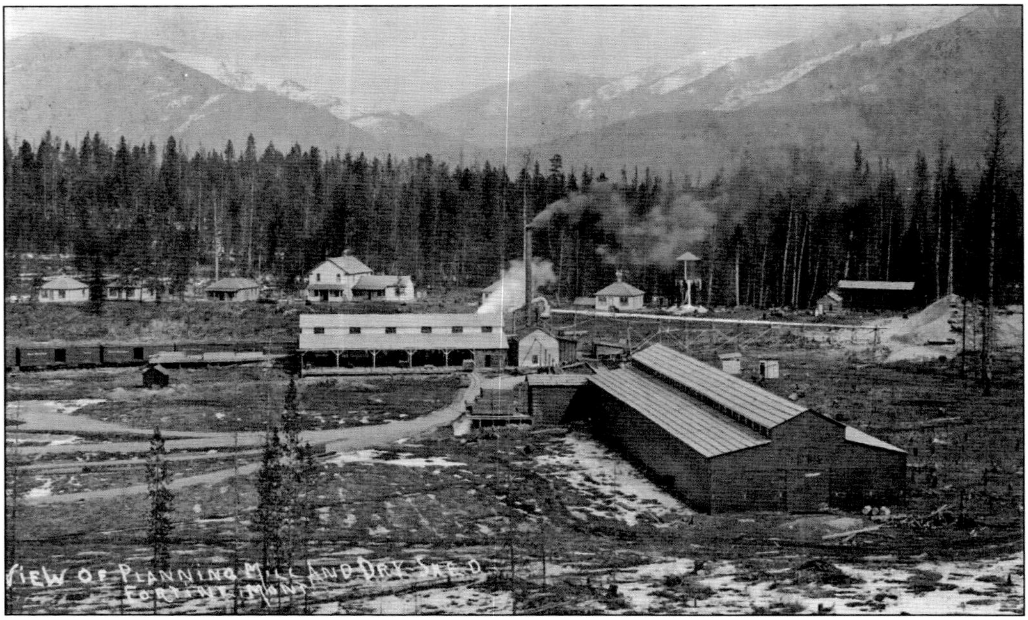

The Eureka Lumber Company, and its successors, was the largest but not the only important lumber mill in Tobacco Valley. C. B. Roberts and A. E. Boorman built an extensive operation on Meadow Creek 4 miles above Fortine (pictured above). The Lincoln Logging and Lumber Company was, at one time, larger than Fortine. Besides a large house for the Roberts family and a number of more modest abodes for the workers, there was a school and a church. The mill also had its own railroad, with the tracks later being removed to Eureka where P. L. Howe used them to build his logging railroad when Roberts and Boorman closed the mill in 1921. Pictured below is the Roberts family. From left to right are Ning Roberts, Annis (C. B.'s wife), Elliott, Olive (Ning's wife) holding Howard, C. B. holding Gladys, and Lavina Jane (mother of C. B. and Ning).

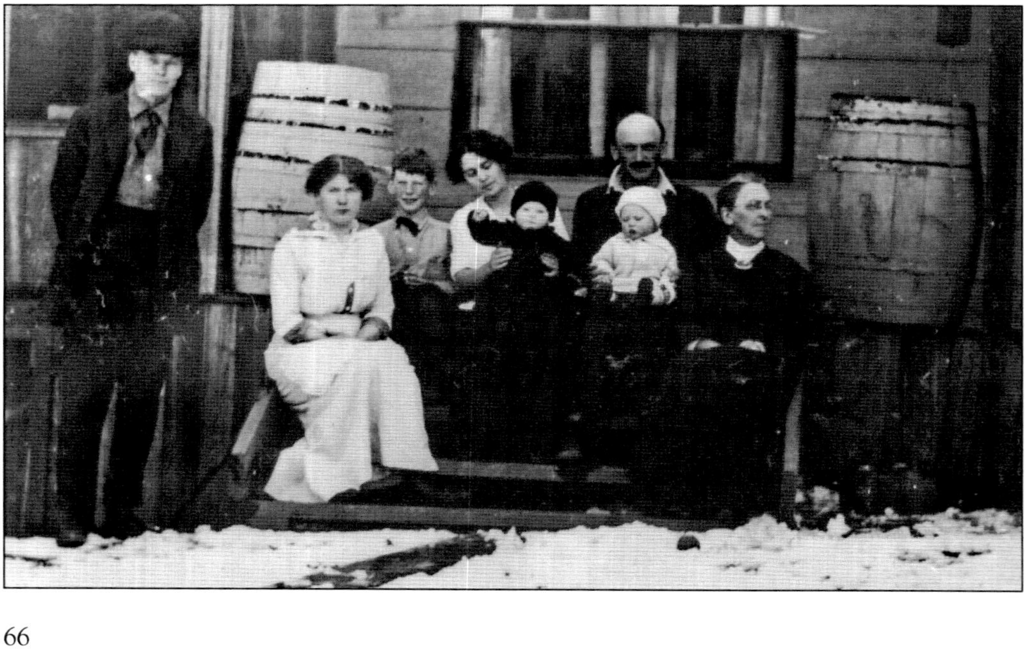

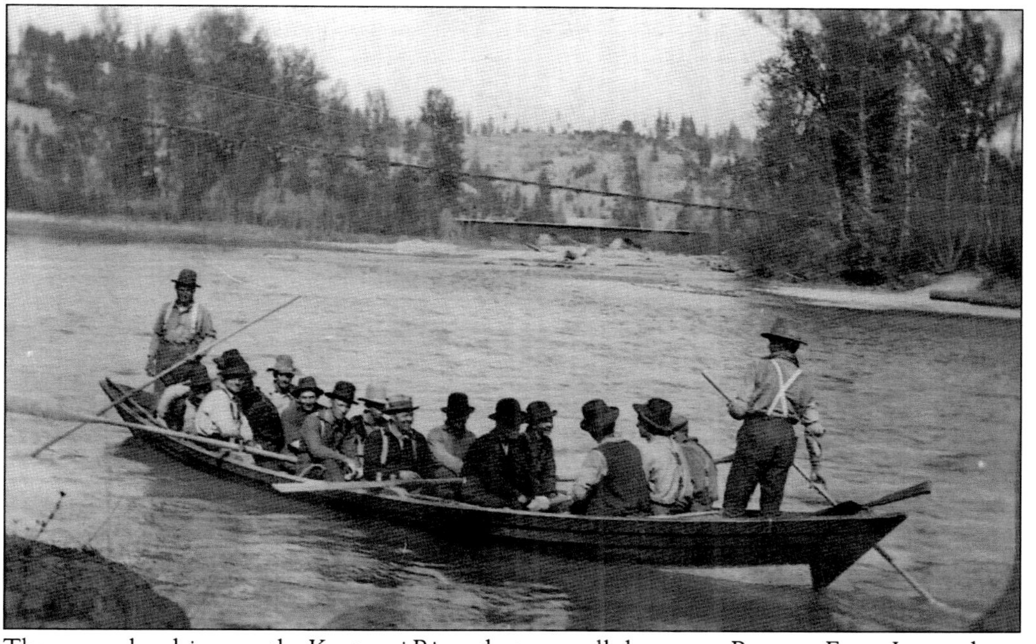

There were log drives on the Kootenai River that went all the way to Bonners Ferry. It must have been some spectacle to see thousands of logs blast over Kootenai Falls. The men were moved in specialized boats called bateaus. Here, in the 1920s, Roy Truman mans the stern rudder. The suspension cable for Byer's swinging bridge to Murray Island is in the center of the image, and the Great Northern Railroad's bridge to Fernie appears in the background.

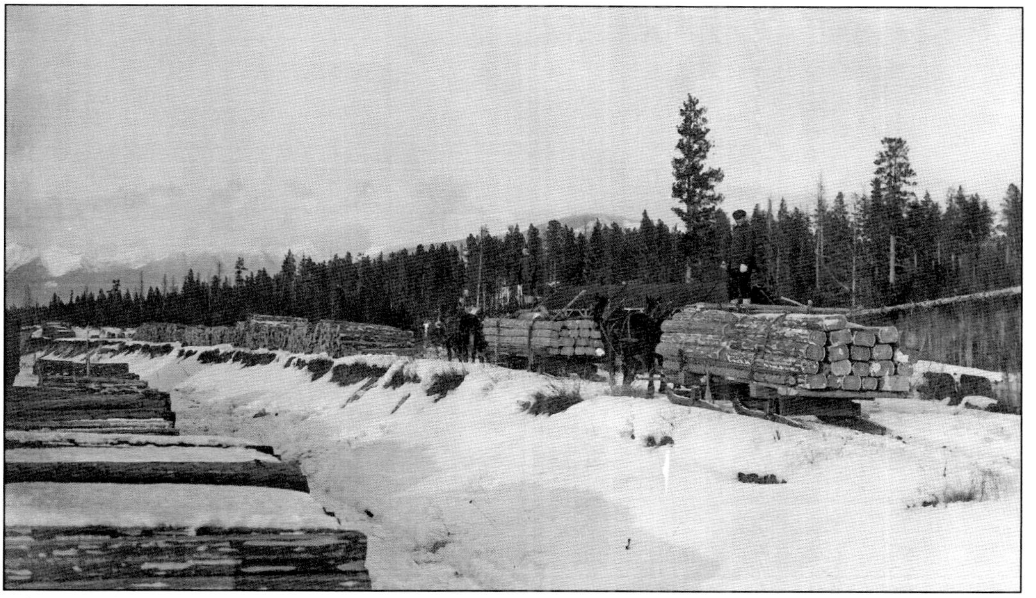

Along with dimension lumber, the number of railroad ties that have been milled and hewn by hand is incalculable. Men who worked harder than a tie hack would be hard to find. They spent their days standing on 8-foot logs chopping two parallel sides with a broadax. Ties were hauled by sled and later by truck to railroad sidings; the Fortine siding is pictured here.

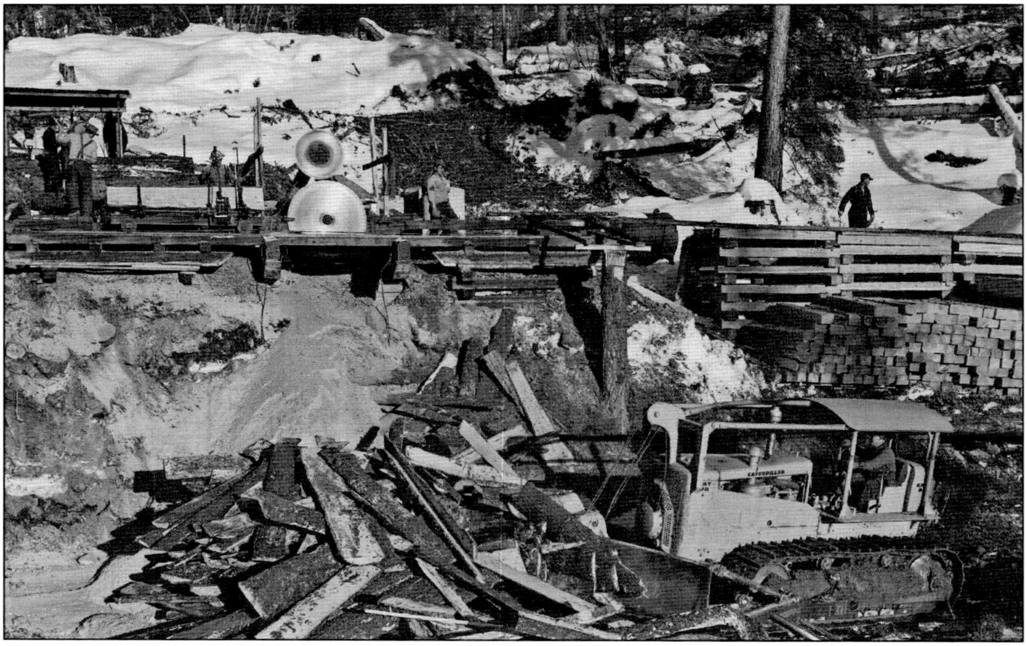

Beginning after World War II, small transportable mills went into operation throughout the area milling cants. A cant was created when an 8-foot-long log was run through a gang of 4-inch saws. The resulting timbers varied in width but were 4 inches thick. Those larger pieces were then trucked to a mill and cut into two-by-four studs. Here Herb Salois is logging for the Tobacco River Lumber Company in 1957. The huge slabs, considered waste in those days, would be salvaged today.

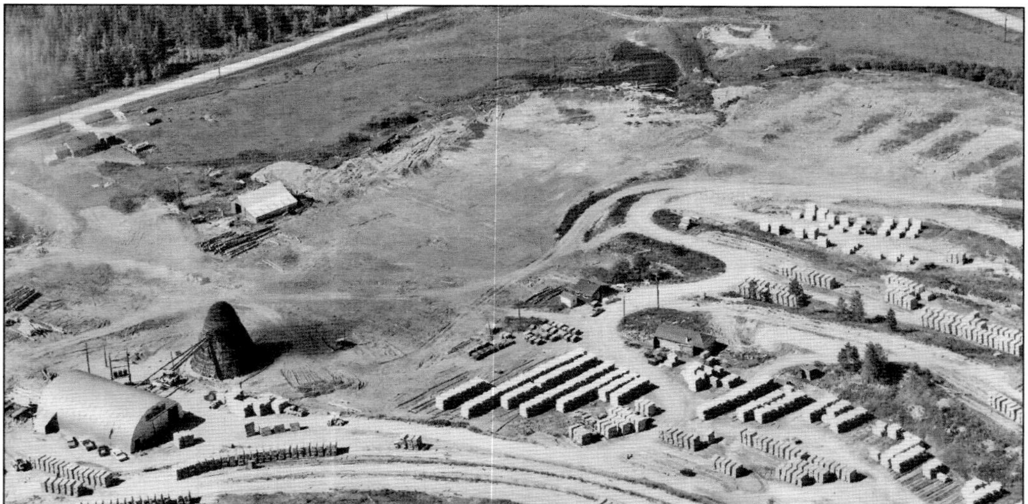

There were seven Osler brothers: Glen, Phil, Dale, Gerald, Wylie, Ervin, and John. They all grew up in the sawmill business. The six oldest went off to war; Glen did not return. In 1946, they resumed the business with their father, Earl, and after milling in several places around Trego and Fortine, they built the mill pictured here near the intersection of Mud Creek Road and Highway 93. The Plum Creek Timber Company bought them out in 1968 and eventually combined it with the Ksanka Mill at Fortine.

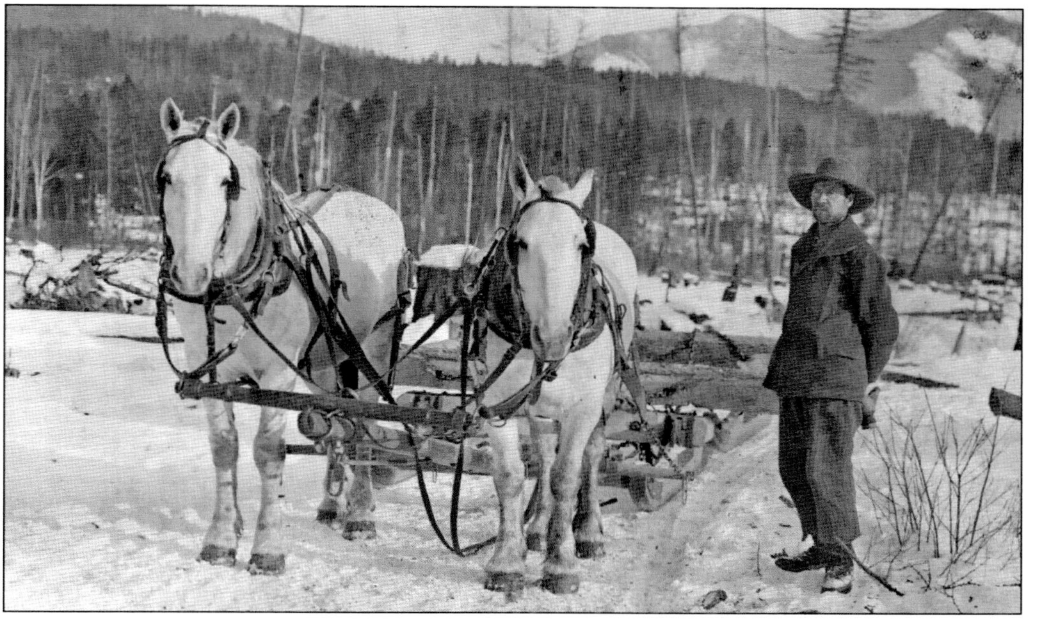

The Pluid brothers, Ernie, Frank, and Chet, came in to log for the Eureka Lumber Company in 1906. Before that they were largely responsible for creating Stumptown, now Whitefish. Ernie is pictured above in the country around Whitefish. The fourth generation of Pluids remains engaged in logging, though much of their equipment sits idle these days. Throughout the 1960s and 1970s, there may have been upwards of six Pluid trucks hauling logs around the Tobacco Valley at any given time. Below, a logging truck is hauling spruce logs from the Wigwam Basin in the 1960s, and it is possible that one of the Pluid boys is driving it.

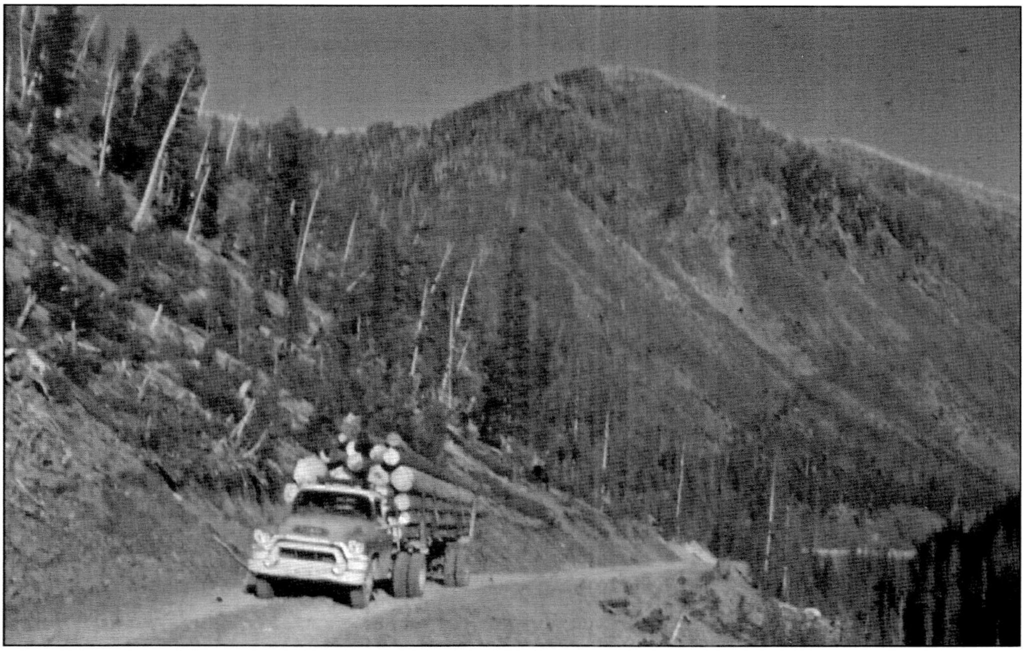

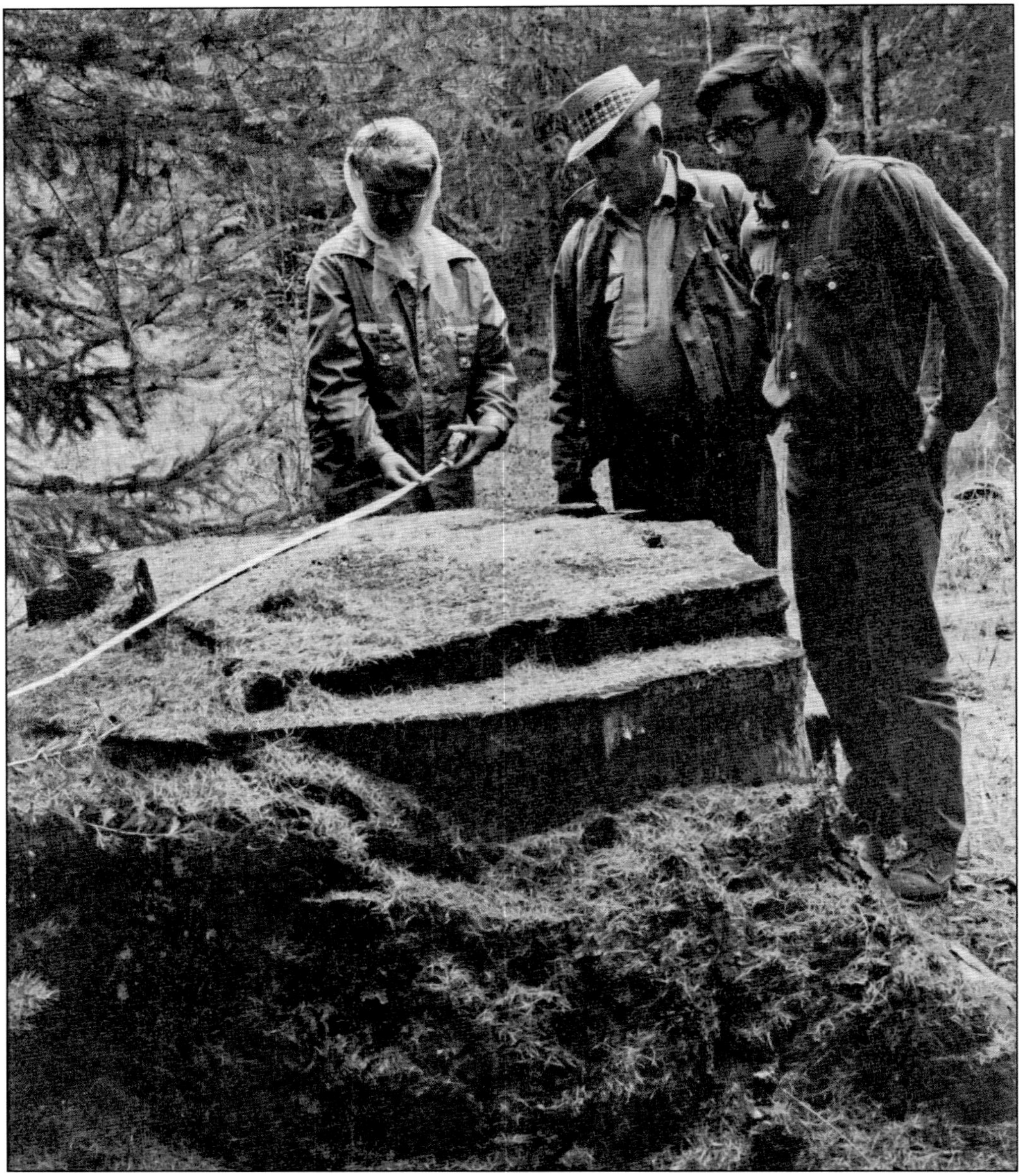

From the onset, the timber industry has had its ups and downs. Throughout the 20th century, it was the mainstay of the local economy, providing employment for sawyers, skidders, teamsters, and mill workers, to mention only the obvious. Such operations demanded much by way of supplies and services as well. As the century waned, so did the large lumber mills; one after another they have curtailed or closed their operations, leaving the valley's economic future in flux. Trees like the one that grew on the stump shown here passed from the scene long ago. There are only a few trees of this size that have survived (although they will return given a few hundred years). In the meantime, there will be arguments about how to make use of a renewable resource while providing future generations with the opportunity to know such giants.

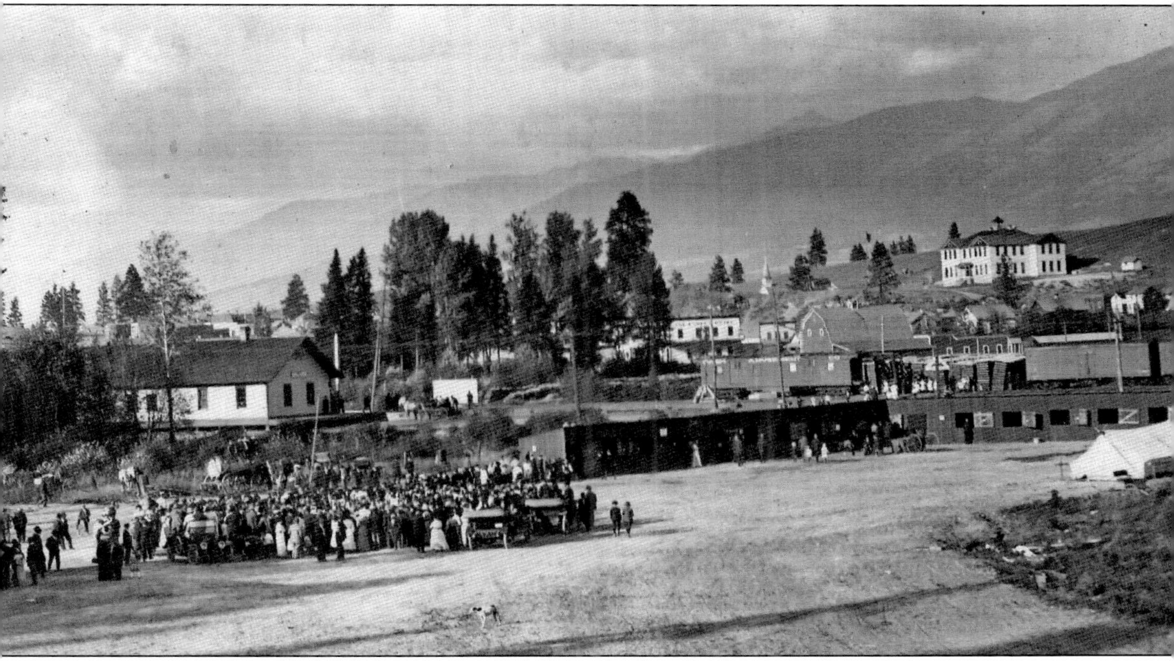

In April 1921, a group of Baltimore investors calling themselves the International Chemical Products Company announced plans to build a facility to extract mucic acid from the butts of tamarack trees left in the woods after logging. Mucic acid was a necessary product in the manufacture of baking soda. A site was chosen across the tracks from the Big Mill. That area also happened to be in use as the county fairgrounds, pictured above *c.* 1915, but a trade was made with Joe Peltier, and the grounds were moved to the present location. The Town of Eureka got on board and extended a water main 2,500 feet to the site. Work began in July, and the *Eureka Journal* reported: "With the arrival here of Dr. S. F. Acree, chemist for the International Chemical Products company, work on the construction of the new plant has been started in earnest. About 30 men and a half dozen teams have been put to work and everything possible will be done to expedite the work and rush the plant to completion."

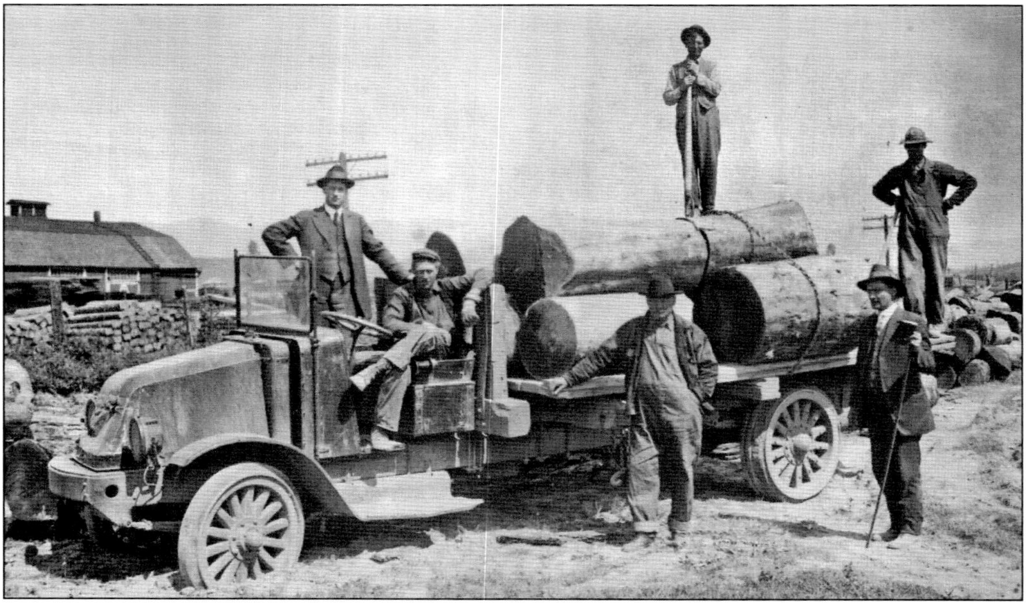

Meanwhile, contracts were let providing for the stockpiling of tamarack butts. Johnny Dahlberg and Claude McCully began hauling butts in with their trucks, the latter bringing 6 to 10 loads a day. The men on and around the truck (pictured above) are believed to be, from left to right, Frank LaMotte, Claude McCully, two unidentified workmen, Dr. S. F. Acree, and unidentified. At least one man used a wagon (shown below), most likely hauling butts that were relatively close to the plant site. LaMotte, the plant manager, wrote on the picture that he sent back home to his family: "A thousand ways to make money in Tobacco Valley." By June there were 500 cords of tamarack butts amassed.

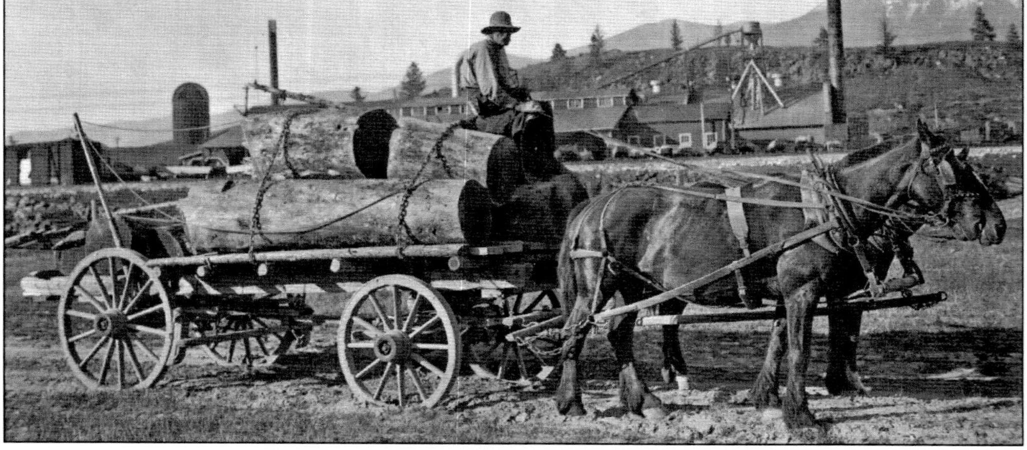

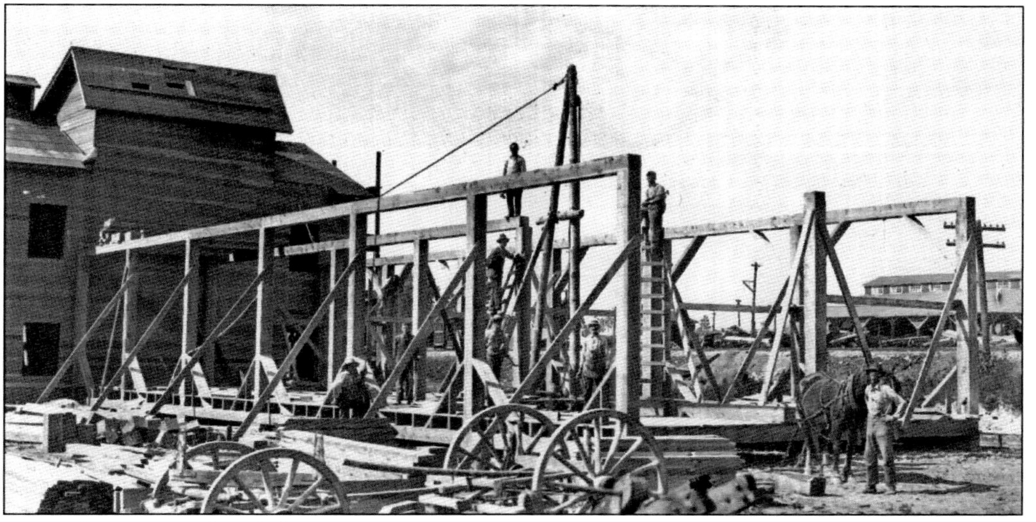

It was time now to build the plant. J. H. Gallinger, a local carpenter and former town cop, was placed in charge of the work—but not for long. The July 14, 1921, issue of the *Eureka Journal* carried the tragic story: "The people of Eureka and vicinity were shocked to learn of the sudden death of J. H. Gallinger, who died as the result of injury from a falling timber at the new plant of the International Chemical Products company. The work, under Mr. Gallinger's direction, had been making fine progress and the walls were rapidly being placed. About four o'clock a sharp gust of wind swept down over the old fair grounds. Mr. Gallinger had just been considering more substantial bracing for the wall. With his back turned, he was struck from the rear by a falling timber of 6x10 dimension and 24 feet long. At the time of his death he was sixty years old, although he had the appearance of one much younger and seemed to be in the prime of life."

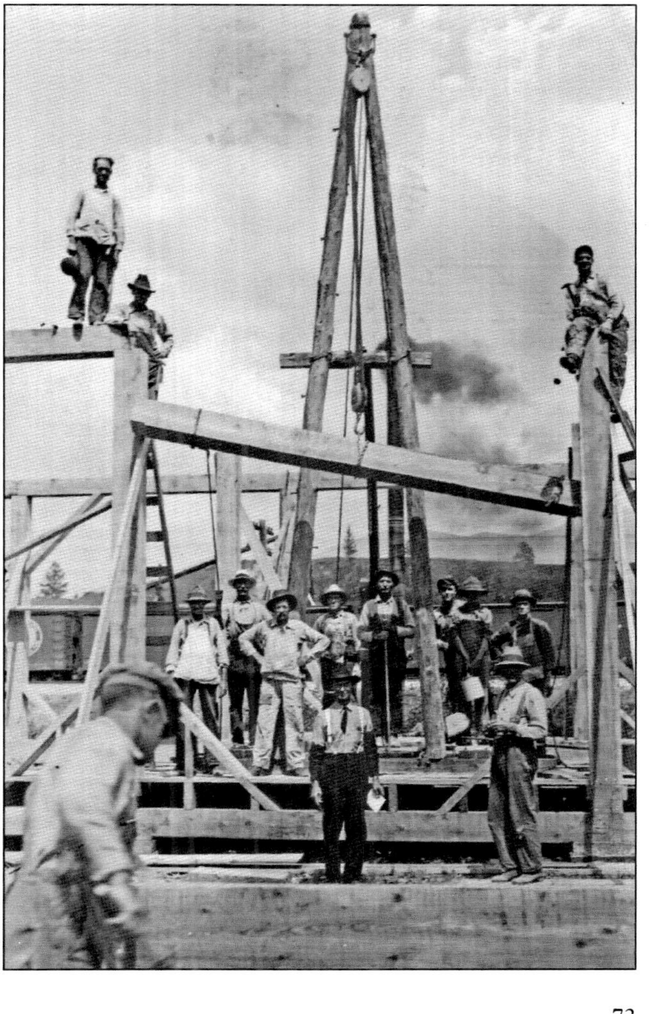

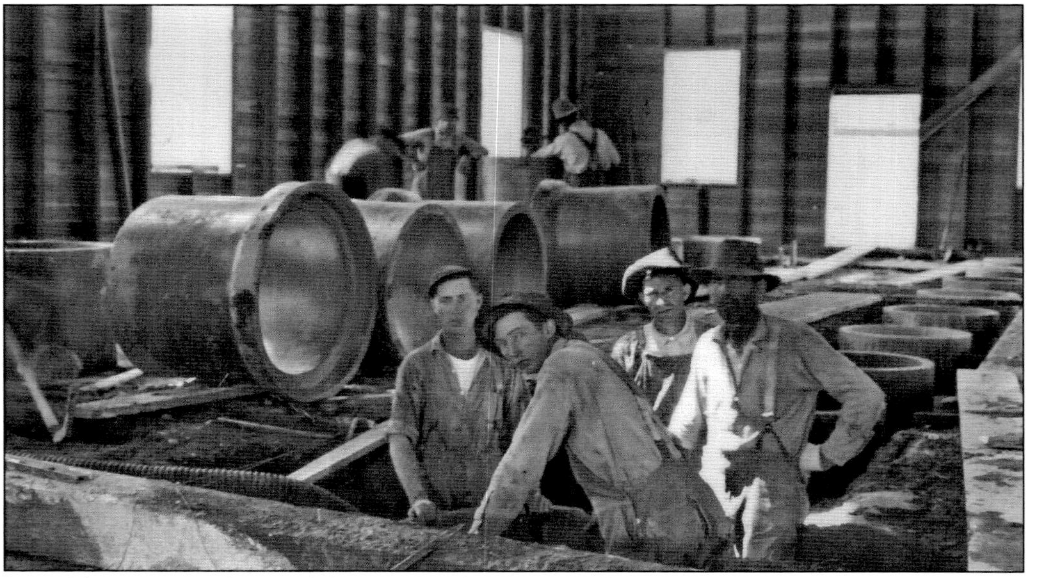

Jesse Oliveria came from California to replace J. H. Gallinger. Dr. John Bucher, having gained distinction during World War I for his work with explosives, came to oversee chemical controls. Large objects arrived by rail, and workmen began to assemble the innards of the plant even as the walls were still going up around them.

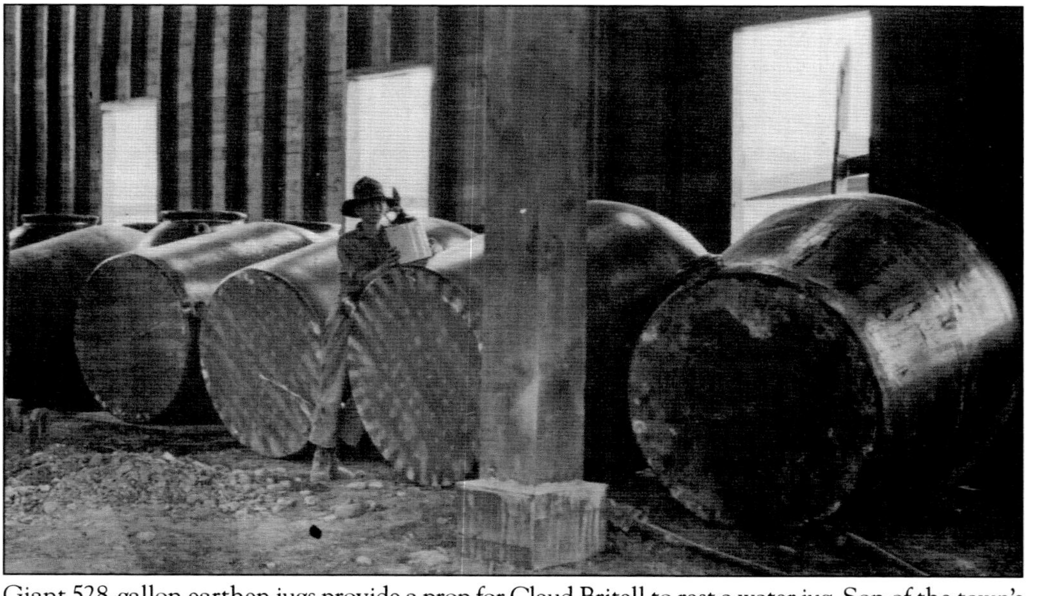

Giant 528-gallon earthen jugs provide a prop for Claud Britell to rest a water jug. Son of the town's family physician, Dr. Olie Britell, the lad was employed as water boy at the plant. As construction went on, night classes were held at the high school to train men to operate the plant, and the town was told that there would eventually be jobs for 1,500 men. High school students taking chemistry classes were offered summer jobs.

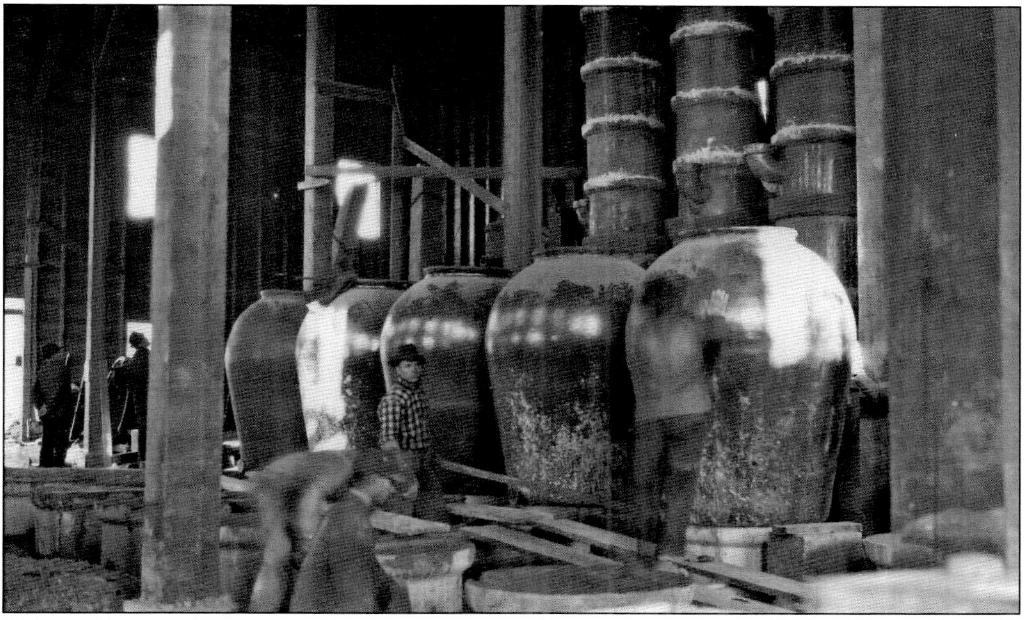

Perhaps the most fascinating object to arrive was a heavy iron retort, a still-like affair with 3-inch walls and weighing 8 tons. The *Eureka Journal* described events as they unfolded throughout 1921. "Unloading was quite a feat, successfully accomplished under the direction of C. E. Davis and hauled to the company's property on the Beutel truck . . . As the plant grows and equipment arrives, the people here are becoming more and more impressed with the magnitude of the enterprise and its activities are being watched with a keen and kindly interest."

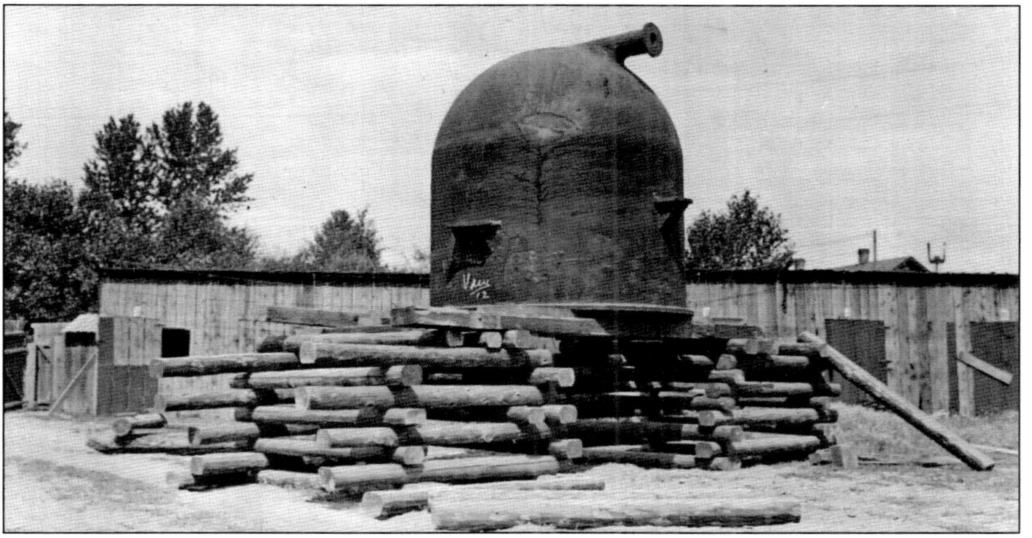

By March 1922, the plant came on line with two shifts of 40 men. At the end of that month, the company shipped its first carload of mucic acid. Over $300,000 had been spent so far, and the town was secure in the knowledge that another industry would shore up the local economy. The comfort was short-lived. In August 1923, a fire at the planer mill of the Eureka Lumber Company destroyed its capacity to generate electricity for the chemical plant. Without power, the operation was forced to shut down.

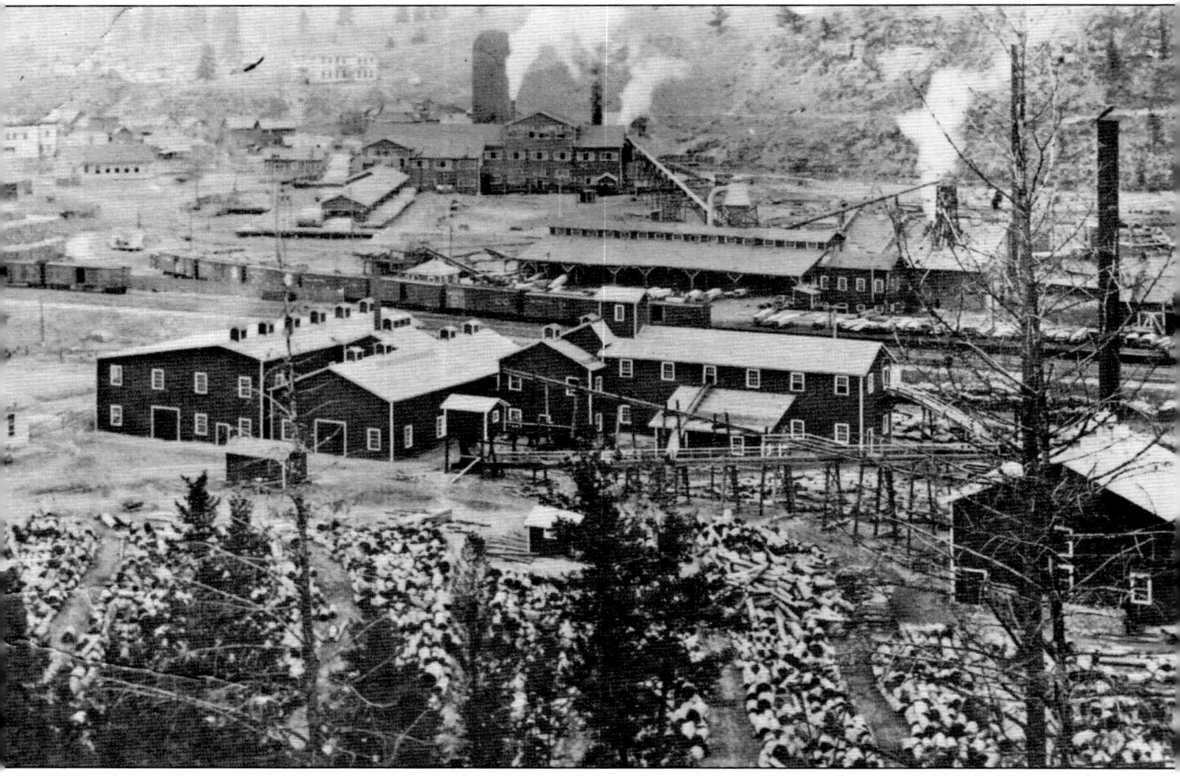

The chemical plant never turned into a paying proposition. It was on again/off again throughout its brief history. It peaked in 1923 and never recovered from the temporary loss of electricity, although power was restored in 1924. Ironically, the Big Mill and the chemical plant sank in the same boat. With the Tobacco Valley as a whole already on the skids, it is no surprise that the Farmers and Merchants Bank failed in 1925. One of the most common refrains to pop up in the *Eureka Journal* throughout the 1920s was that problems had been solved and the plant would soon be up and running. Eight months passed between the announcement that a plant would be built until the first product was shipped. It would be eight years before the hopeful pronouncements disappeared from the newspaper. The last one appeared on February 14, 1929: "Dr. S. F. Acree arrived on No. 1 . . . It is quite probable that he has a plan whereby the plant can be operated on a paying basis and a reorganization of the proposition under his direction is expected." The *Eureka Journal* ceased publication two months later.

Six

CHRISTMAS TREE CAPITAL OF THE WORLD

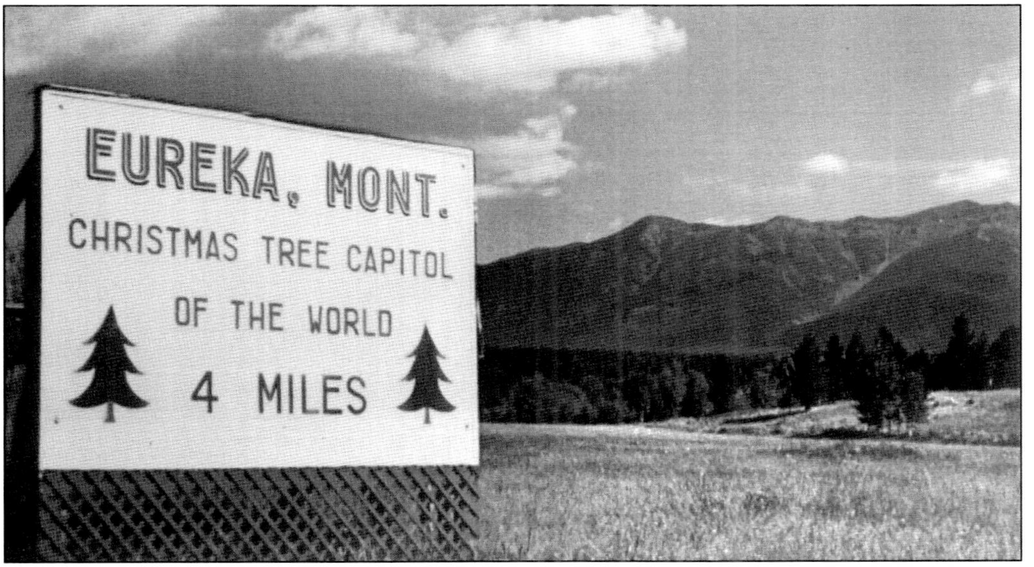

At the beginning of the 20th century, timber was cut from thousands of acres in the mountains and foothills of the Tobacco Valley. Nobody saw it coming, but when those stands regenerated, there was acre after acre of pretty little Douglas fir seedlings that grew naturally into perfect Christmas trees. Better yet, because of Tobacco Valley's geographic location, these trees got hit by hard frosts before it was time to harvest them, thus setting the needles. Tobacco Valley Christmas trees hold their needles long after those grown on plantations have littered the living room floor with theirs. By 1948, there were 300 freight cars loaded with 1.8 million trees leaving the valley. *Collier's* magazine published an article in December 1948 lending credence to the seemingly outlandish claim.

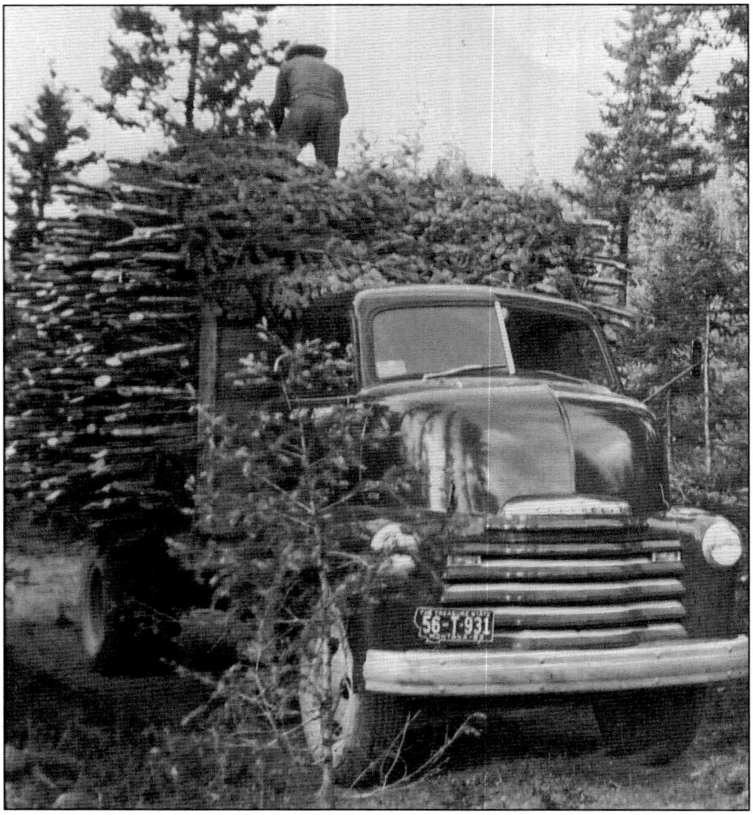

Christmas trees were typically cut with an ax, and more than a few tree cutters had scars on their feet and shins to prove it. When hauling, weight was less of a problem than volume. In 1935, Harold Butts (at left) piles them precariously high in preparation to haul them to a yard. Howard Butts (below, left) and Jim Butts are on their way to a waiting boxcar with trees that have been tied into bundles for shipping. It was 1942 and Howard Butts, who does not appear to be dressed for the occasion, died fighting in World War II. (Both, courtesy of Darris Flanagan.)

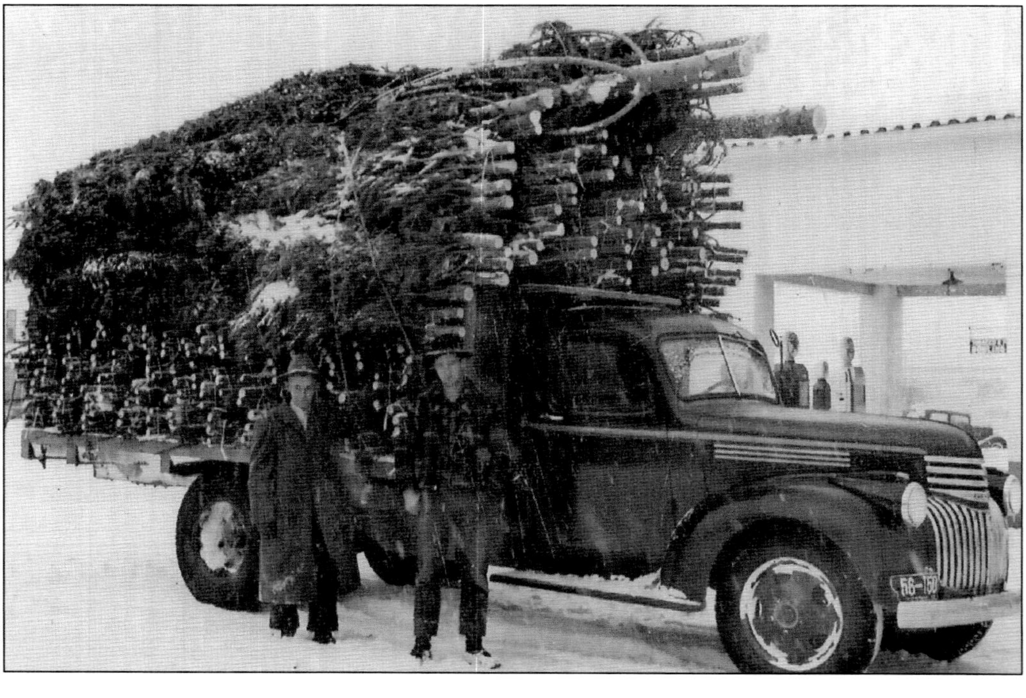

Couples from around the valley went to work cutting and hauling Christmas trees each fall. Husbands commonly cut while their wives and children dragged the trees. Once in the yard, the trees had to be graded and sized. Elsie Helms worked in the Hofert yard, which was located along the Great Northern tracks behind the Peltier Oil Company.

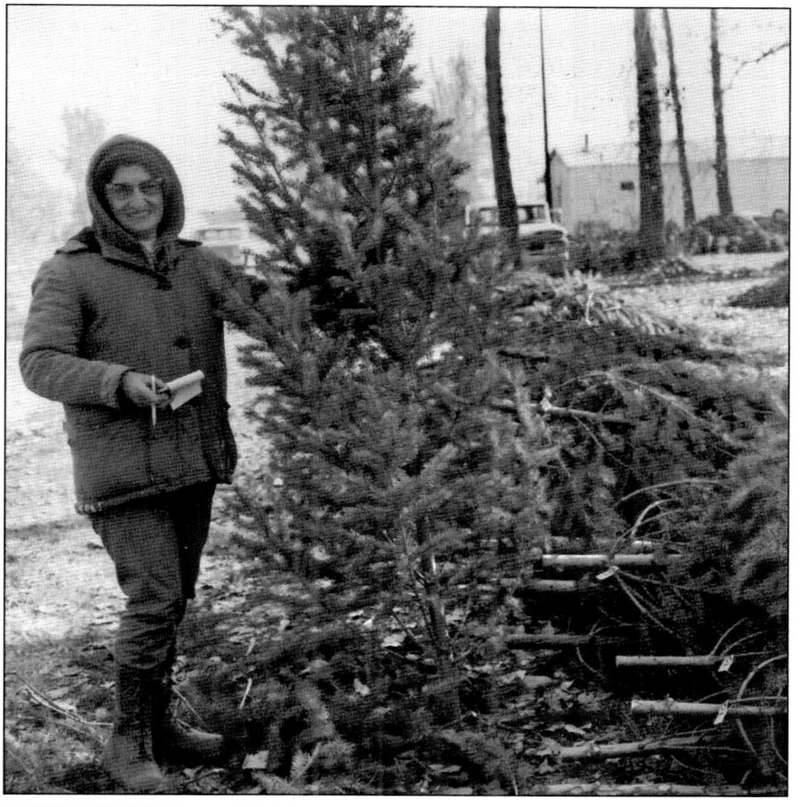

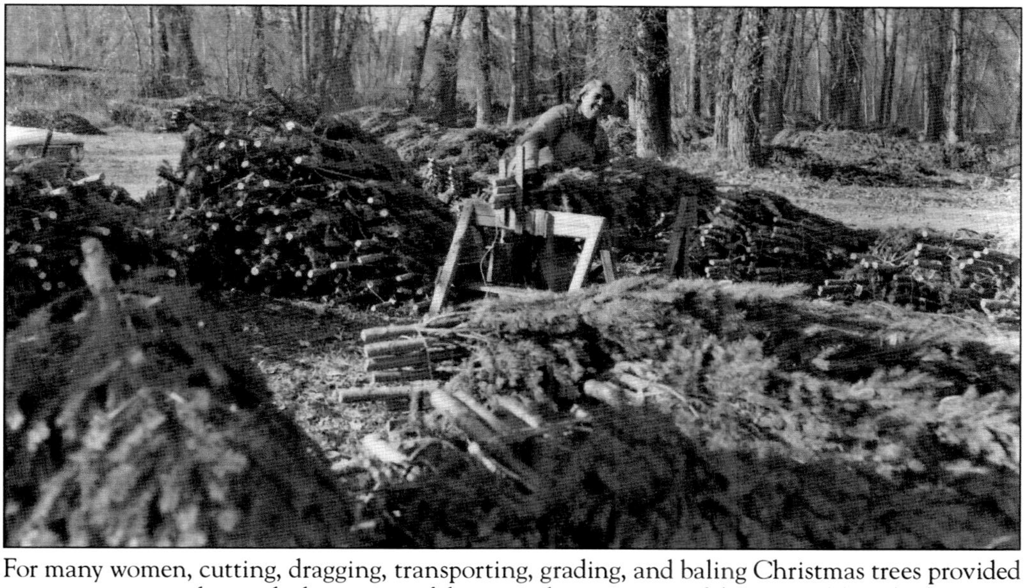

For many women, cutting, dragging, transporting, grading, and baling Christmas trees provided opportunity to work outside during one of the most pleasant times of the year. Although plantation and artificial trees have made deep inroads in the wild Christmas tree market, many women are still employed in the fall making wreaths and evergreen roping. Here champion baler Lois Workman, with a smile on her face, ties trees at the Hofert yard in the 1950s.

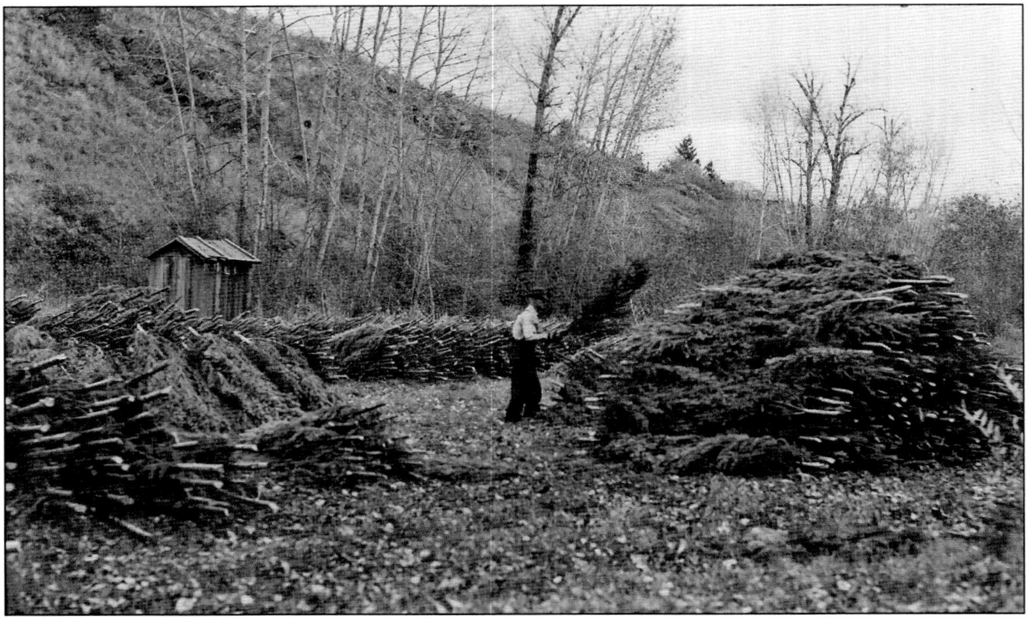

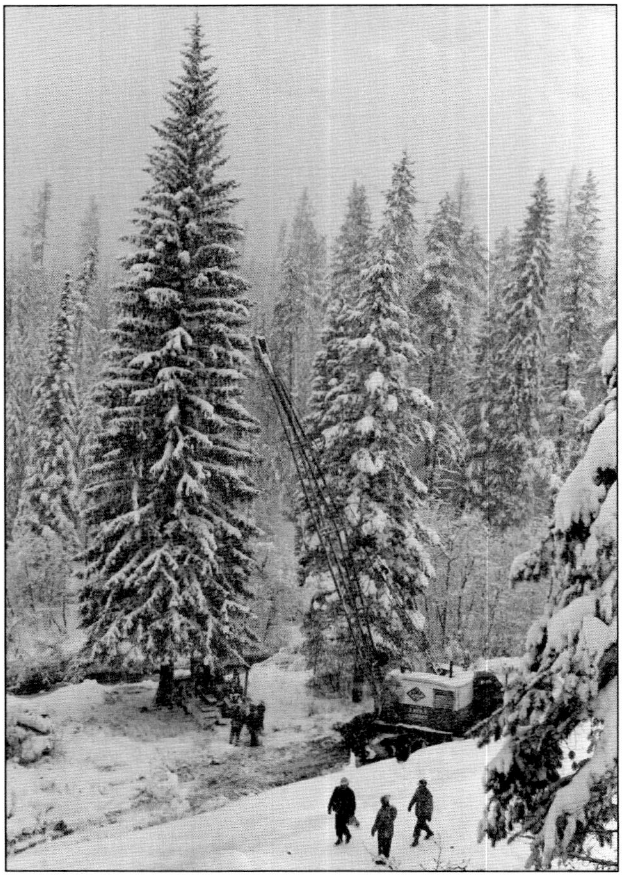

Christmas tree harvesting remained important to the economy of Tobacco Valley for the better part of 40 years. By the 1970s, much of the stumpage had grown into harvestable timber. Besides, plantation and artificial Christmas trees had eroded demand for wild trees, which were not always perfect. Through a number of those years, particularly in the 1940s, Slim Anderson managed the Hofert Christmas tree yard.

In 1958, Lincoln County was chosen for the honor of providing the national Christmas tree. It was harvested from the Kootenai National Forest near Libby. Here powerful machines used a gentle touch to get this 100-foot tree on the ground and then onto a truck for the cross-country push to Washington, D.C.

Seven

UNCLE SAM PLAYED A HAND

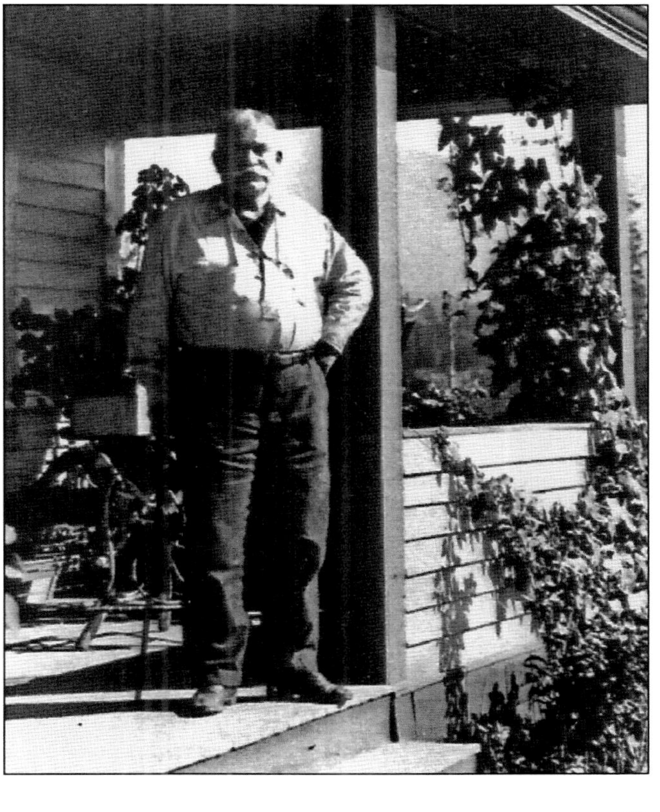

Fred Herrig was one of a kind. He arrived in the United States aged 15 and was soon packing, trapping, and living the cowboy life in the northern plains. In 1893, he went to work at Teddy Roosevelt's Elkhorn Ranch in South Dakota. After about five years, he returned to Montana. He had not been here long when Colonel Roosevelt sent a telegram asking Herrig to join him for an adventure in Cuba. In 1900, Herrig went to work for what would ultimately become the U.S. Forest Service. He was the first ranger at Ant Flat, assuming duty at that lonely outpost in 1903. He pursued the affections of Freida Wilke, a widow with five young boys. Being just what she needed, they married and had one son of their own. Herrig retired in 1927 but never left the Trego/Fortine area.

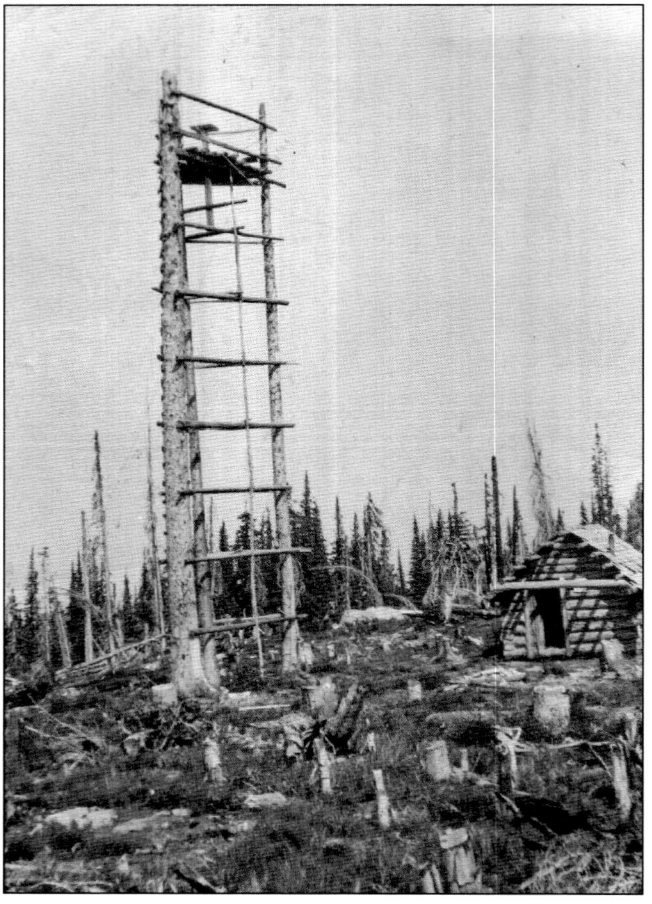

Forest fires raged throughout the inland northwest in 1910, devastating vast stands of timber. The U.S. Forest Service set about fighting fire as if it were the devil itself. It took until after World War I for them to come up to an effective level of efficiency, due in large part to the men and technology that came out of the war. There were men to be put to work, and in 1920, they cleared off the top of Pinkham Mountain, except for three trees. Then they built Pinkham Mountain's first lookout tower (at left). The men who manned the lookouts were trained to hike to the fire and, using basic tools, extinguish it. Should their efforts fail, a larger fire would likely develop, which required men, supplies, and a camp. That is when men like Frank Marston (below) became critical to the effort. Here, in August 1926, he is packing supplies to a camp in the aftermath of a fire that swept through Stryker.

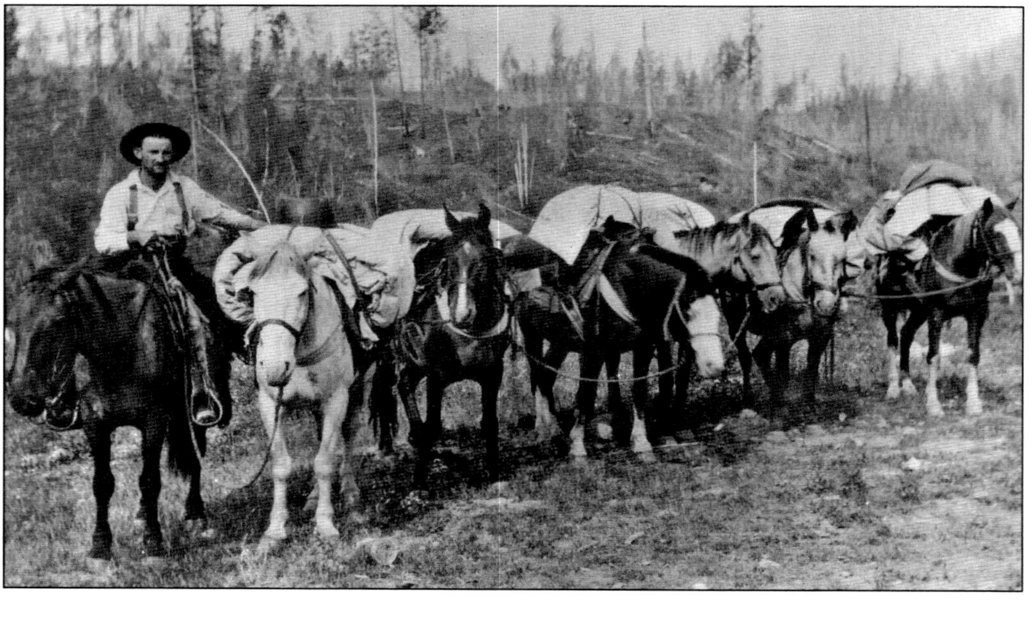

Ross "Shorty" Young, born in 1873, arrived in northwest Montana as a young man. He chose the rugged life, working at trapping, prospecting, and eventually for the U.S. Forest Service. Late in his career he was posted on Roberts Lookout, a short distance from Fortine. Pete Klinke remembers the Fortine boys harvesting fresh produce from their parents' gardens and taking it up to Shorty, who would treat them to rice pudding in return. Shorty also let them burn up lots of .22 ammunition when they came to visit. Shorty was an accomplished gunsmith capable of making his own telescopic sight. He died in 1945 and is buried at the Fortine Cemetery.

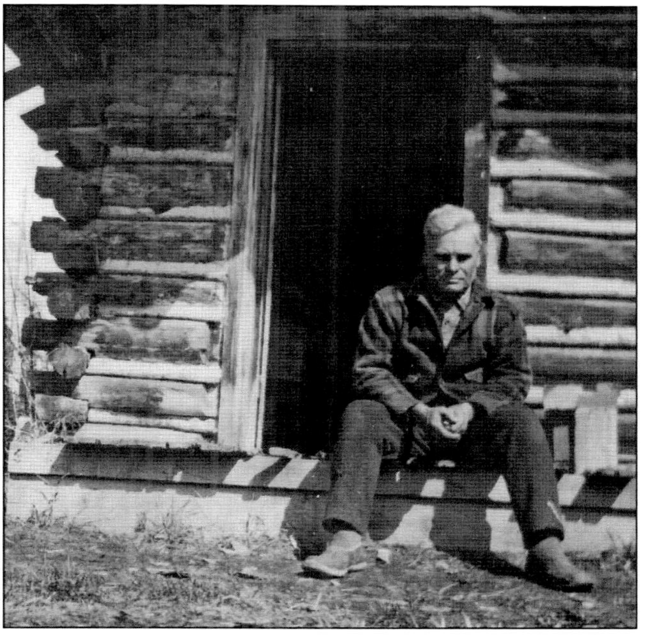

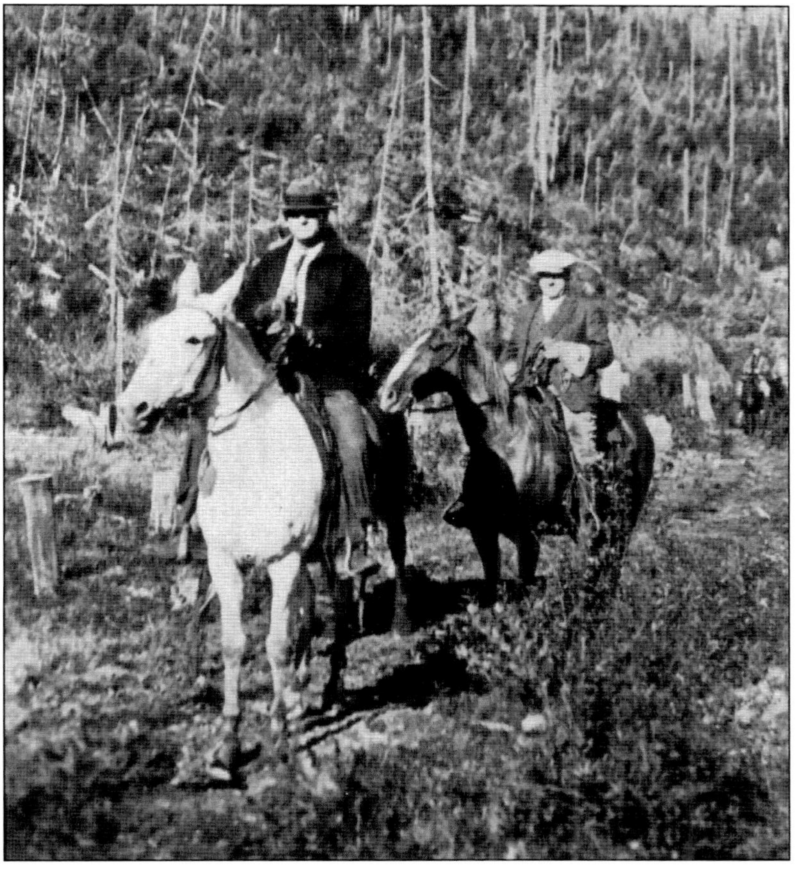

Early forest rangers put in a great deal of saddle time. Ray Woesner, seen here in front, went to work for the U.S. Forest Service in 1909, and cut his teeth on the fires of 1910, where he was assigned to the Point of Rocks Ranger Station, at that time part of the Blackfoot National Forest. He spent eight years at the Bunch Grass Ranger Station and several at Ant Flat. The other rider is unidentified.

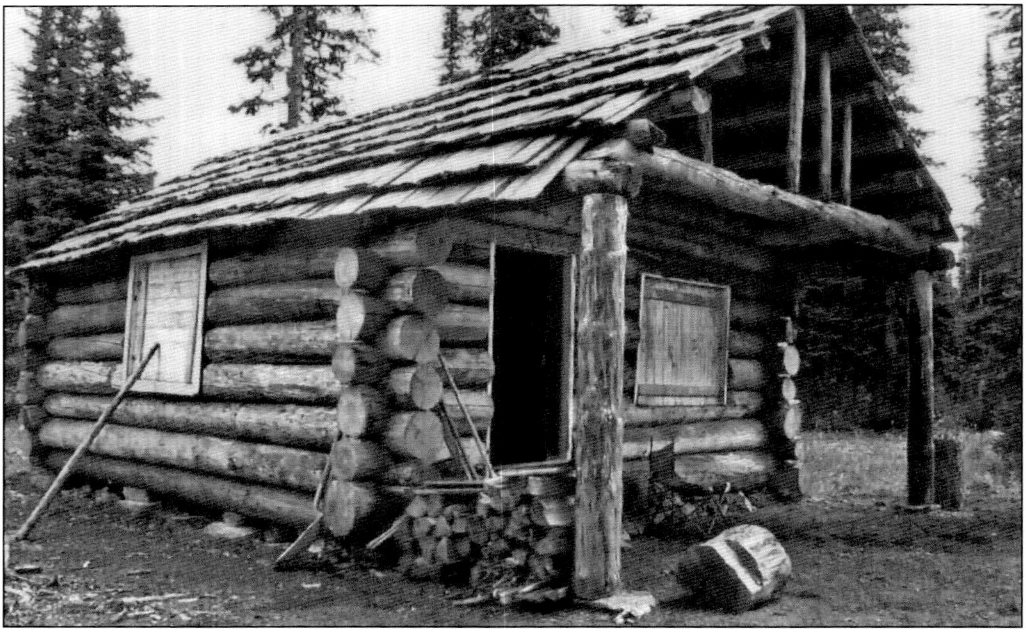

Having a need for a stopover for the U.S. Border Patrol officers who traveled by horseback between the North Fork and Roosville, a cabin was built in the Wolverine Basin. Wolverine Cabin was erected in 1944 with the capable guidance of Boots Coombs. The cabin remains popular with hikers and snowmobile enthusiasts, and even Border Patrol agents visit there more often these days.

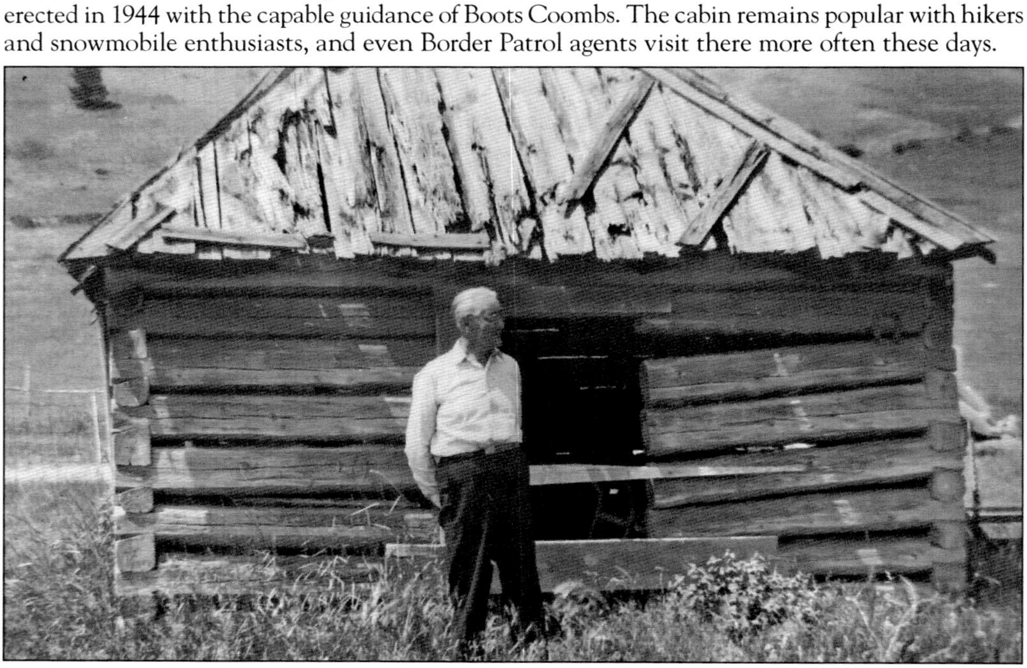

Jim Sinclair was born in Eureka, but ended up a Canadian, working for their customs and immigration for 20 years, retiring in 1961. He worked the Roosville crossing, which was gated at night until the 1980s. He sometimes went out and opened it to allow Eurekans who had attended a dance back across the line. Sinclair is seen here inspecting the first Canadian Customs building at Roosville, abandoned in 1914. Sinclair Creek is named after his father.

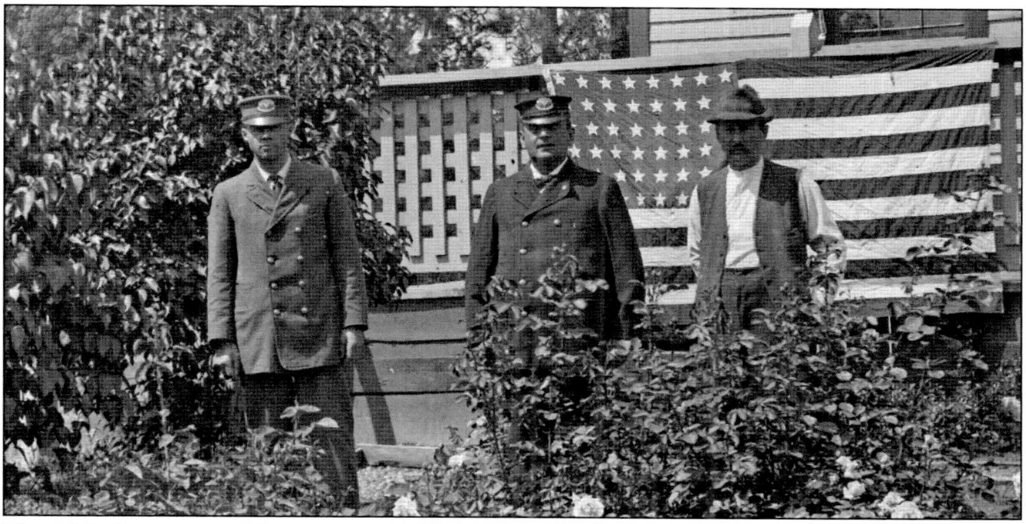

The U.S. Customs and Immigration office was originally located at Gateway. Pictured here in 1914, the officers are, from left to right, Art Fleming, J. E. Brice, and Bill Hoover. Fleming was the superintendent during the Prohibition era. Between booze-laden coal trains crossing at Gateway, rumrunner boats floating down the Kootenai River, and bootleggers with their heavily loaded Hudsons crossing at Roosville, he was kept on his toes.

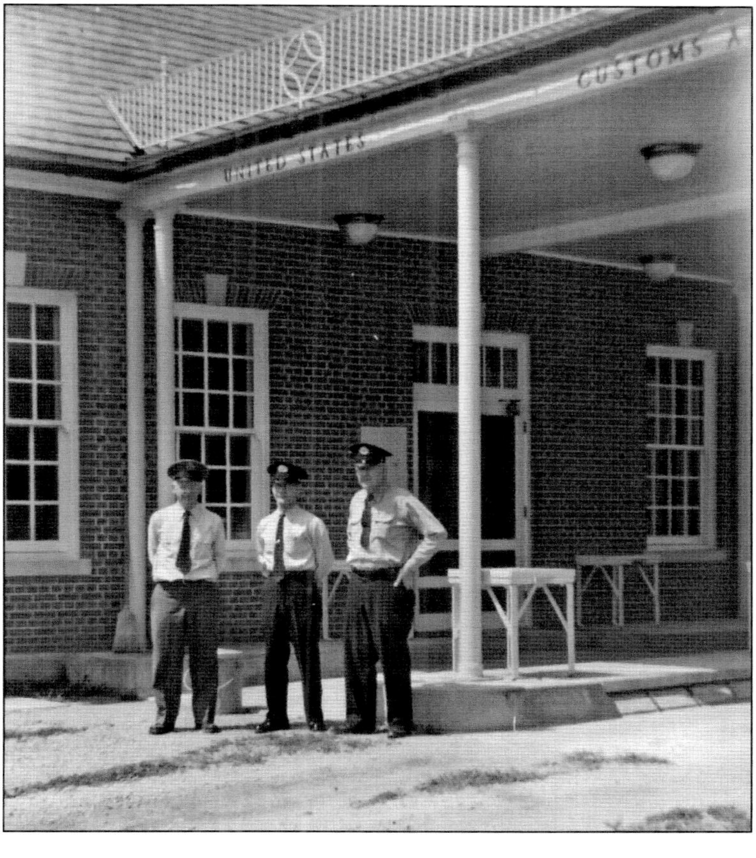

In 1957, it was a small matter to enter the United States, but there were no terrorists, bootleggers, or BC Bud with which to contend. Only a handful of officers were needed to man the crossing. Locked at night, the gate was opened early enough in the morning to allow Canadian students attending school in Eureka through to catch the bus. From left to right are William Howe, Hugh Biggar, and Tom Weatherly.

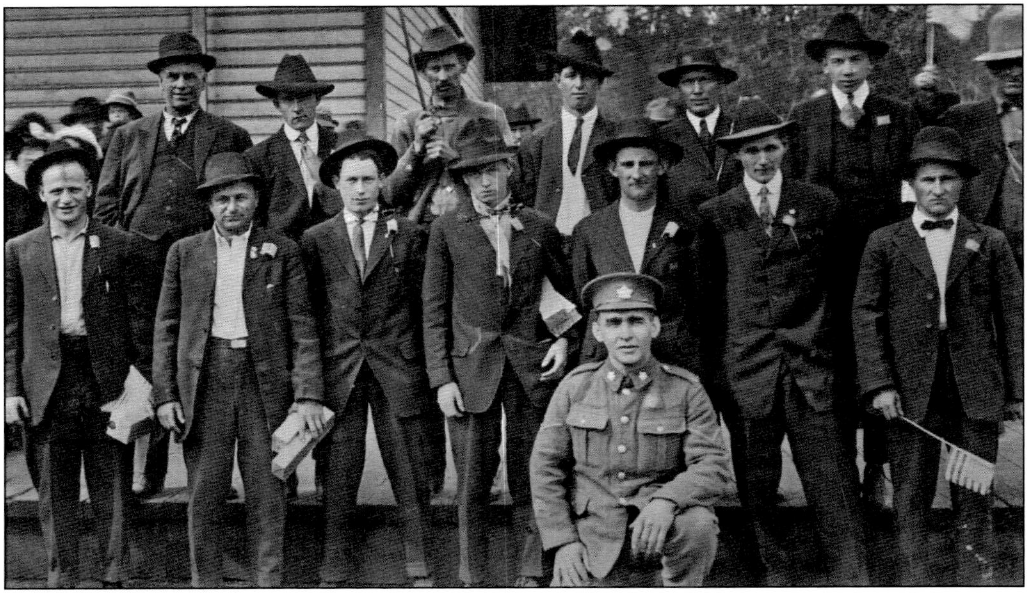

There was another way that the government provided employment. When both world wars fired up, men from the Tobacco Valley were quick to sign up. Above, inductees are off to fight the Great War in May 1918. (It was not called World War I until World War II came along.) Some of the men are holding two packages, one of which is probably cigarettes. Each man is also wearing a flag on his lapel. From left to right are (first row, kneeling) unidentified; (second row) four unidentified, Guy Brock, unidentified, and Roy Brock; (third row) unidentified, William Baker, and five unidentified. Twenty odd years later, Tobacco Valley residents were at it again as well-wishing friends and anxious family members went to the depot to see the boys off (shown below). Fathers and sons from left to right in 1942 are Maurice and Xennie Bernhard, Clarence and George "Shorty" Rich, and Glen Roose Sr. and Jr. (Below, courtesy of Juanita Rich Butts.)

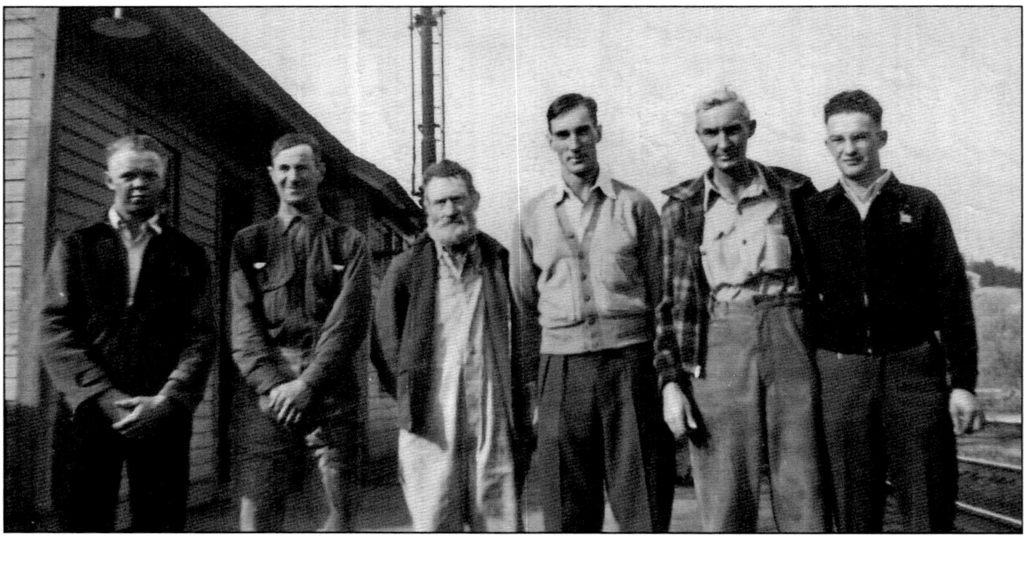

Eight

The Basics
Churches and Schools

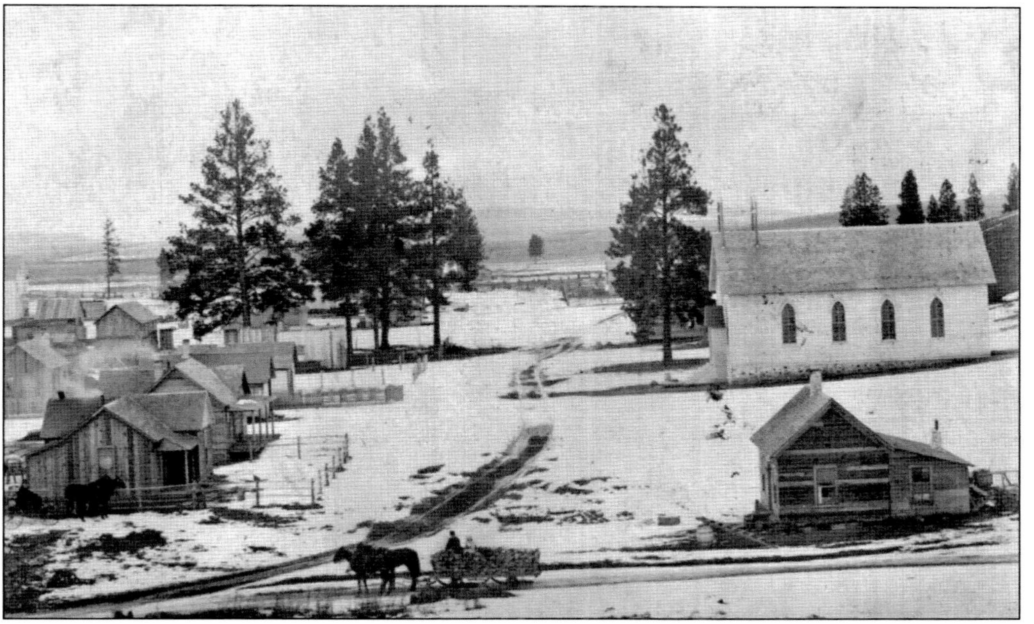

The Catholics were the first denomination on the Tobacco Plains; a mission was built for the natives in the late 1850s. Roughly 50 years later, construction began on Second Avenue East for the first Catholic church in Eureka. Pictured here in about 1911, the photograph shows a belfry under construction. January 1912 was a good month for church bells in Eureka with both the Baptist and Catholic bells going into action. A new church, presently in use, was completed in 1968. The old church was moved with the intent of creating some apartments but ended up being razed.

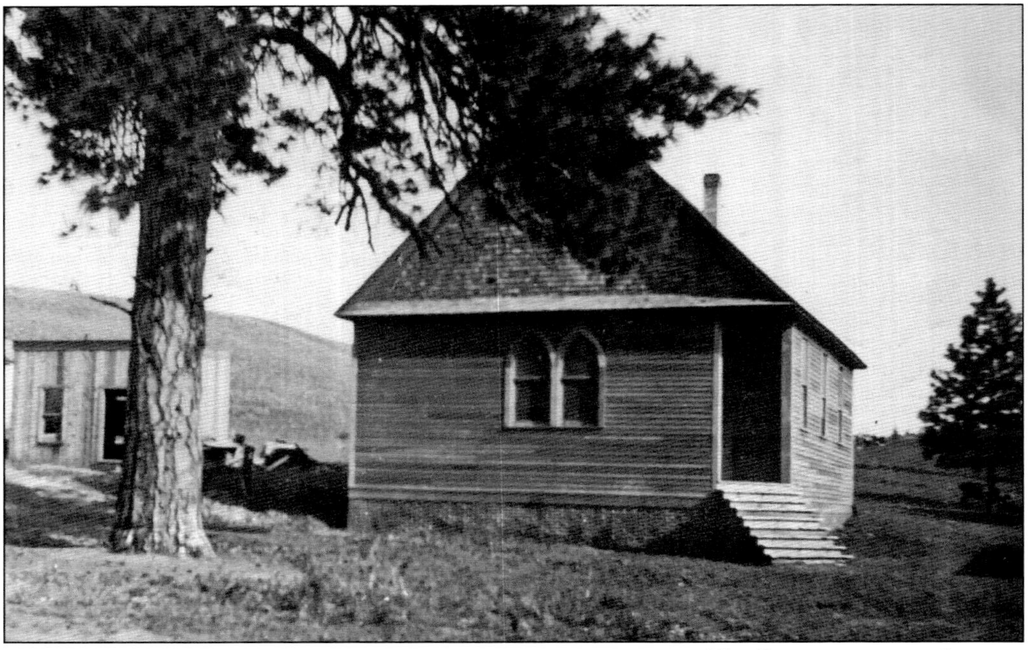

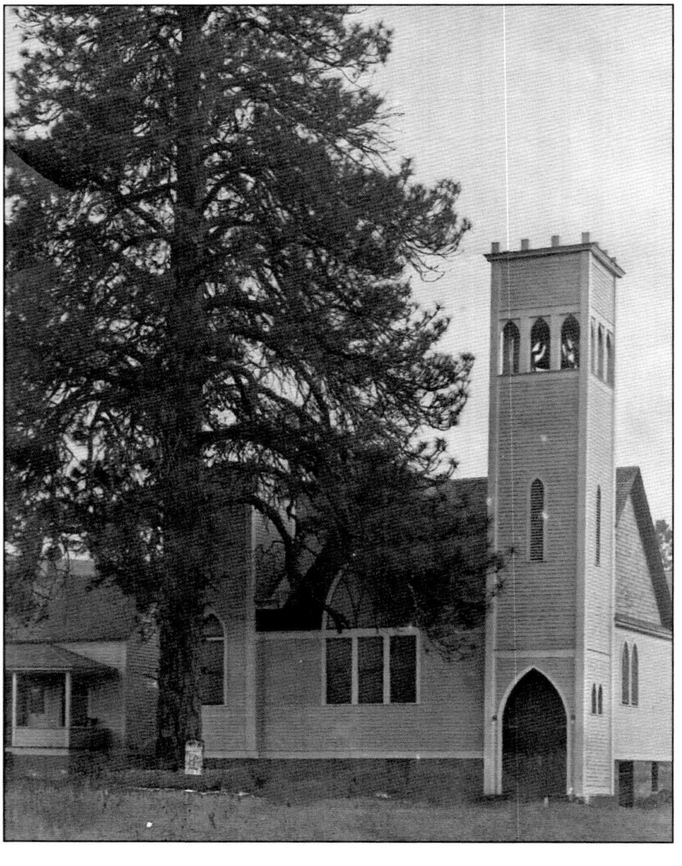

The Baptists organized in 1906 and promptly built a chapel on Third Street East (pictured above). By January 1912, they had built a larger church that surrounded the original chapel (shown at left). The church survives today as the Kootenai Fellowship. The Baptists and Catholics both installed their bells in January 1912. At 1,800 pounds, the Baptist bell weighed twice as much as the Catholic one and pealed two weeks earlier. It cost $300, and Jim Hill of the Great Northern transported it from Ohio free of charge. The *Eureka Journal* reported: "When erected the church will have a bell of which it can feel justly proud and which can be heard for miles around." The Baptists built a new church in Midvale in 1975, but they took their bell with them, and it continues to summon the faithful to this day.

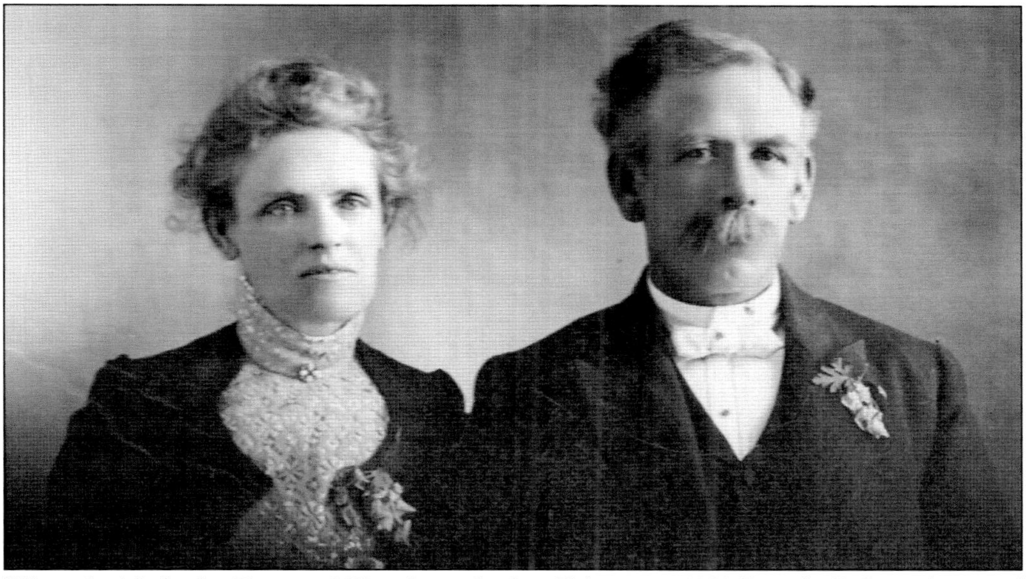

When the Methodist Episcopal Church was built at Tobacco in 1901, Rev. A. C. Snow (pictured above with his wife) came to serve as pastor. One of his first official acts was to marry Frank Baney and Eva Mills. The people also built a parsonage, which was moved to Eureka in 1904, for Snow and his wife. They placed it beside the newly constructed Methodist Episcopal Church, now the Creative Arts Center, where it remains to this day.

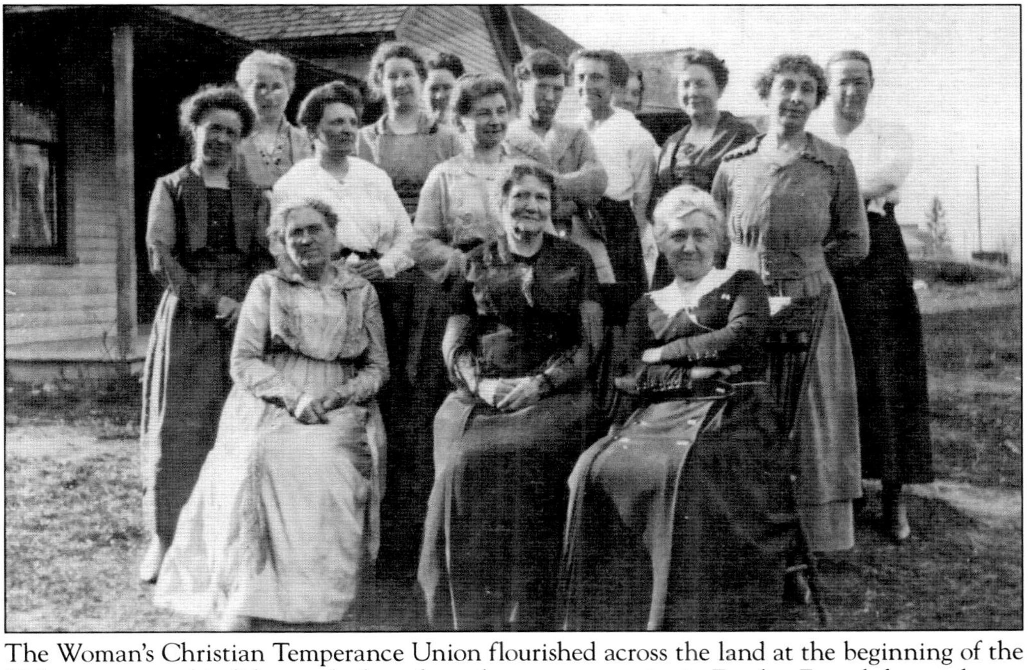

The Woman's Christian Temperance Union flourished across the land at the beginning of the 20th century, and it did not take long for a chapter to organize in Eureka. From left to right are (sitting) Anna Harvey, unidentified, and Mary Campbell, known by all as Aunt Mary; (standing) Cora Sampson, Lina Clark, three unidentified, Marie Mosby, unidentified, Mrs. Charles Rogers, two unidentified, Lillian Albee, and Aliph Drake.

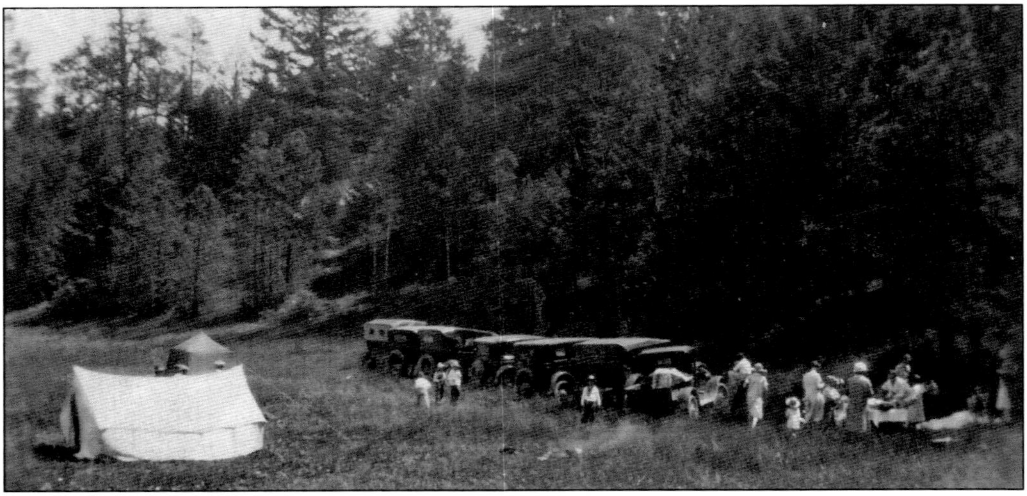

This photograph is titled "Sunday school picnic at Tetrault Lake, 1927." The lake was a favorite bathing spot, which is the word they used in 1927 for swimming. It later became known as Carpenter Lake because the Carpenter family lived around it. In recent years, though, the name was changed back to Tetrault. At left are a tent and a cabana where bathers could change their clothes in privacy.

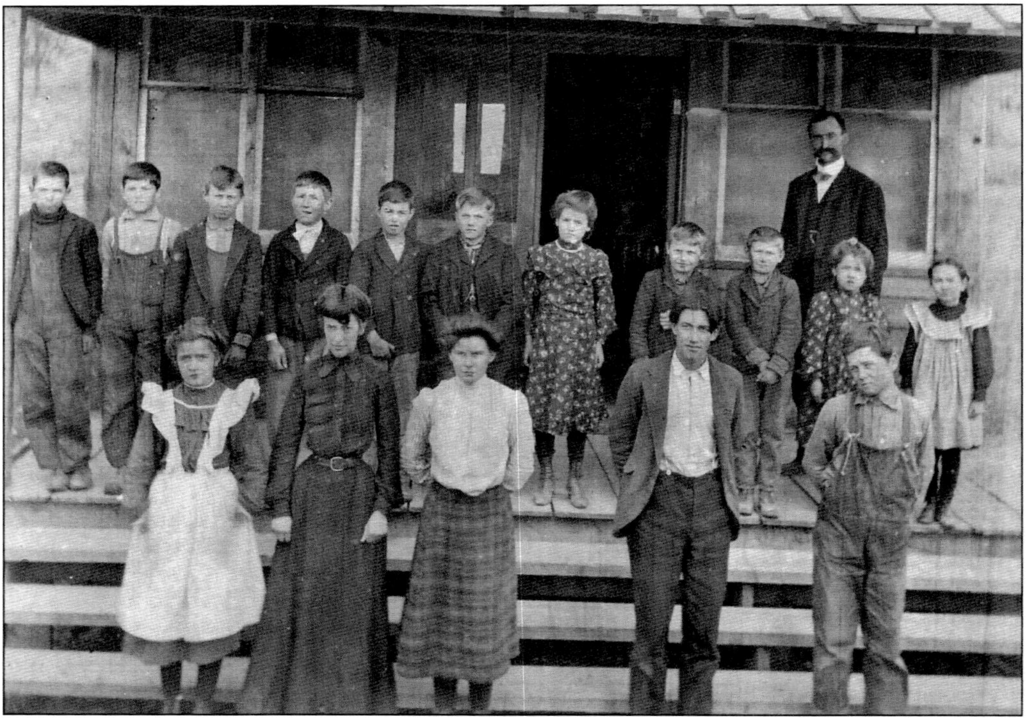

Mary Carpenter came to the Tobacco Plains in 1901 with six sons and one daughter. All of them took up homesteads, mostly around Tetrault Lake, which explains how the lake came to be known as Carpenter Lake for many years. One of her sons, Sam, a schoolteacher, was hired to teach the Tobacco Valley's first school at Gateway. A year or so later, he came to teach in Eureka. That class is pictured here.

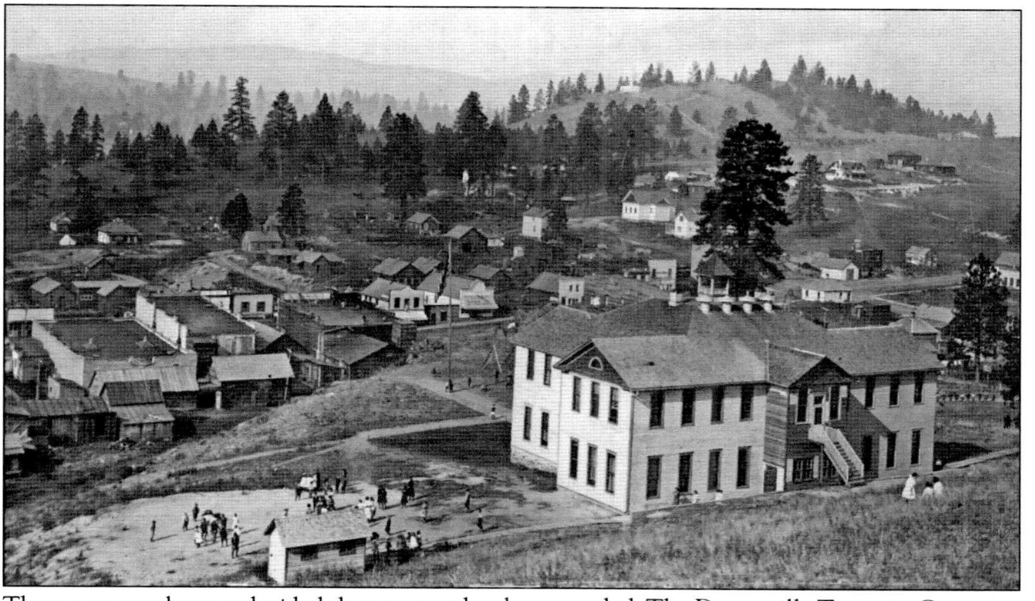

The townspeople soon decided that a new school was needed. The Deweyville Townsite Company donated a commanding spot just east of downtown. On January 16, 1904, the *Tobacco Plains Journal* noted, "A movement was started this week to establish a public school at this place. We can't have too many schools and like evidences of civilization."

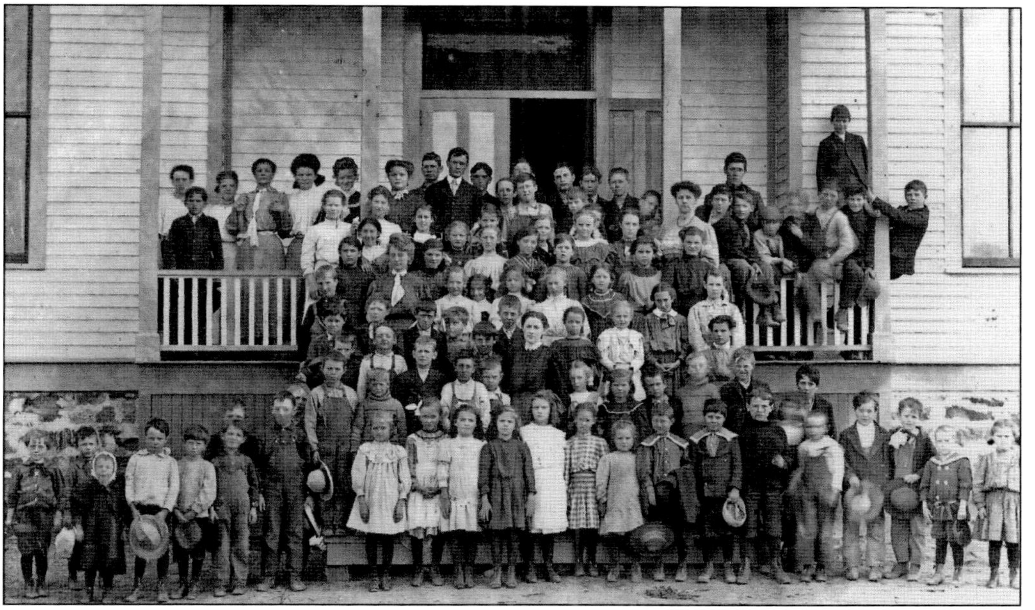

The Eureka Grade School was the town's most recognizable landmark from 1904 to 1923. Students are pictured here in about 1910. When the Roosevelt School was built in 1921, this building was turned into apartments. It burned to the ground in the wee hours of November 13, 1923. There was a birthday party, and some boys may have dropped a cigarette. Others theorized a spark from a stove that was moved into a hall to accommodate dancing was the cause.

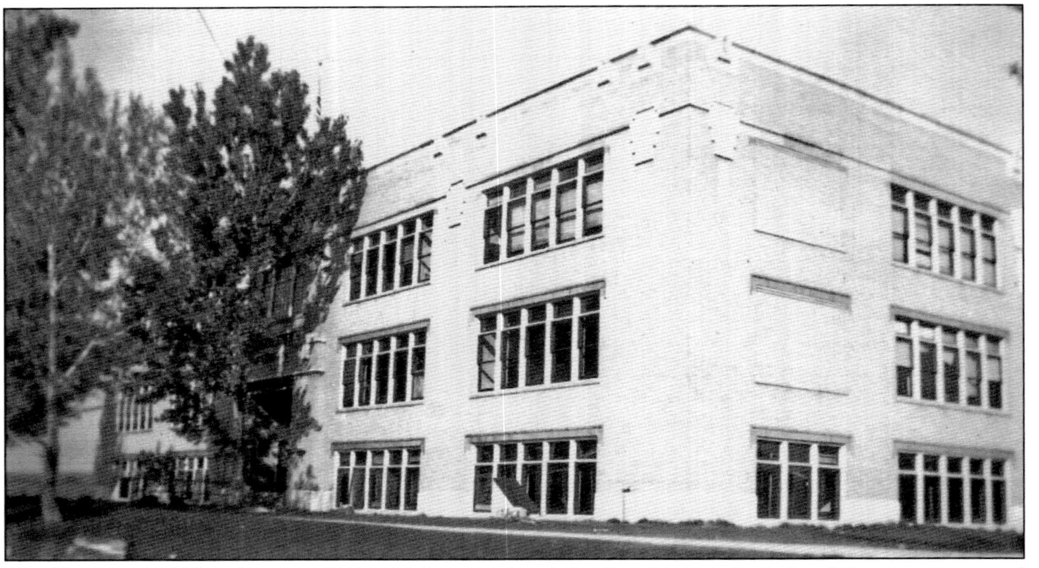

The Roosevelt School was built in 1921 to replace the Eureka Grade School. It was so named in honor of Teddy Roosevelt, and because the newly built, federally funded highway, also with Roosevelt's name, passed near it. The sturdy brick edifice saw many students pass through its portals during the next 82 years. The venerable school building, deemed unsafe in 2003, was razed to make room for the new high school.

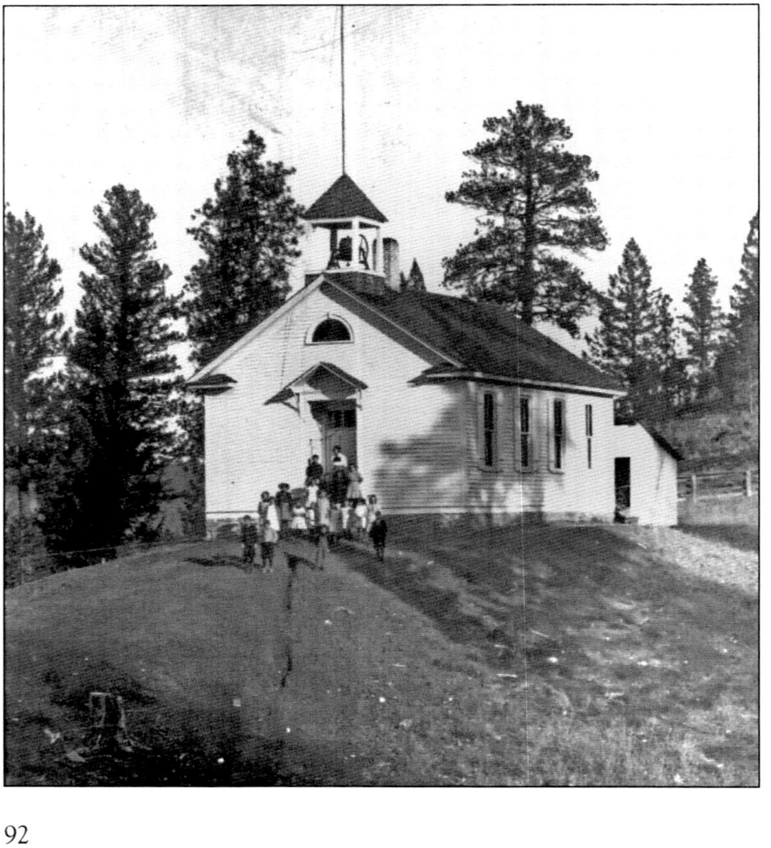

The Rexford School was built in 1912 on a bench above town. To raise money for an organ and a clock, the school decided to hold a dance and auction off supper boxes. It so happened that it coincided with an election campaign, and several Democratic candidates attended to support the school. Frank Baney was the auctioneer and, applying the gavel with a heavy hand, raised nearly $100 for the school—enough to buy the organ and clock.

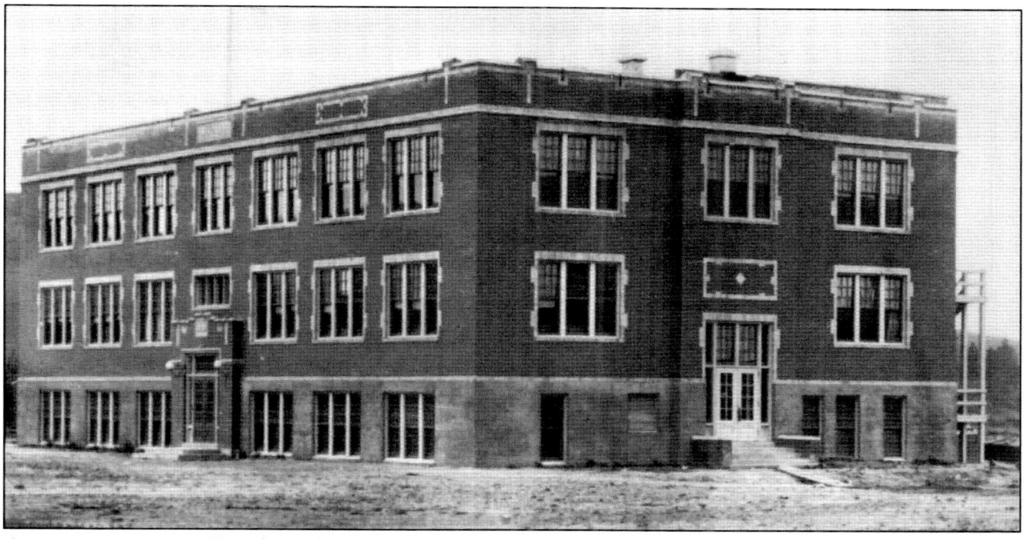

As a concession to Eureka, after a bitter battle for the county seat, the commissioners chose to build a high school in the Tobacco Valley. Lincoln County High School was ready for occupation by February 1919. That October, the Whitefish Booster Club visited Eureka and the new school. The *Eureka Journal* reported: "This tour terminated with a call at the new Lincoln County high school . . . Every advantage is offered young men and women to obtain a complete and practical education. A gymnasium contributes to its modernity, providing also shower baths for both sexes after basket ball and other games and exercises. There is also a motion picture machine, the younger generation getting good, clean, wholesome entertainment and instruction from this source at five cents per. This is the only county high school in the state located other than at the county seat."

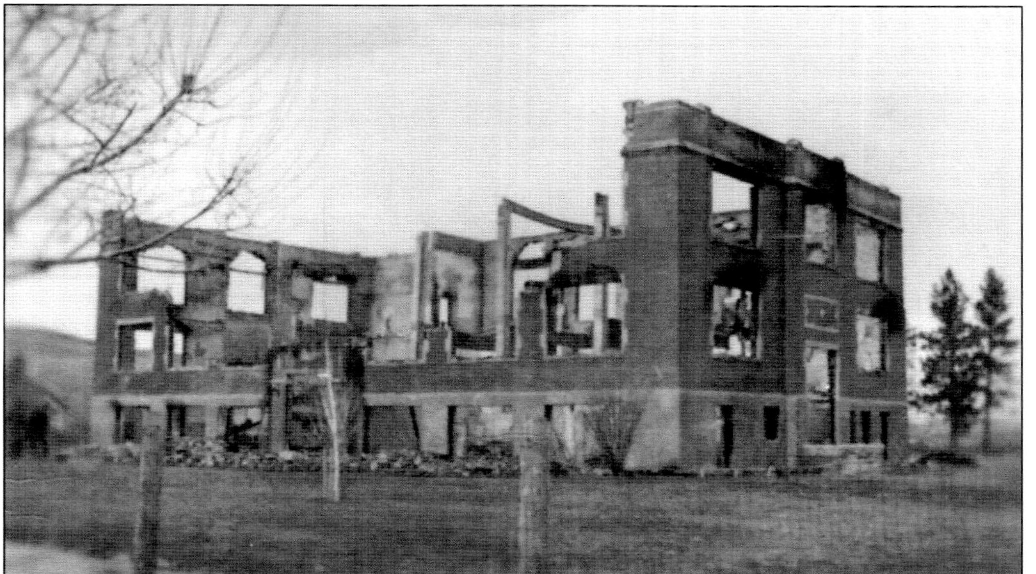

One cold winter night, 16 years after its completion, Lincoln County High School was destroyed by fire. A new building was erected in the same spot, graduating its first class in 1937. That building is presently in use as Eureka Junior High School.

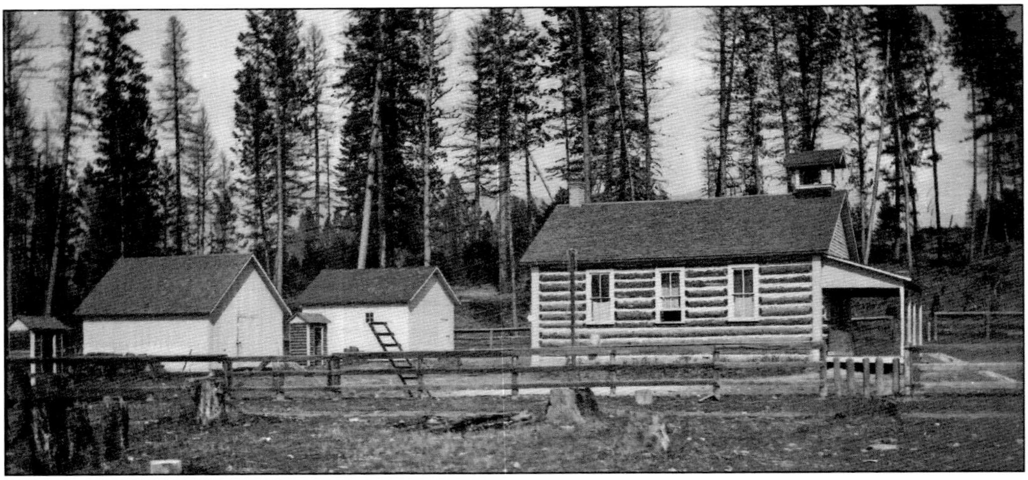

Pictured above is the Trego School as it appeared in the early 1920s. Below, these laughing students attended there in 1921. From left to right are (first row) ? Dennis (brother), ? Dennis (sister), Lenore Ritter, ? Wilson (hands on her face), Bjarne Erickson, Howard Falgren, ? Erickson, and ? Erickson; (second row) six unidentified and Evelyn Falgren, her face framed by two Erickson sisters in the front row. The children attending Trego School, then as now, enjoyed sled riding at recess. There are six Erickson children in the picture, and one of the four girls, Ruth, wrote in her memoirs that her brother Bjarne once brought a sled to school that his grandfather had made for him. Some older boys stole the sled and pushed it through the ice on Fortine Creek. The Erickson children searched along the creek the half-mile that it ran from the school to their home but never found it. (Both, courtesy of Evelyn McCurry, née Falgren.)

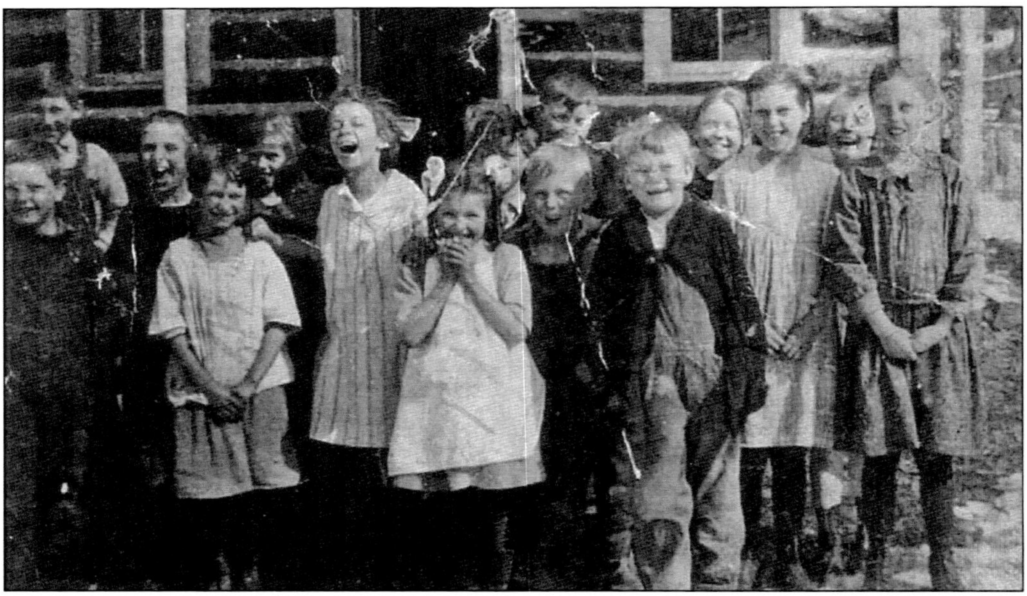

Nine

An Interesting Cast of Characters

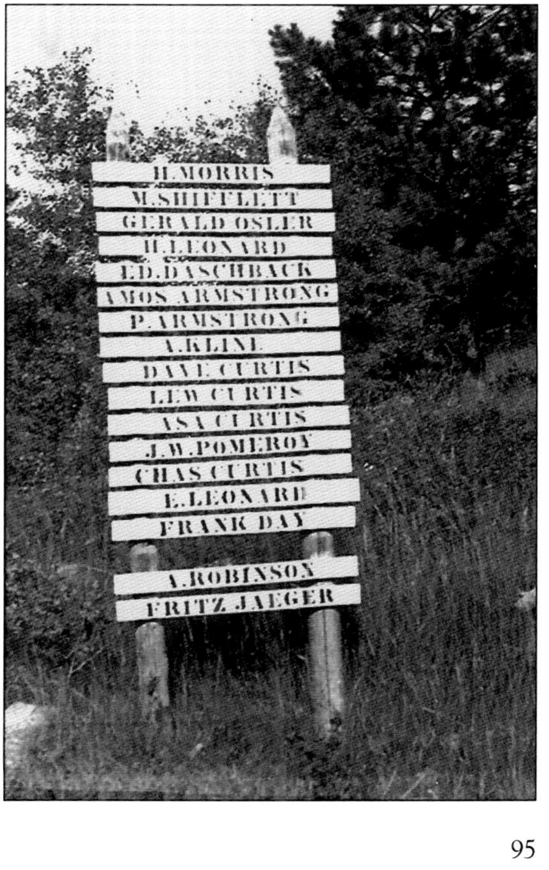

One of the most steadfast organizations in the first half of the 1900s was the Grange, and Grange halls existed all across America. It provided farm families a place to focus their social needs and advocated for them in a world that was becoming increasingly urban. In 1957, the Tobacco Valley Grange decided that its members might benefit from having their names placed on signs and those signs to be located at strategic places on roads that served the various farms and ranches. This sign was placed close to the spot where the Deep Creek Road leaves Highway 93 near Fortine.

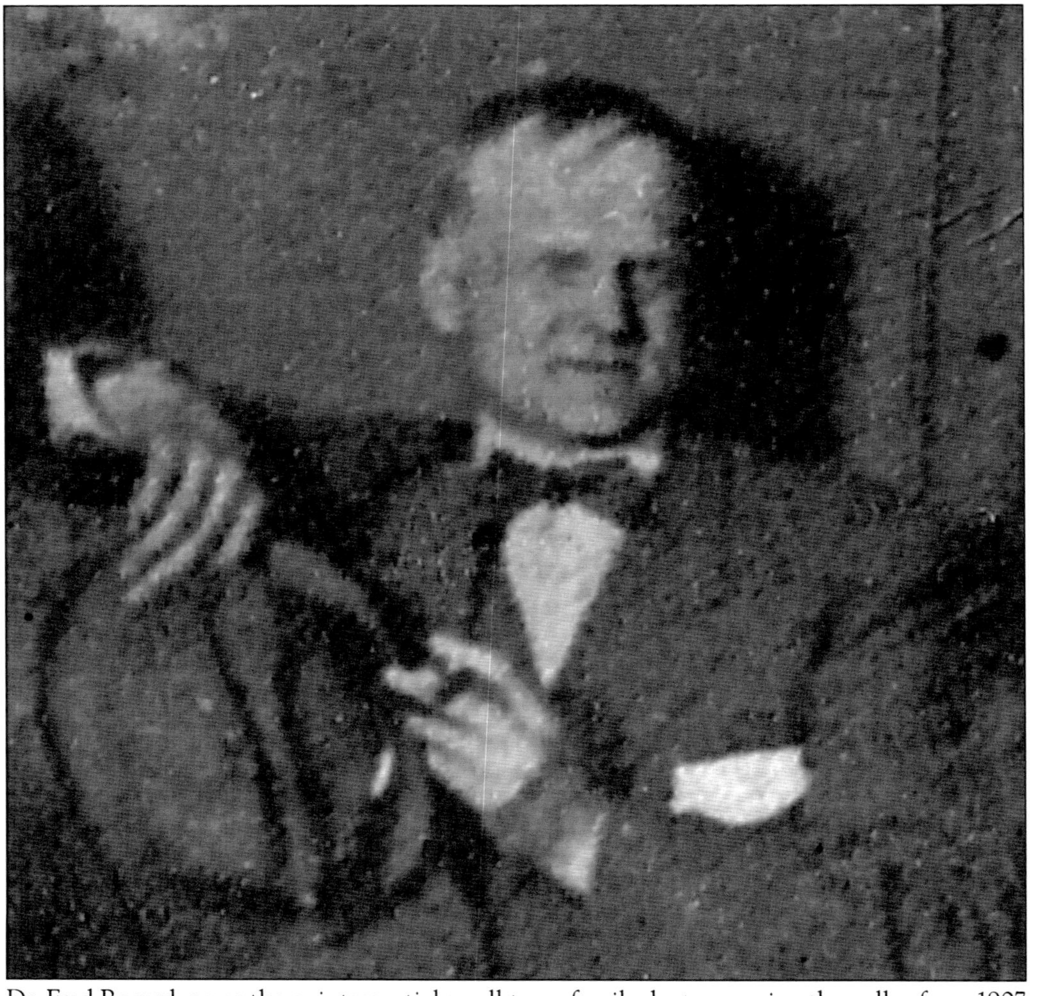

Dr. Fred Bogardus was the quintessential small-town family doctor, serving the valley from 1907 to 1919. By 1916, he had built Eureka's first hospital and installed an X-ray machine. Bogardus owned the second car in town, a 30-horsepower Buick. To say that in his 12-year tenure he saw it all is not an overstatement. Gleaned from the *Eureka Journal* are reports of injuries he treated, including all manner of sawmill and logging accidents, knifings, gunshots, explosions, buggy wrecks, car wrecks, and people kicked by a horse. He amputated limbs, removed an eye, relieved a depressed skull fracture, and gave a number of blood transfusions. He was in charge when nearly 50 people died in the influenza epidemic of 1918. He once removed a pin from the esophagus of a young seamstress. An emergency in Rexford prompted Bogardus to hitch a ride on a helper engine. Two miles from town, he was forced to make a spectacular leap into the snow when the helper engine met an eastbound freight train. Dr. Bogardus died of a rare skin disease, erysipelas, six years after leaving Eureka. He was not yet 50.

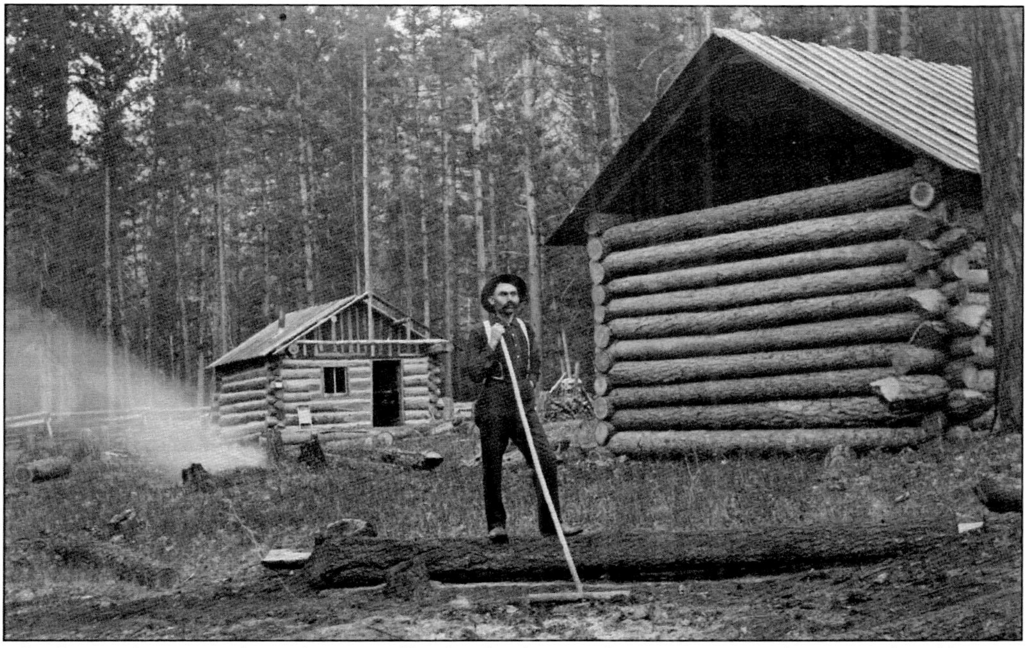

Charles Ford came to the Tobacco Valley for the dream of proving up on a homestead and having Uncle Sam hand him a deed to 160 acres. He had to live on the place part of the year, and he had to make improvements. Nothing else is known about Ford except that, from the photograph, it appears as though he is well along his way to fulfilling his requirements.

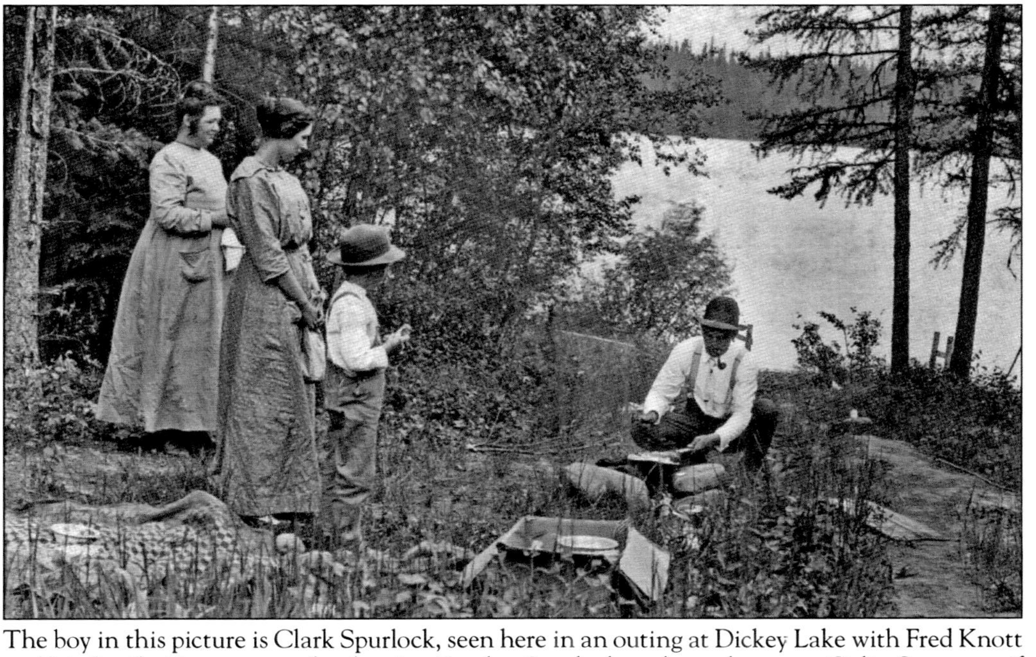

The boy in this picture is Clark Spurlock, seen here in an outing at Dickey Lake with Fred Knott and his family. Some years after leaving Eureka, Spurlock took on the name Colin Stuart, as if Clark Spurlock lacked punch, and wrote the novel *Shoot an Arrow to Stop the Wind*. The novel was set in the ranch lands on the northeast side of the valley.

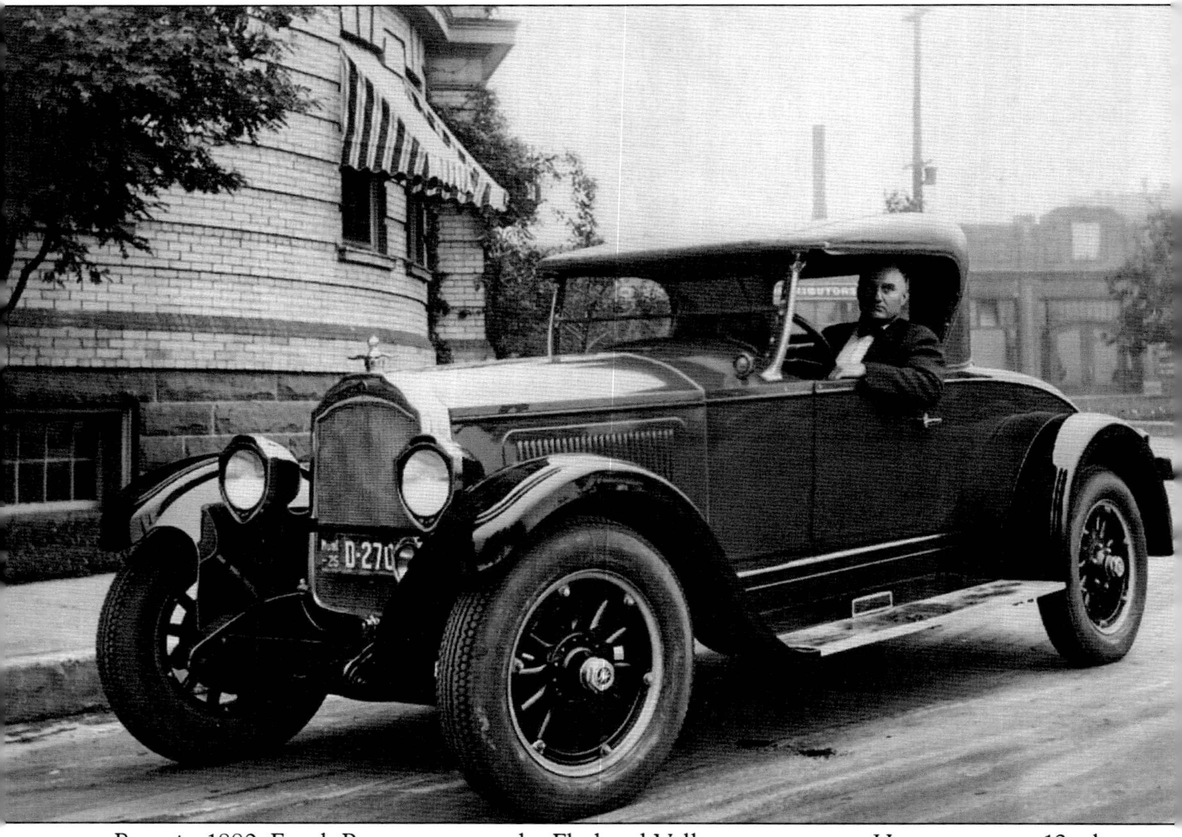

Born in 1880, Frank Baney came to the Flathead Valley at age seven. He was not yet 12 when he tagged along with a trapper to Tobacco Plains. Hanging around Mills Spring resulted in him marrying one of the Mills girls, Eva. He was appointed as deputy sheriff in 1907, and when Lincoln County formed in 1909, he was elected its first sheriff. With the exception of a brief stint as game warden, Baney served until 1947. The *Western News* once wrote of him: "Fearless as a lion . . . he never paraded his power or made offensive use of his authority." And the sheriff typically got his man. In 1927, two desperados fatally shot a Great Northern depot agent. Leaving Libby after midnight, Baney arrived on the scene by 3:00 a.m. Noting the caliber of rifle the robbers used, he developed a list of locals who owned such a gun, then went to the home of one man to procure his rifle. Baney test fired it, establishing that the rifle made marks on the cartridge casing matching those found at the scene. Two suspects who had borrowed the innocent man's rifle were soon in custody.

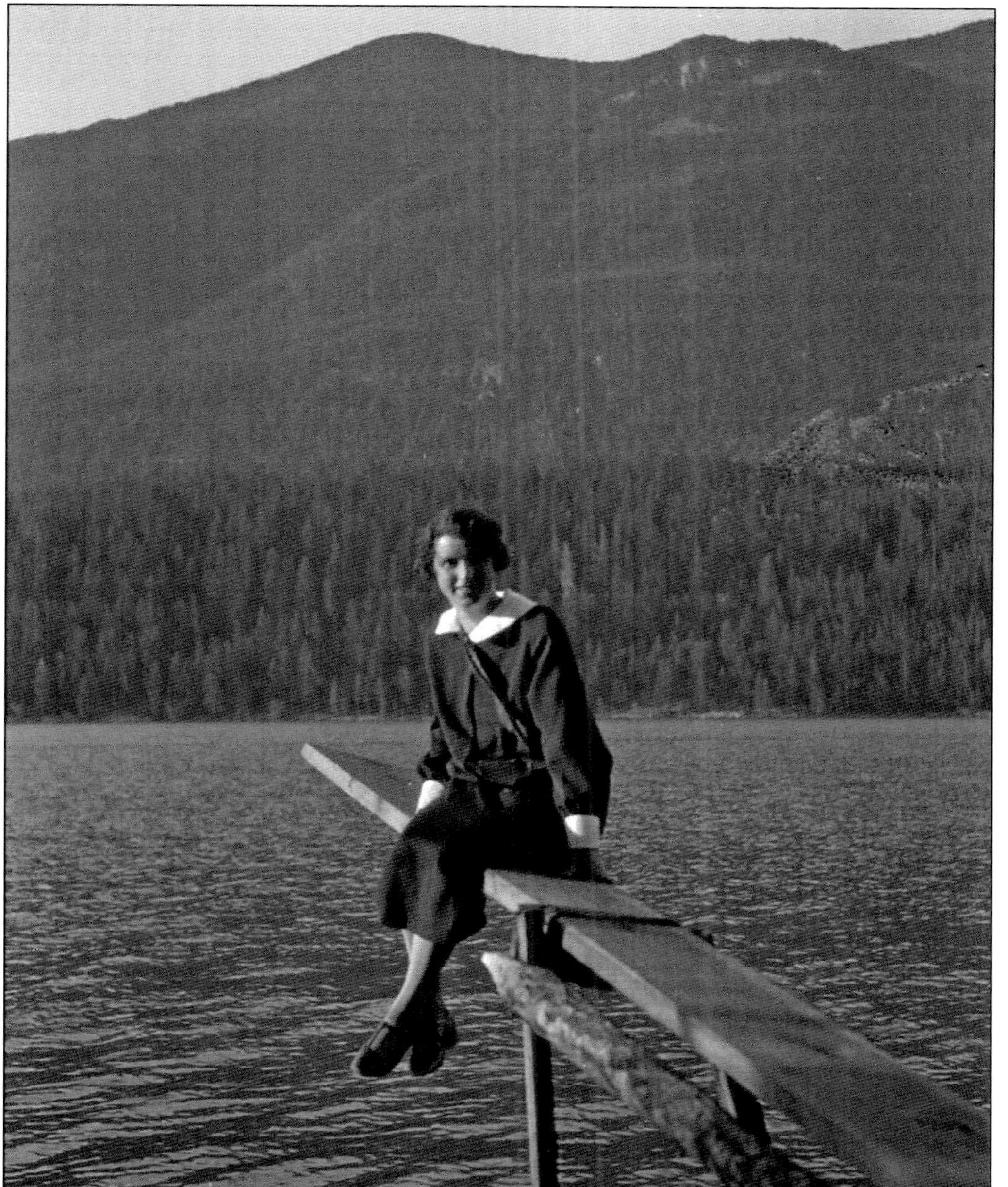

Eva Baney, having born a son named Force, died in 1922. She was not yet 50 but had been ill for years, suffering from tuberculosis. In 1924, Sheriff Frank Baney married Victoria Dunston. She bore him two children, June and Duke. Seen here at Dickey Lake around 1927, Victoria commonly accompanied Baney as he exercised the duties of his office and often rode with him to deliver inmates to Warm Springs or Deer Lodge. One May day in 1925, Baney was looking for a man who had stolen a car and other items. Victoria was with him, and when they arrived at the Bull River Bridge, they spotted two men crossing it. The *Eureka Journal* reported: "Mrs. Baney took the wheel and Mr. Baney took the other side to enable him to get out quickly if necessary." Alas, the man fled, and the sheriff fatally shot him.

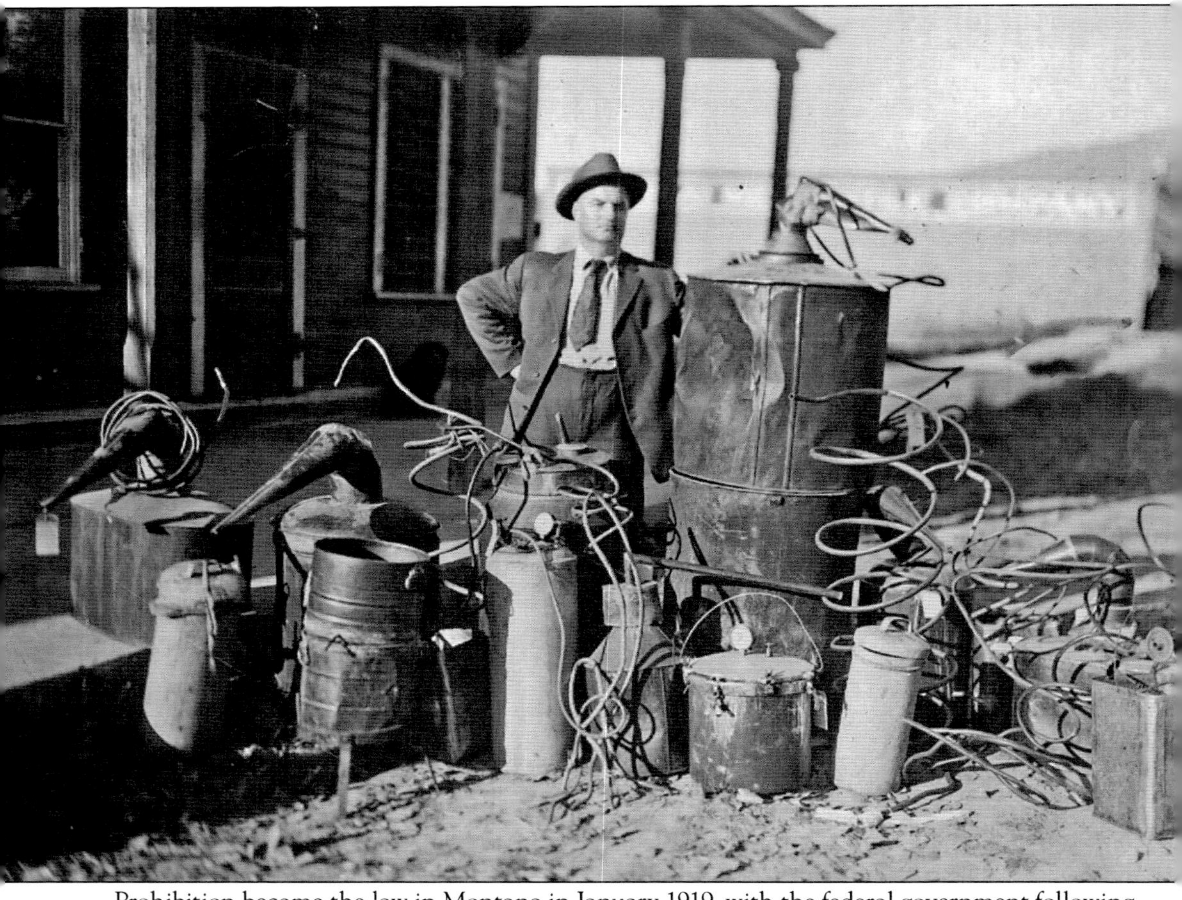

Prohibition became the law in Montana in January 1919, with the federal government following suit one year later. The Feds were slow in coming up to speed, so enforcing the liquor law fell to local law enforcement. Given that the Tobacco Valley was the only route out of Canada for scores of miles both east and west, cross-border bootlegging became the norm. In addition to that, there were many people around who knew how to make whiskey. Sheriff Frank Baney, a temperate man, took a serious approach to the problem. A few of his successes are pictured above. In 1921, the venerable sheriff nearly died when he took a .45 slug in his chest, shot by a drunken itinerant. In 1926, Montana repealed its Prohibition law, which meant that from then on its peace officers could no longer arrest its citizens for liquor violations. The federal government tried for seven more years to control alcohol, throwing in the towel in 1933. Sheriff Baney lived for three years after retirement, dying in 1950.

Frank Garey (center) and his sons, Jim (left) and Webb (right), were involved in Tobacco Valley activities from 1903 until well into the 1930s. Frank Garey served on the school board and was a Glen Lake ditch commissioner, a county commissioner, and quite active in Republican party politics. He was also known for his proactive stance on new road construction. That Jim secured the Ford franchise for Eureka may have been a factor.

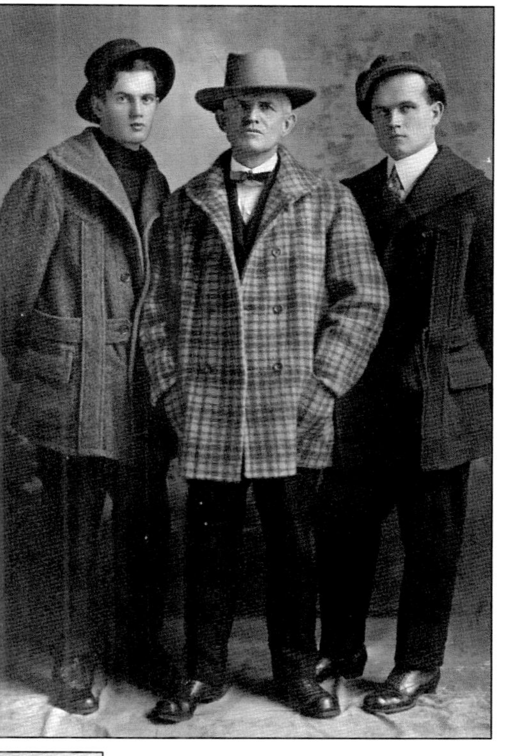

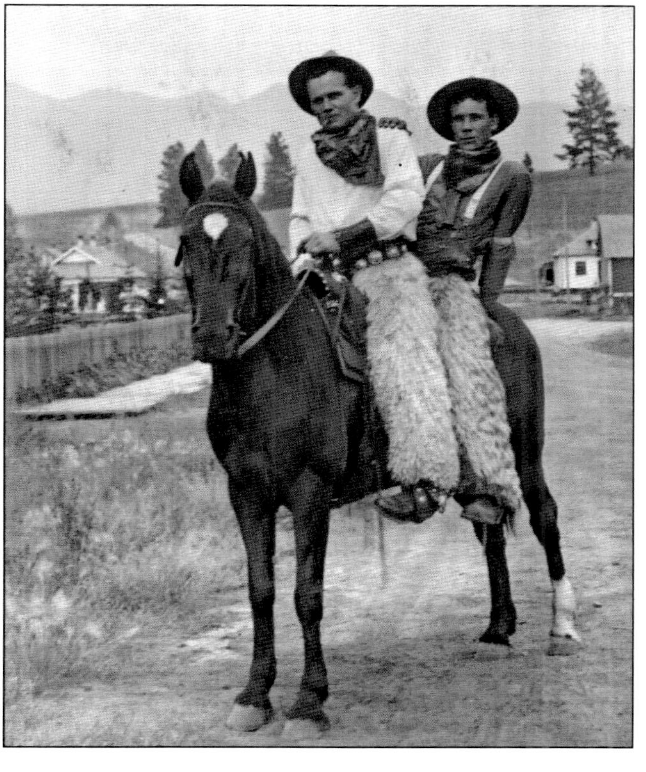

Webb Garey, by all accounts, was engaged in rum-running. The story is told that he had a mare that could be led across the border, packed with Canadian whiskey, then turned loose to return on her own to Garey's barn, where her foal was kept. Garey's ranch was about one mile west of Four Corners on Highway 37. Webb is in front, and Jim, Webb's brother, is mounted behind him around 1915.

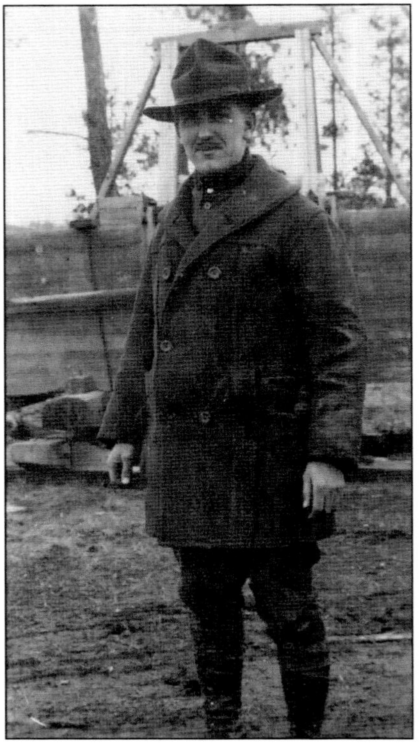

Frank Sabin was part of the mainstream business community for more than 30 years. Early on he contracted with the Eureka Lumber Company to supply its logging camps. He operated a hardware store in Eureka until 1947 when he set returning soldier Ott Olt up in the business. Sabin retired from the Eureka business scene in 1960 when he sold the Majestic Theatre. He died about one year later. (Courtesy of Mike Gwynn.)

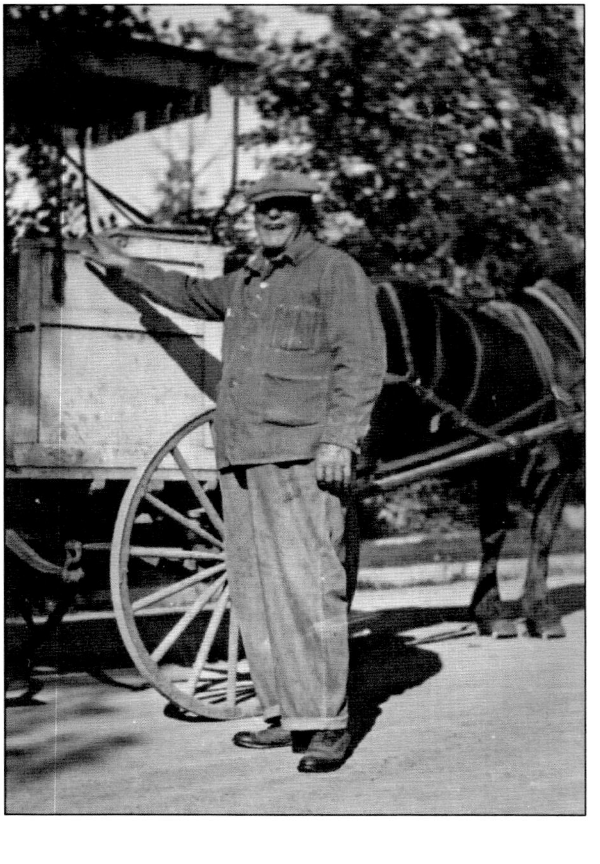

Arthur and Terecia Purdy came to Tobacco Valley around 1900 and bought the Colin Sinclair homestead. It remains in the Purdy family today, and the barn Arthur built still stands along Sinclair Creek. Purdy founded the Meadow Home Dairy. Throughout the 1920s, Purdy or his son Lynn delivered milk door-to-door. Fourth-generation Purdys supplied Eureka with fresh raw milk into the 1980s.

Jim Whilt (left) was a man of contrasts. At one time he captured mountain lions, which he sold to two-bit zoos and menageries. Later he worked as an interpretive guide at Glacier National Park. Known locally as the "Bard of the Rockies," he wrote several volumes of poetry and one book for children entitled *Our Animal Friends of the Wild*. He may also have flaunted the Prohibition law.

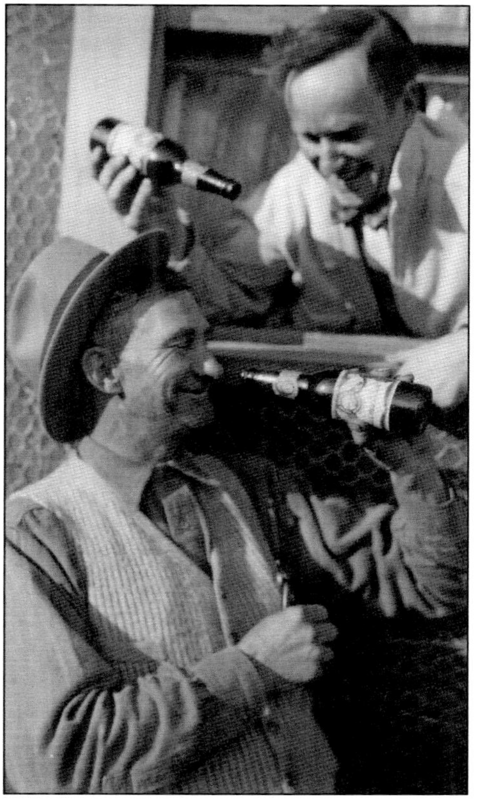

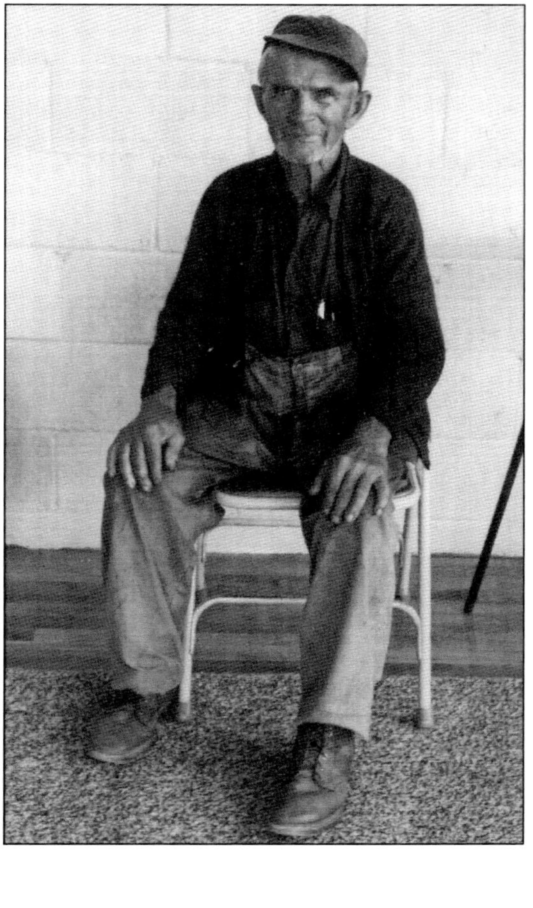

Fritz Yeager was one of many bachelors who spent their lives at some remote location in the mountains east of Tobacco Valley looking for a mother lode—gold, silver, copper, lead, it did not matter—but none of them ever found the object of their desire. As shown on the Grange sign on page 95, Yeager lived at the last place up Deep Creek. "Just a little further," he kept telling people.

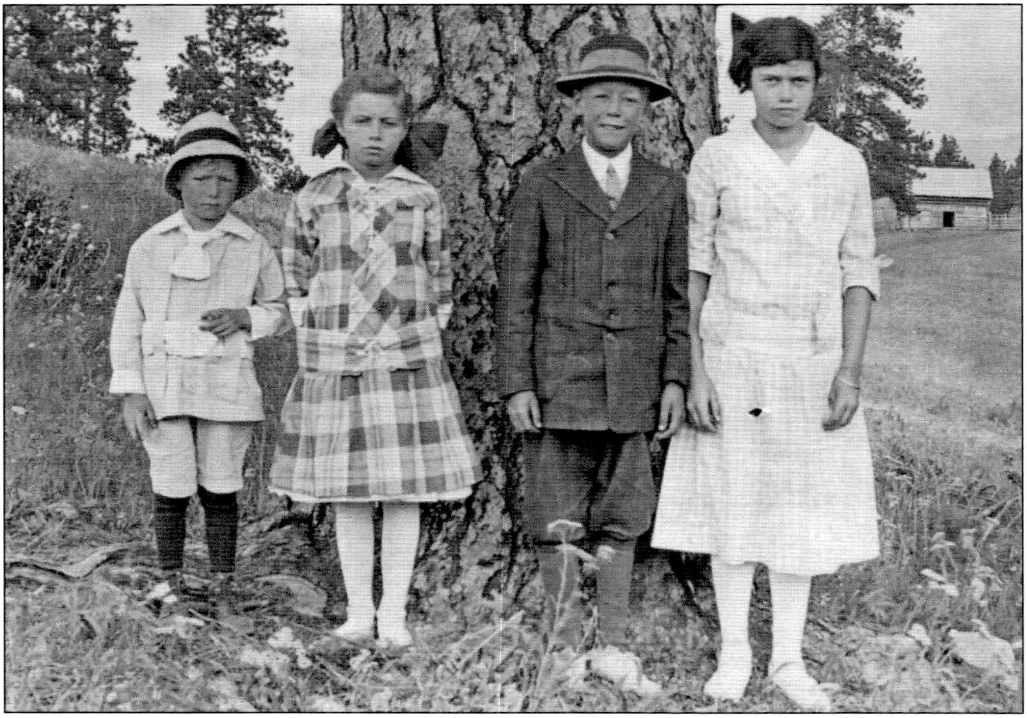

This photograph might have been taken on Easter Sunday. From left to right are two unidentified, Howard Helms, and Dorothy Raber. Helms spent his entire life on the Tobacco Plains, and his father's ranch is still held intact by the fourth generation. In a 1992 interview Helms recalled, "We run a few cattle at that time . . . I've rode ever since I was knee high to a duck. I'd ride up into Canada to check them."

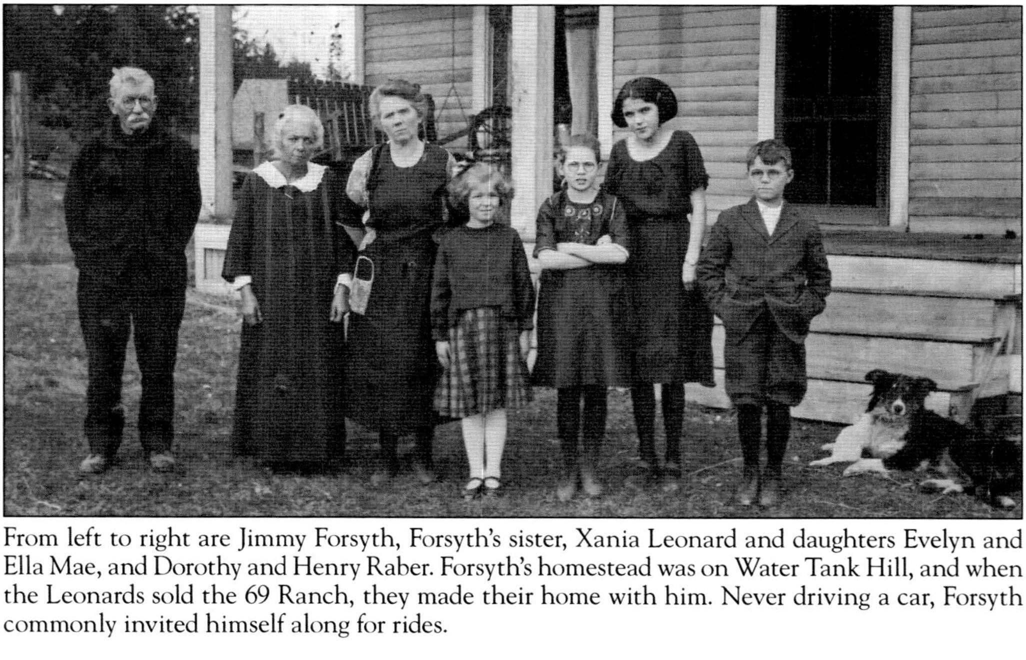

From left to right are Jimmy Forsyth, Forsyth's sister, Xania Leonard and daughters Evelyn and Ella Mae, and Dorothy and Henry Raber. Forsyth's homestead was on Water Tank Hill, and when the Leonards sold the 69 Ranch, they made their home with him. Never driving a car, Forsyth commonly invited himself along for rides.

Fred and Lucy Knott had their home on the heights of Eureka's west side. There they raised three girls and a boy. Knott was an avid amateur photographer and took a number of the pictures that appear in this book. It is fair to say that he was also a passionate fly fisherman. Though he often traveled into Washington building dams, Lucy and the children always stayed in Eureka.

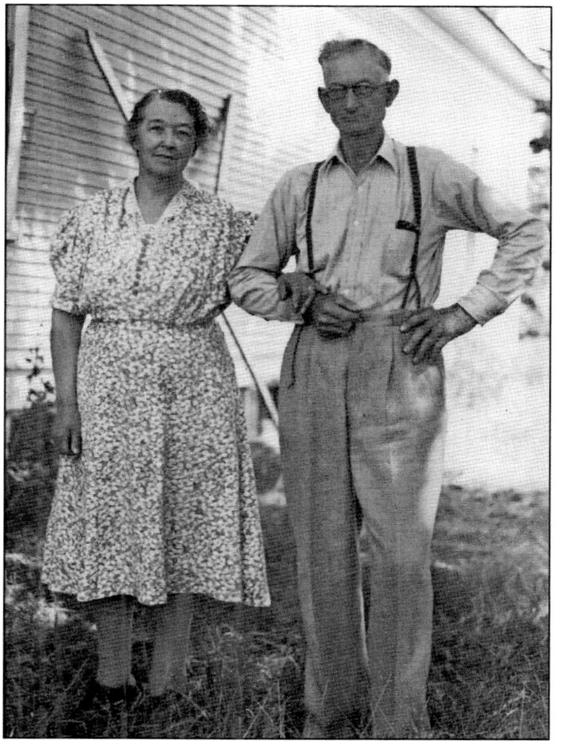

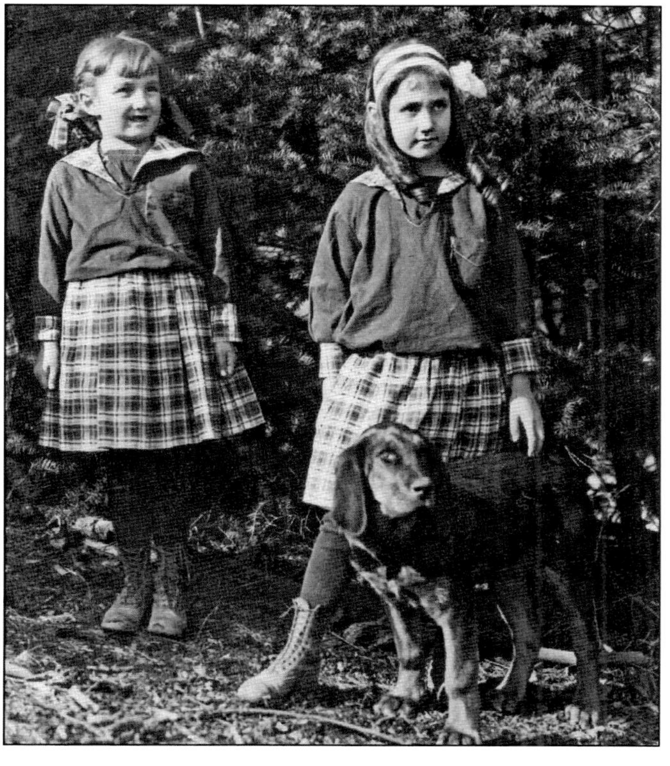

One of Fred Knott's favorite subjects was his daughters. Phyllis Americana is on the left, and Winifred is on the right. Clara Belle and son Forest are not pictured. Phyllis has spent her whole life in Eureka, except for a few years in the mid-1940s when she lived in Los Angeles, where she helped build P-51 Mustangs.

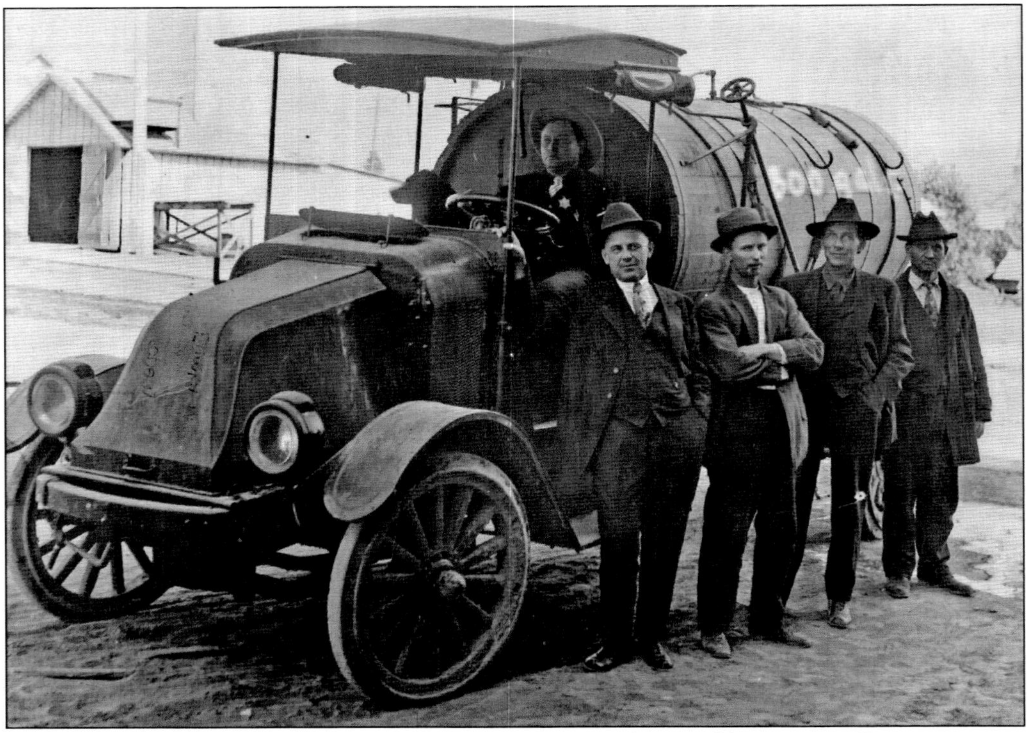

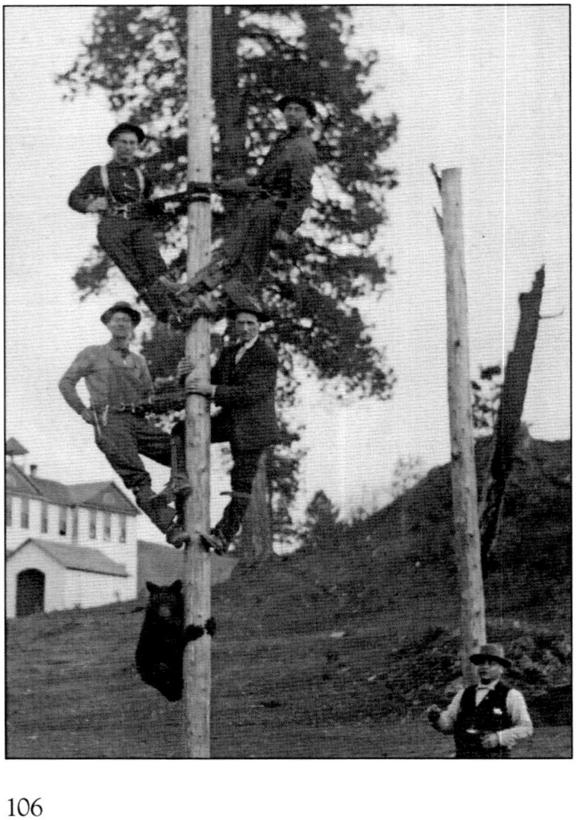

After World War I, small towns across America started receiving trucks, thanks to the generosity of Uncle Sam. Eureka's sprinkler truck, pictured here *c.* 1919, was probably used primarily to control dust, but it surely hauled water for fires as well. The chief of police, Calix Dugas, is at the wheel. Standing from left to right are city attorney H. G. "Greely" Pomeroy and councilmen William Schuck, Frank Thomas, and F. L. R. McCoy.

Calix Dugas (standing) was one of Eureka's most colorful characters. This photograph from a postcard dated 1909 possibly refers to a bear cub captured the previous year. The *Eureka Journal*, June 12, 1908, read: "An Indian from near Rexford brought a bear cub to town (which was) added to the Dugas zoo. This collection is assuming a varied assortment of animals . . . expected to hobnob with each other in peace and harmony."

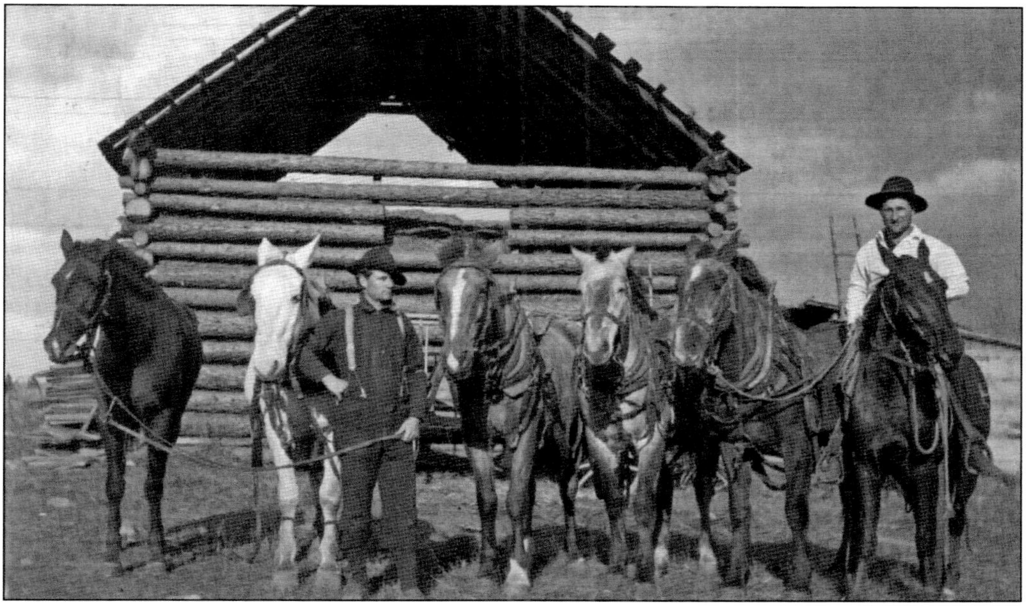

Albert Brock is believed to be the man standing, and Roy Brock is mounted. Their parents, Wellington and Sara, proved up on the West Kootenai, raising eight children there. Roy remained in West Kootenai his entire life, raising racehorses in the 1950s.

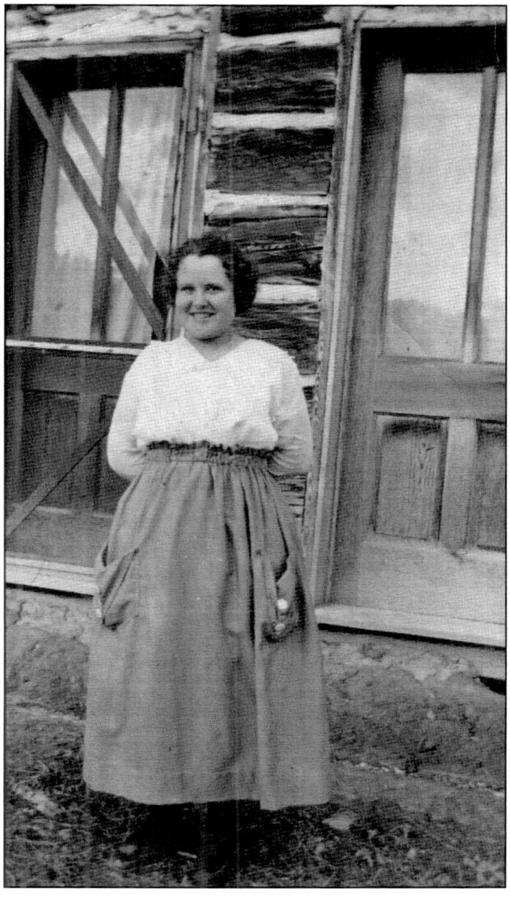

Gladys was the youngest of Wellington and Sara Brock's children. Born in 1900, Gladys married Ernie Sahnow and left the area, but she returned in the mid-1980s to spend her declining years in the Tobacco Valley that she loved.

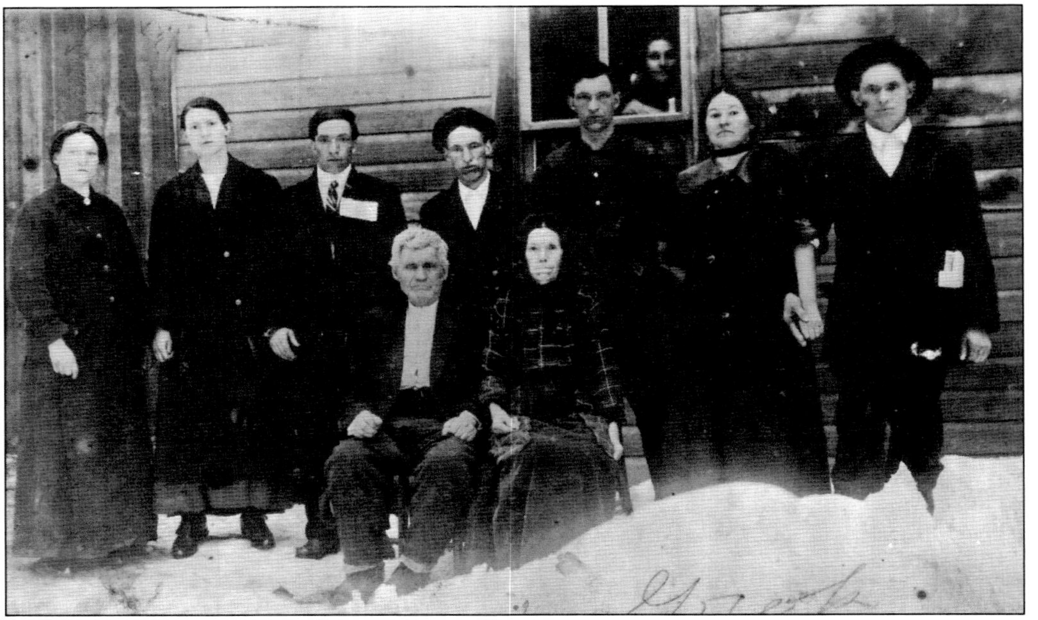

William and Almeda Stacy, along with their seven grown children, came to Montana from West Virginia in 1905. Several of them took up homesteads on Pinkham Creek. William Stacy chose his homestead on the west side of Virginia Hill, recognizable today as the area around the Pinkham School, which is now a community hall. Indeed, it was Stacy who deeded the land for the school to the district. Below are, from left to right, Jim Roberts, Lockey Roberts Stacy, Sylvester Stacy, Bess Stacy, and Andy Stacy at work in the family garden around 1915.

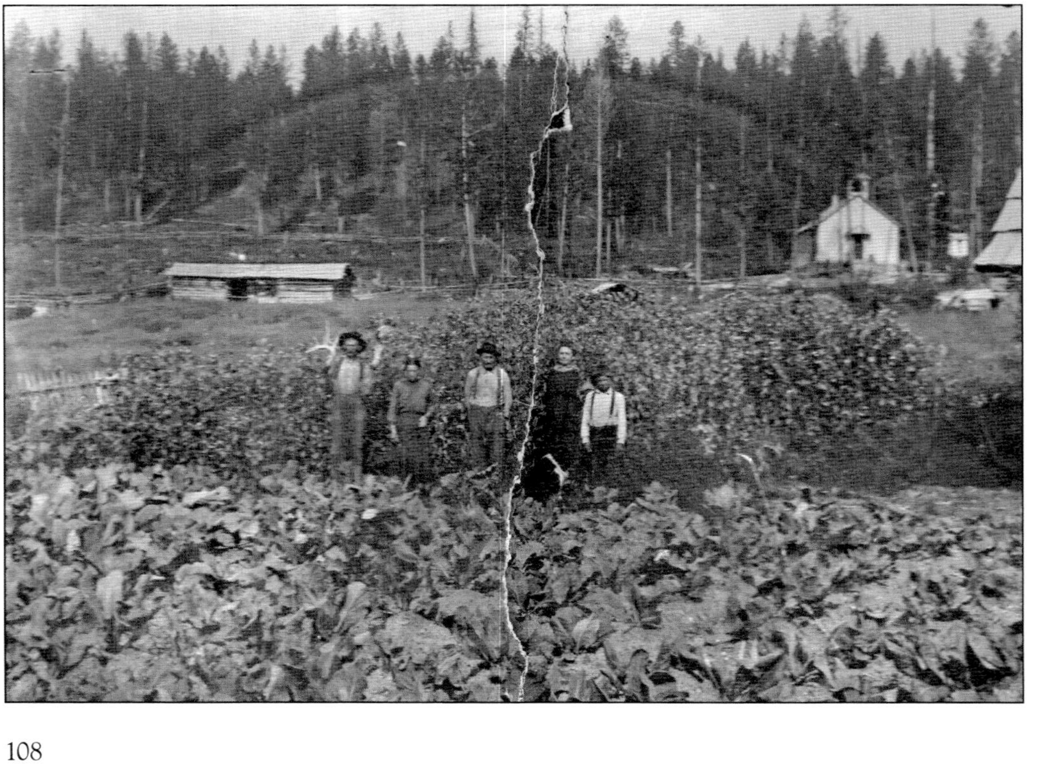

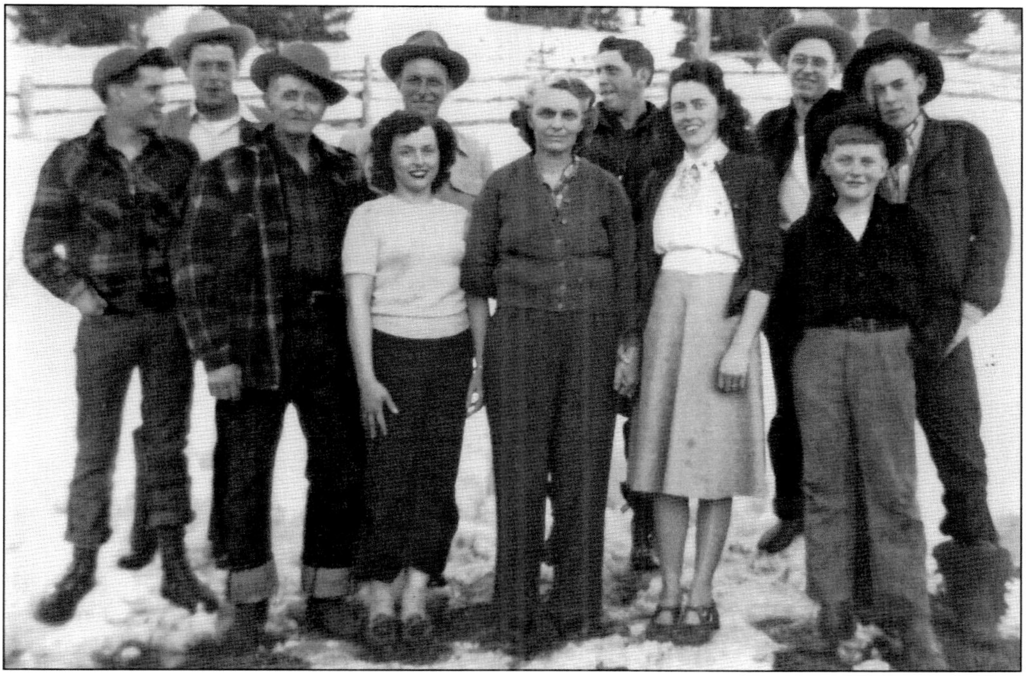

Will and Nanny Workman were the first homesteaders on Pinkham Creek, coming from West Virginia in 1903. In 1913, their oldest son, Charlie, married Alta Kinney, and they took out their own homestead across the creek from his parents. Charlie and Alta Workman had nine children, most of whom literally lined Pinkham Creek with their homes. Pictured here from left to right c. 1948 are Roger, Wayne, Charlie, Ellegene, Lynn, Alta, Sid, Lula, Chuck, Jack, and Harry.

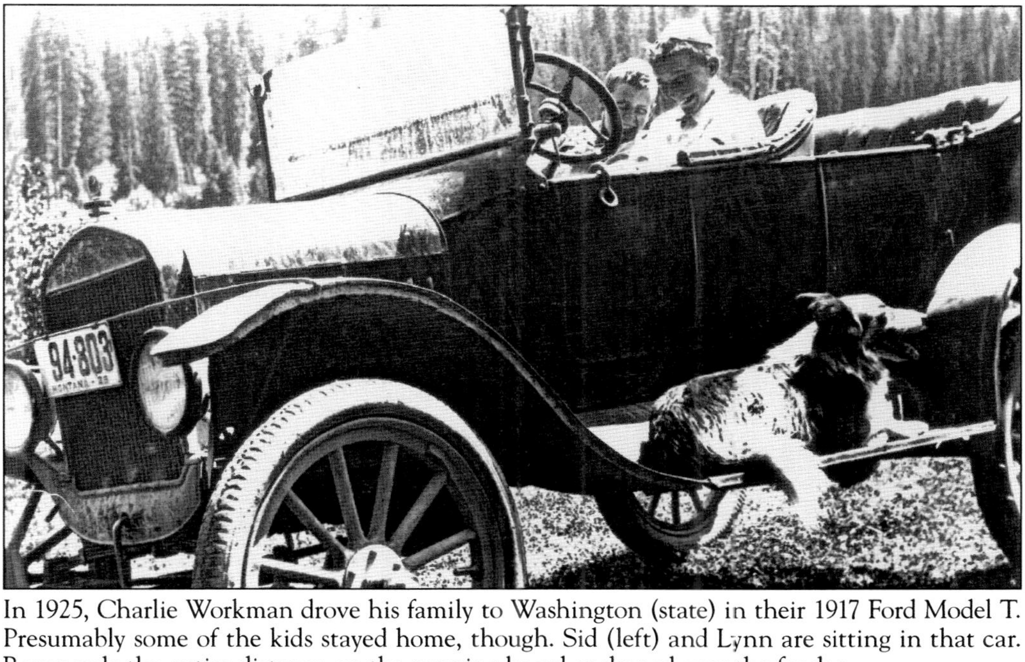

In 1925, Charlie Workman drove his family to Washington (state) in their 1917 Ford Model T. Presumably some of the kids stayed home, though. Sid (left) and Lynn are sitting in that car. Rover rode the entire distance on the running board or draped over the fender.

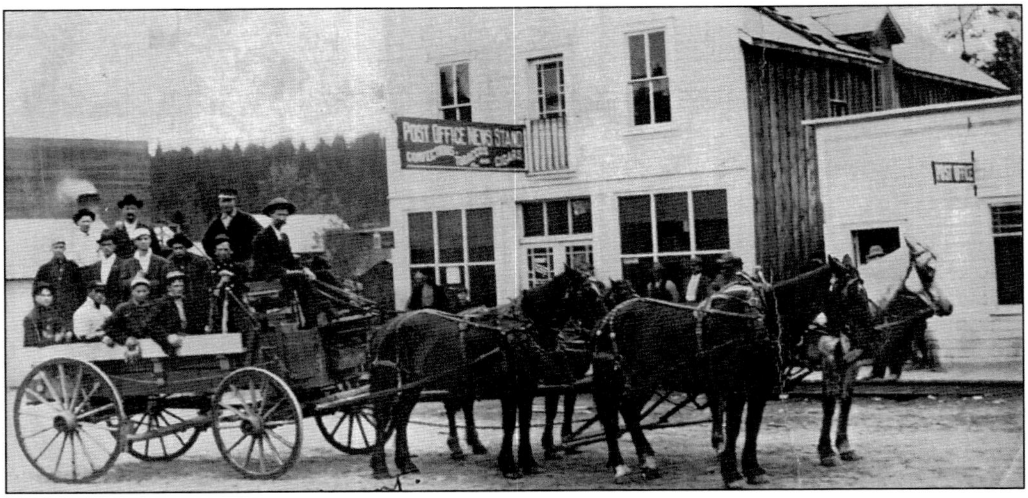

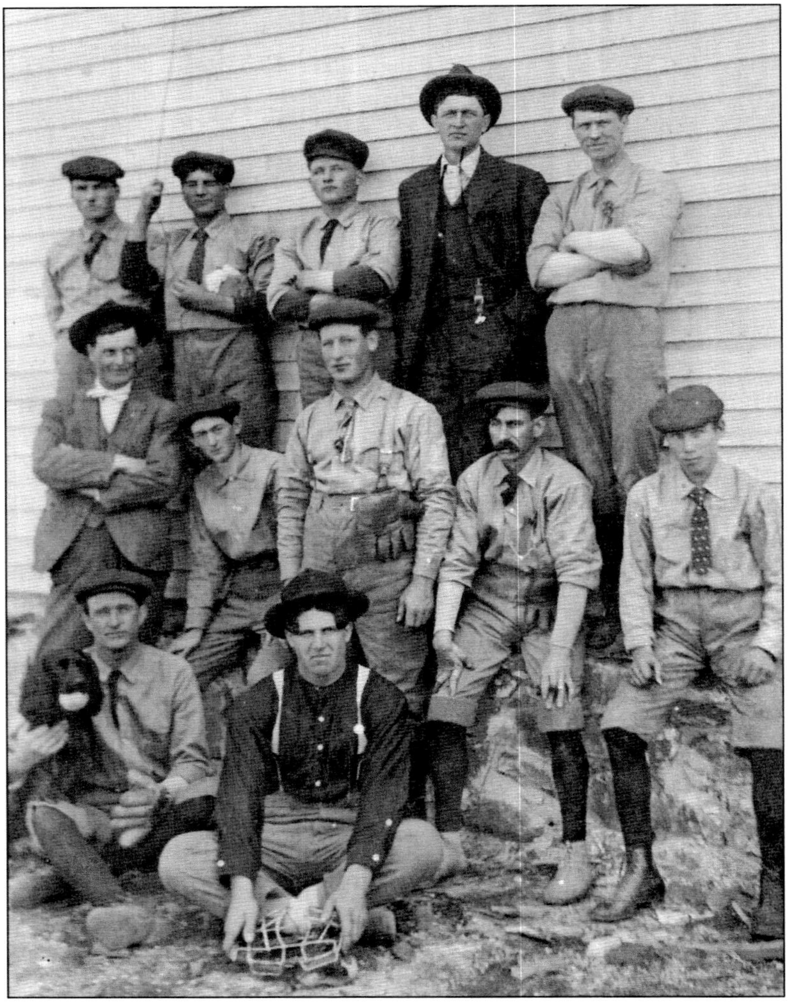

Most towns, no matter their size, had baseball teams. The Eureka team (pictured above) is on its way to Fernie in 1905. Presumably the wagon is intermediate in that effort, and they will eventually board the train. When Marston formed a baseball team, shown at left in 1907, it must have required every man in and around the town. Included in the picture are Dan and Joe Tetrault, Clarence Flanagan, Everett Paxton, Joe Greenburg, and Frank Laderoot. Only Laderoot, fourth from the left in the second row, can be located with certainty. Note the dog on the left. He was known for his wicked spitball.

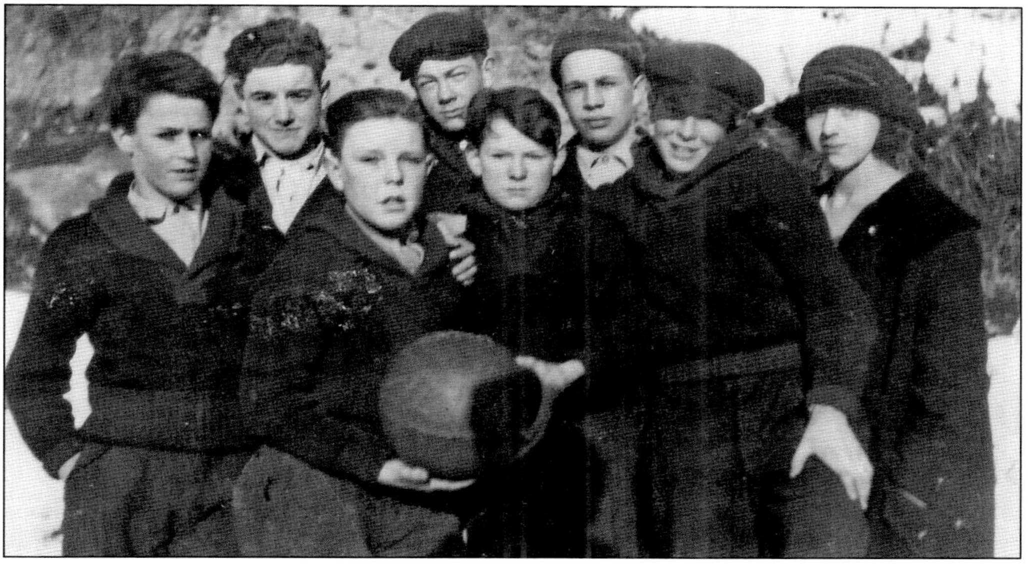

Pictured above *c.* 1920, these young basketball players all seem to be wearing matching sweaters, with the unidentified girl at far right being the exception. From left to right are possibly Lewis Fetterly, unidentified, Manley Schagel, Robert Hendrickson, three unidentified boys, and an unidentified girl. The 1924–1925 Lincoln County High School basketball team (shown below) from left to right are (first row) ? Gill, unidentified, and Bud Madden; (second row) unidentified coach, Lewis Fetterly, unidentified, and Manley Schagel. Fetterly was a star athlete, excelling at track, football, and basketball.

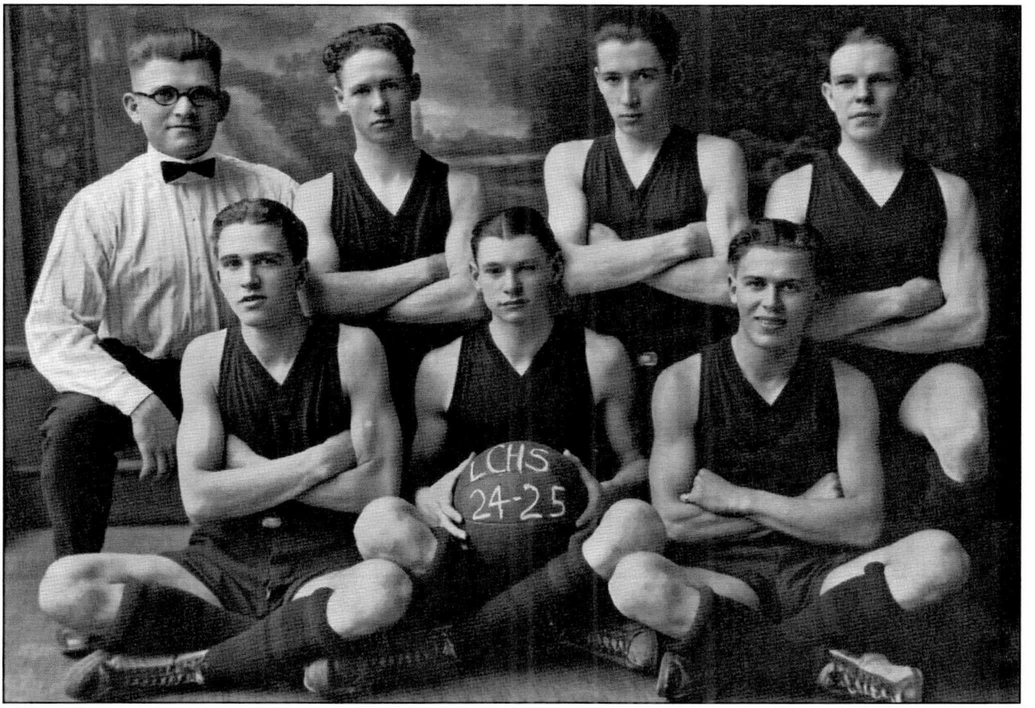

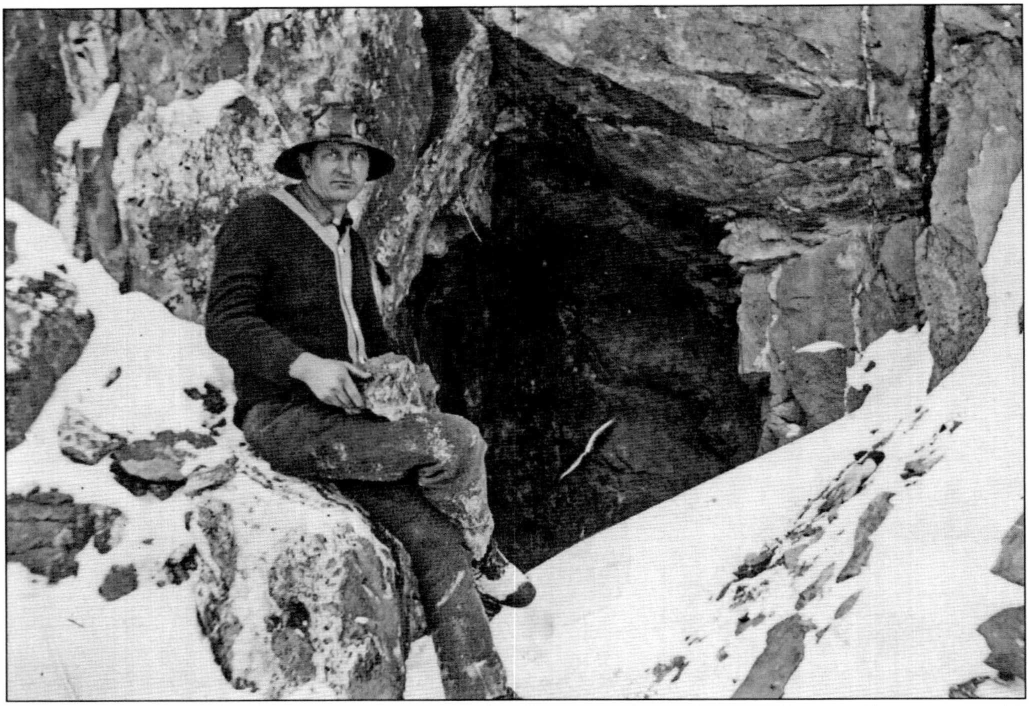

Joe Tetrault arrived before 1900, taking up land surrounding a body of water that eventually became Tetrault Lake. Tetrault's main interest was mining, and he put forth a serious effort at extracting copper ore. He formed the Twin Peaks Mining Company, an entity that transported an impressive amount of supplies and machinery into the mountains to the east. He also dug a 225-foot tunnel on the north side of Poorman Mountain.

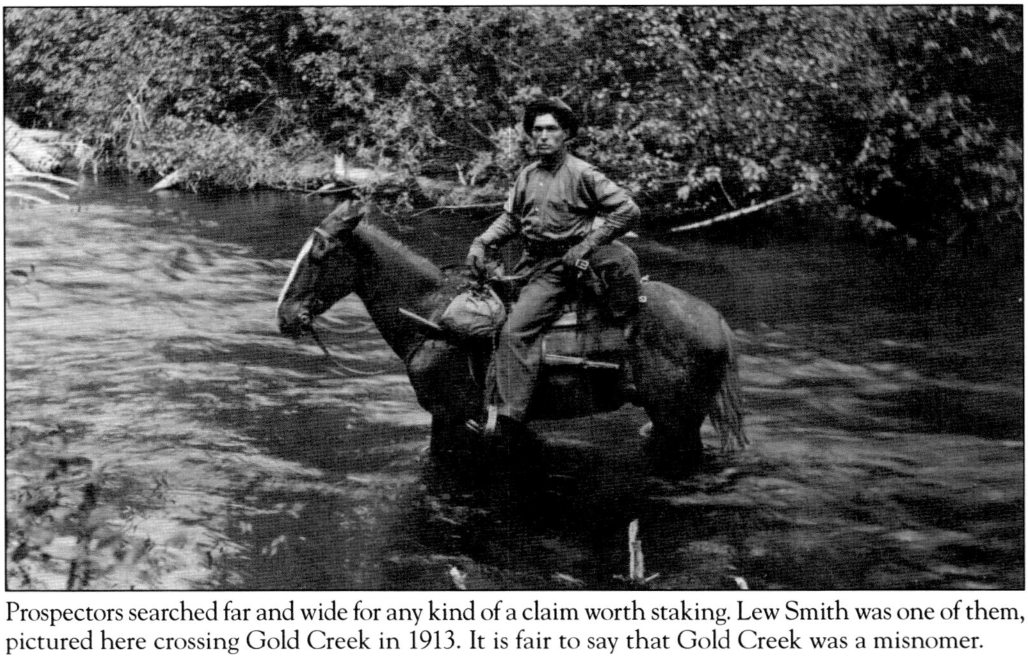

Prospectors searched far and wide for any kind of a claim worth staking. Lew Smith was one of them, pictured here crossing Gold Creek in 1913. It is fair to say that Gold Creek was a misnomer.

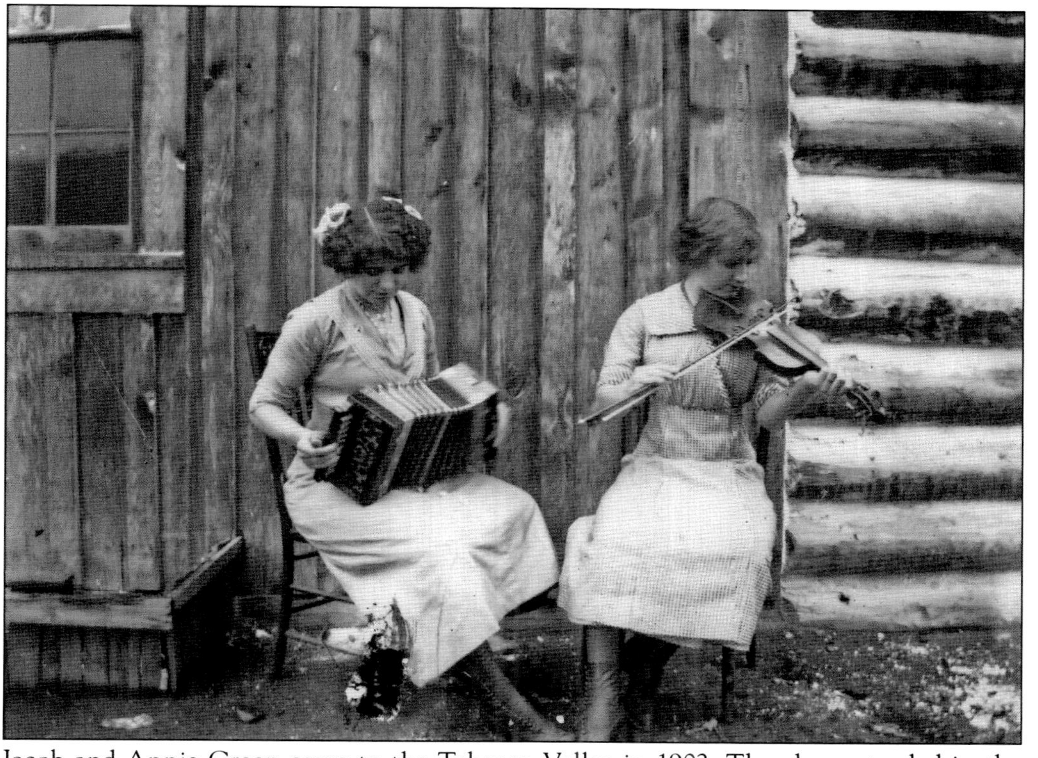

Jacob and Annie Green came to the Tobacco Valley in 1902. They homesteaded in the shadow of Black Butte where they raised eight children. At least two of them were musically inclined. Inez Belinda (left) married Clarence Dierman, and Ora Belle Marie (right) married Celos Baillargion.

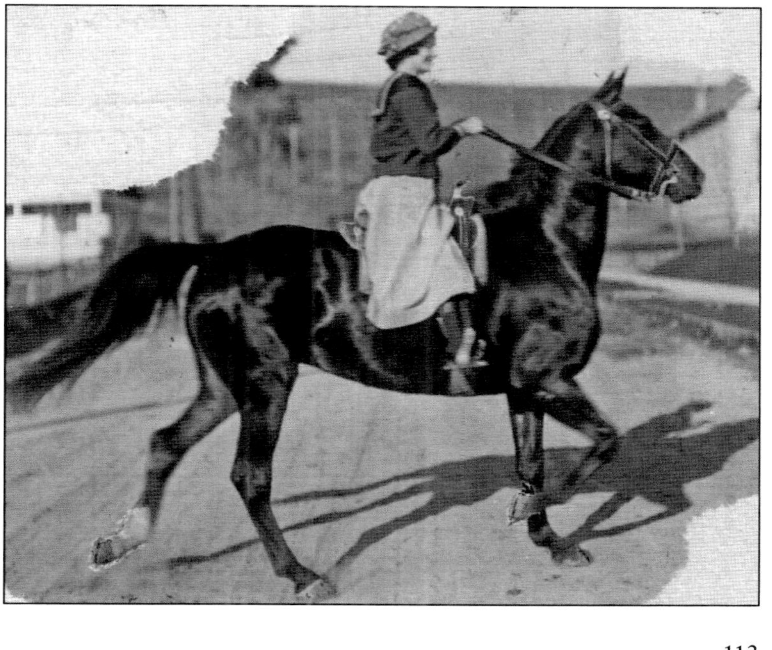

Addie Brock, daughter of Wellington and Sara, grew up in the West Kootenai. Merlin Scott wanted to marry her before he shipped out to France in 1917, but she made him wait until he returned. He trained Star, a five-gaited gelding, for her as a wedding present. When she was widowed at a relatively young age, she married Clifford Irwin. Addie Irwin lived to be 101.

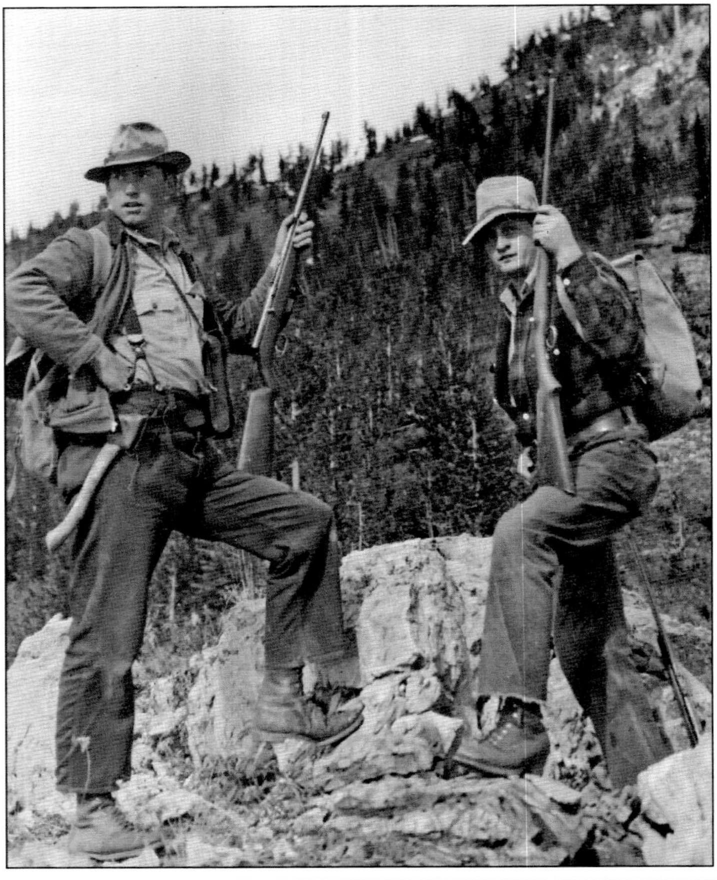

Lloyd West (left) and Bud Moses, shown here c. 1935, spent a large amount of time ranging around what is now known as Ten Lakes Scenic Area. To find the Ten Lakes Scenic Area, one can head due east and find it at the top of the ridge. Glacier National Park is on the eastern horizon.

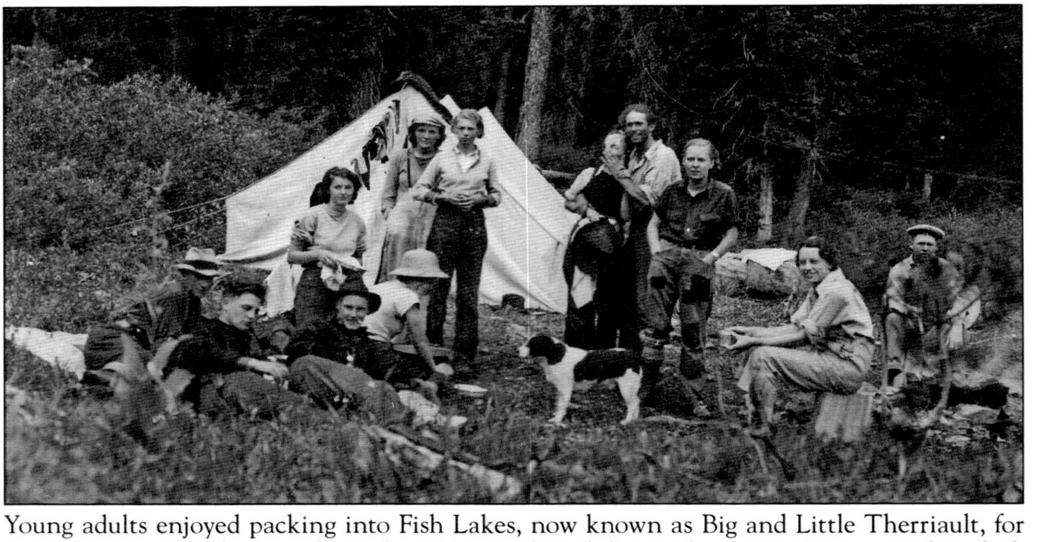

Young adults enjoyed packing into Fish Lakes, now known as Big and Little Therriault, for campouts. Pictured here in the early 1930s are, from left to right, Jimmy Moses, unidentified, Gene Shea, Ruth Shea (kneeling), Nell West (wearing the pith helmet), Nellie Mae Tripp, Neva Bolen, Reva Shea, Lloyd West, Nettie French, and two unidentified.

Art and Frances Fleming came to Eureka about 1914 from a border town in eastern Montana. They are shown here at their Gateway home with Fleming's sister Goldie looking on. Art advanced to the position of superintendent of U.S. Customs and retired in the Tobacco Valley.

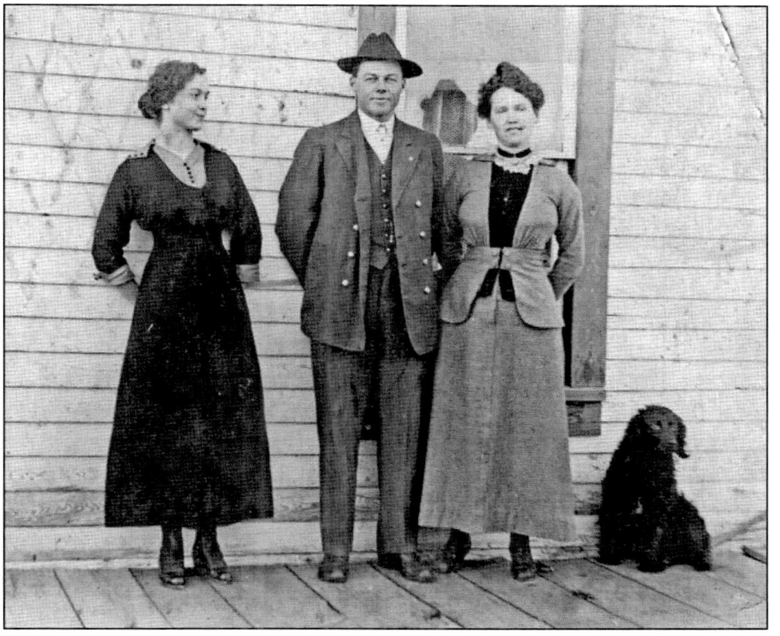

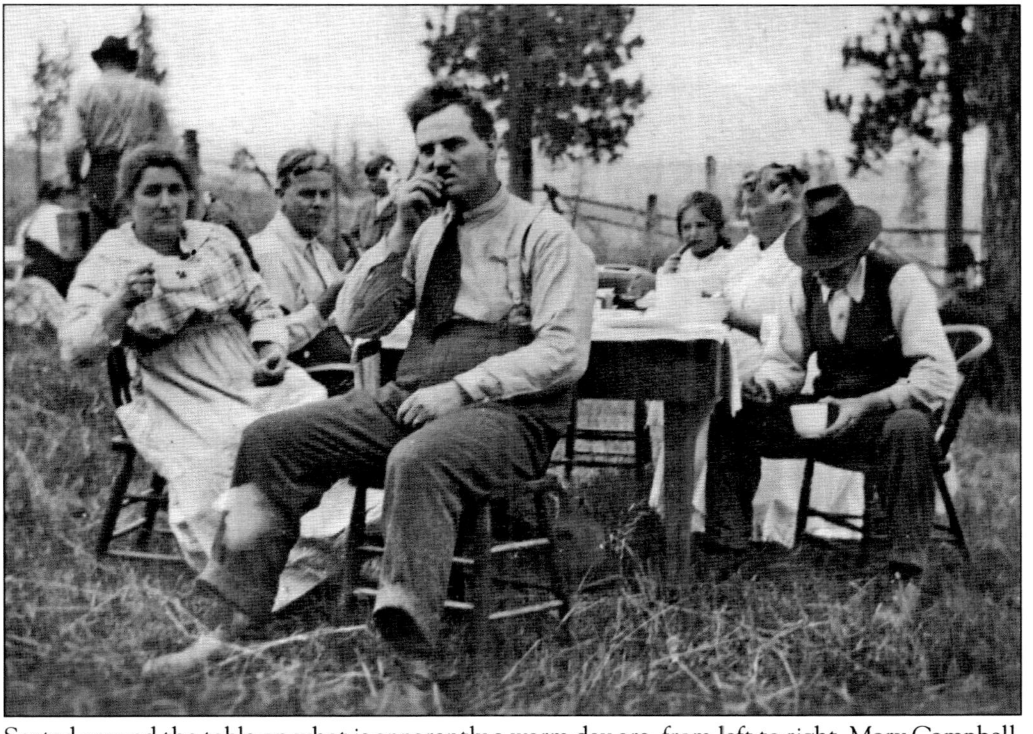

Seated around the table on what is apparently a warm day are, from left to right, Mary Campbell, unidentified, Frank Baney, Evelyn Rock, and two unidentified. It could have been a summer picnic or a funeral. Enos and Mary Campbell arrived early in the valley, Enos being the nephew of Johnny Campbell who first saw the country in the 1860s. Everyone in town knew them as "Aunt" Mary and "Uncle" Enos.

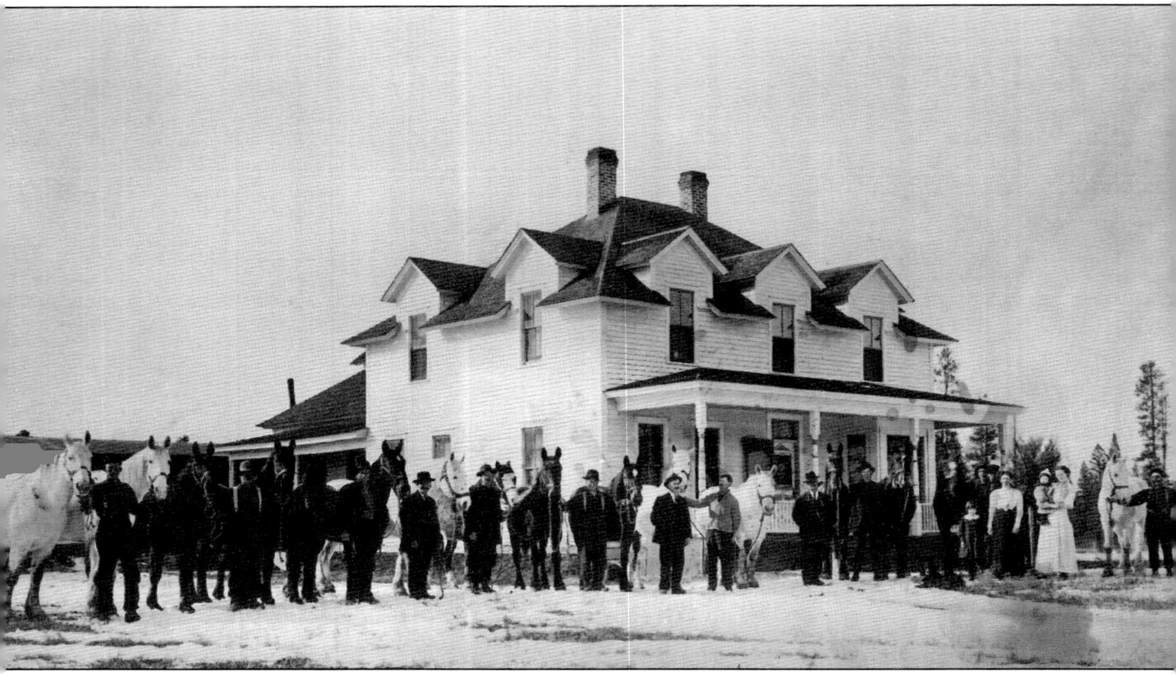

Swan John Dahlberg arrived in Tobacco Valley in 1900 at the age of 40 and began acquiring land. Having already performed on contracts for the Great Northern Railroad, he was awarded the contract to build a line from Jennings to the coalfields near Fernie, British Columbia. Dahlberg later built railroad lines throughout the Inland Northwest. He also went in to the sawmill business, gaining a reputation as a major employer and benefactor. By 1902, Dahlberg was building a prominent house north of Grave Creek, naming it Fairview. He is seen here standing in the middle in front of the white horse with its head up. Fairview, now owned by the Flanagan family, stands along Highway 93 right where it was built. When economic calamity visited the valley in 1924 and the Big Mill closed, Dahlberg's finances turned sour, and that September, he directed his lawyer to draw up a will. On October 6, he stopped his car on a railroad crossing he had built and waited for the fast mail train to end his problems. (Courtesy of Darris Flanagan.)

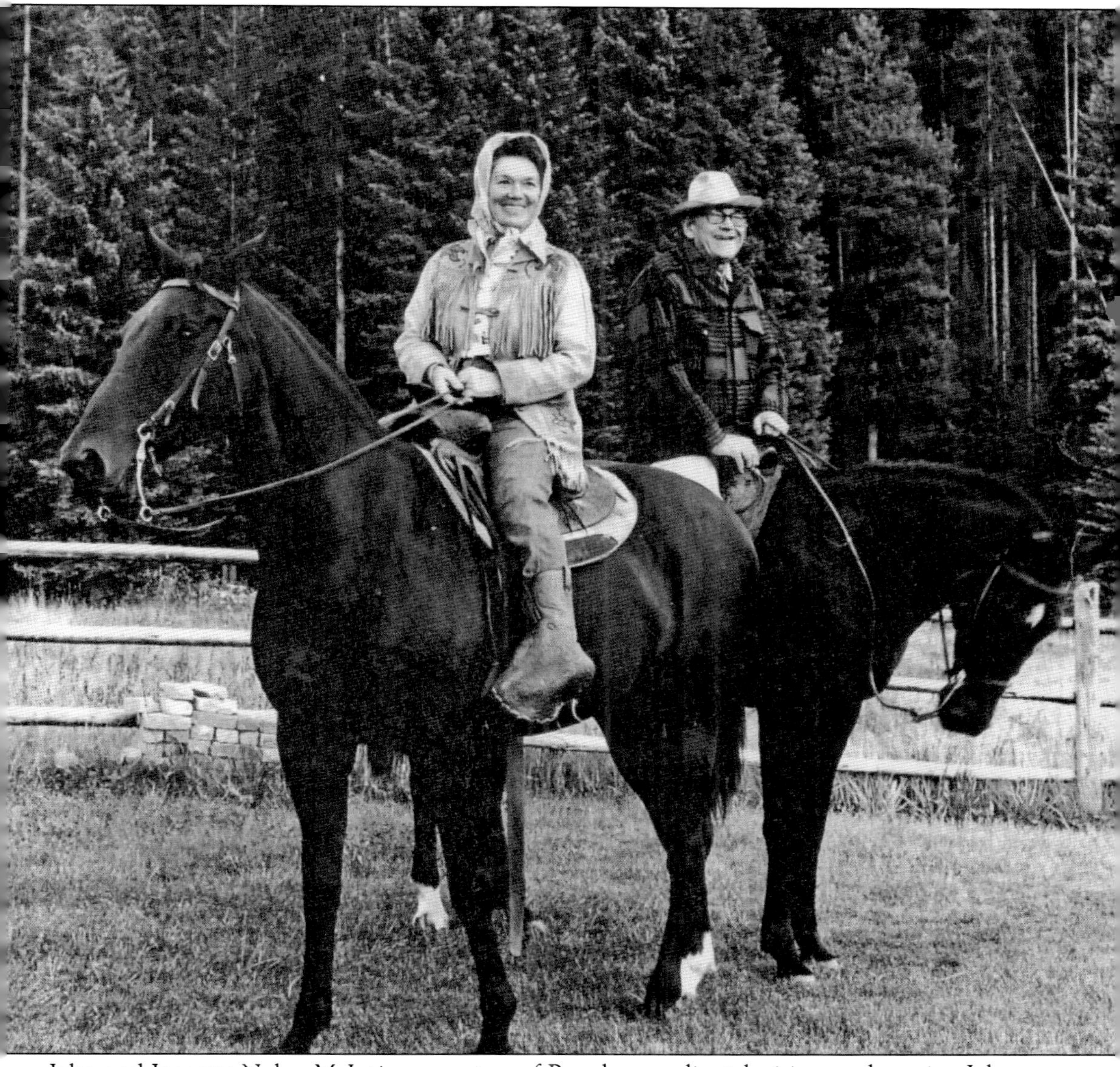

John and Jeanette Nolan McIntire were stars of Broadway, radio, television, and movies. John grew up in Kalispell and Jeanette in Beverly Hills. They met while doing radio with Orson Wells. They married in 1937, and McIntire, pursuing his dream of living in some of Montana's last wilderness, moved his city-bred wife to Yaak country, where they adopted the countryside and its people. While their two children were in high school, they moved to a small ranch near Indian Creek. Occasionally they would attend the Majestic Theatre when one of their movies premiered there. Both lived in the Yaak for the remainder of their lives, leaving only to make a movie or tape their television shows. John McIntire was best known as the wagon master on the series *Wagon Train*. Jeanette had a *Gunsmoke* spin-off called *Crazy Sally* and later a leading role in the series *Rawhide*. (Courtesy of the author.)

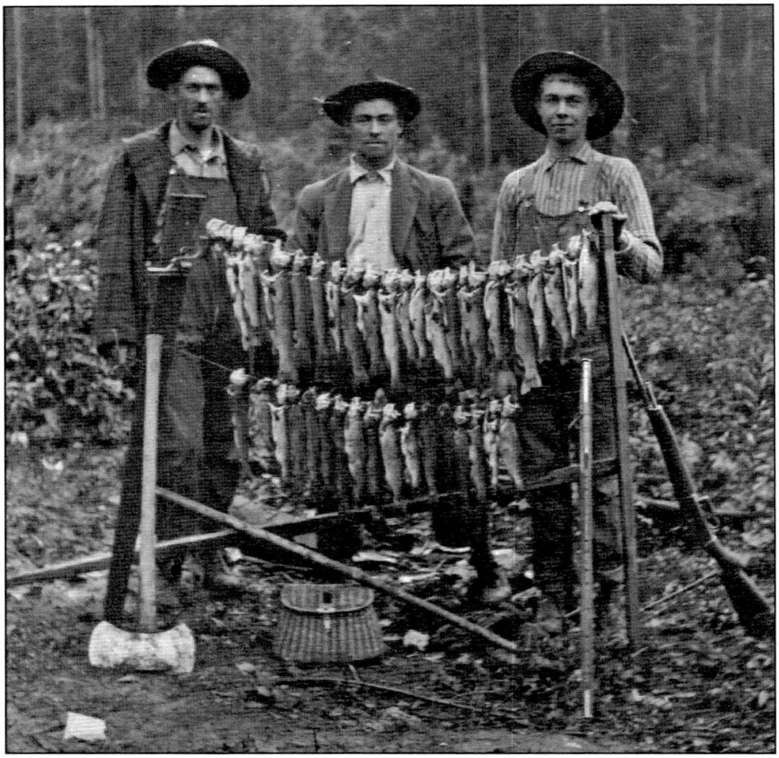

Burr and Jennie Alverson came from Wisconsin in 1906. They went over into Washington and Idaho for a few years, but then returned to a homestead east of Glen Lake. Pictured at left, from left to right, Burr, Grover, and Fred Alverson have a good day at Little Fish Lake. Below, Jennie Dice Alverson (left) and Delephine Alverson Wright may have packed in with the men.

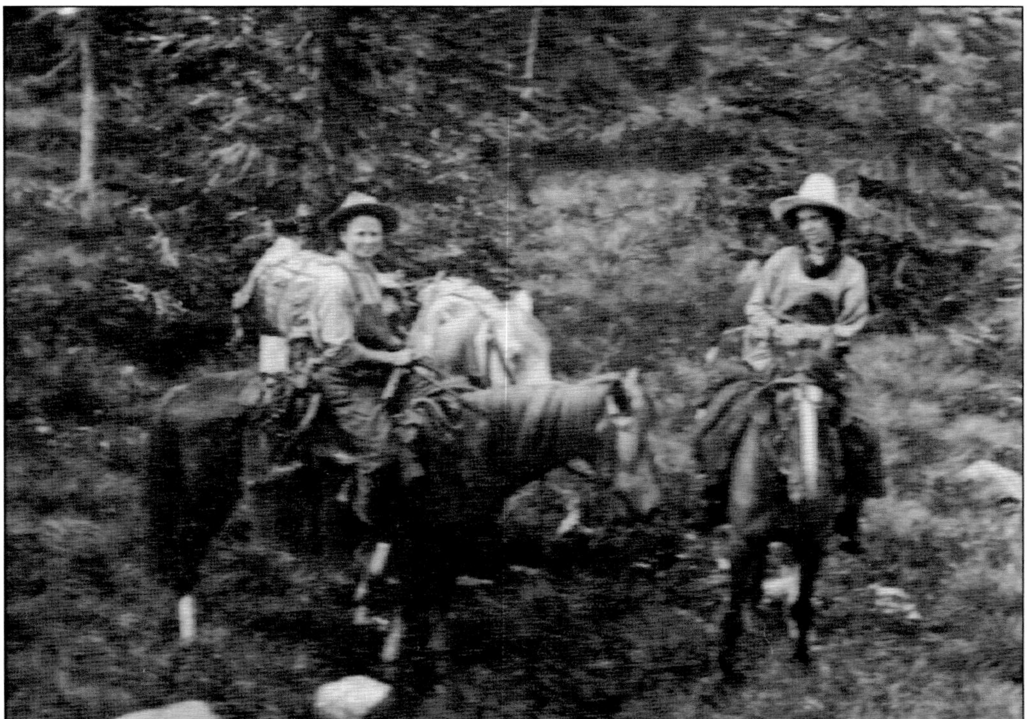

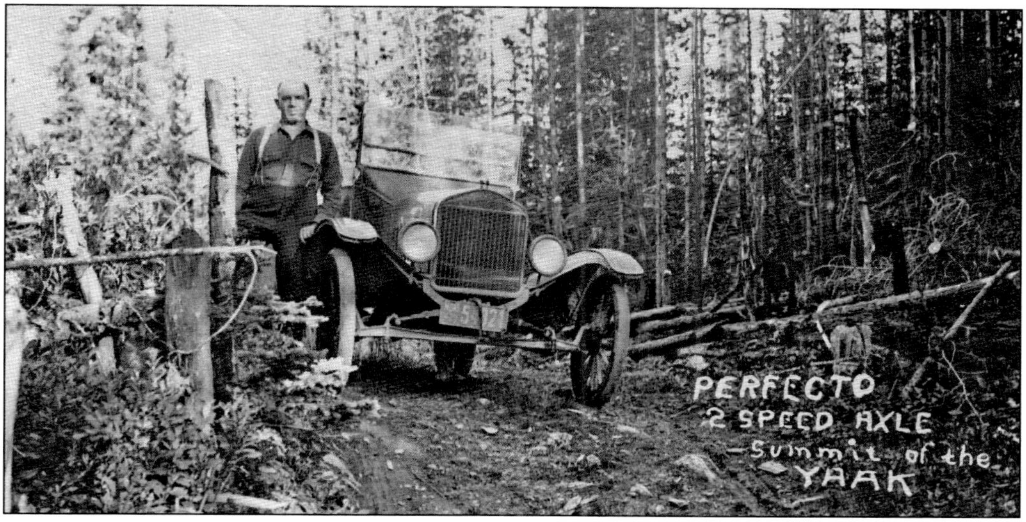

Billy Schagel grew up in Eureka with several brothers and sisters. His father was a millwright for the Eureka Lumber Company. Their home was located adjacent to what is now Schagel Park, the small park beside the ambulance barn, which was also part of the Schagel property, which was later donated to the town by Schagel's sister Helen. Above, Schagel was one of the first to coerce his Ford Model T to the top of Dodge Summit after the county pushed a stump road into the Yaak in 1921. Below, Schagel and an unidentified man look over the remains of Schagel's Model T on a less successful outing.

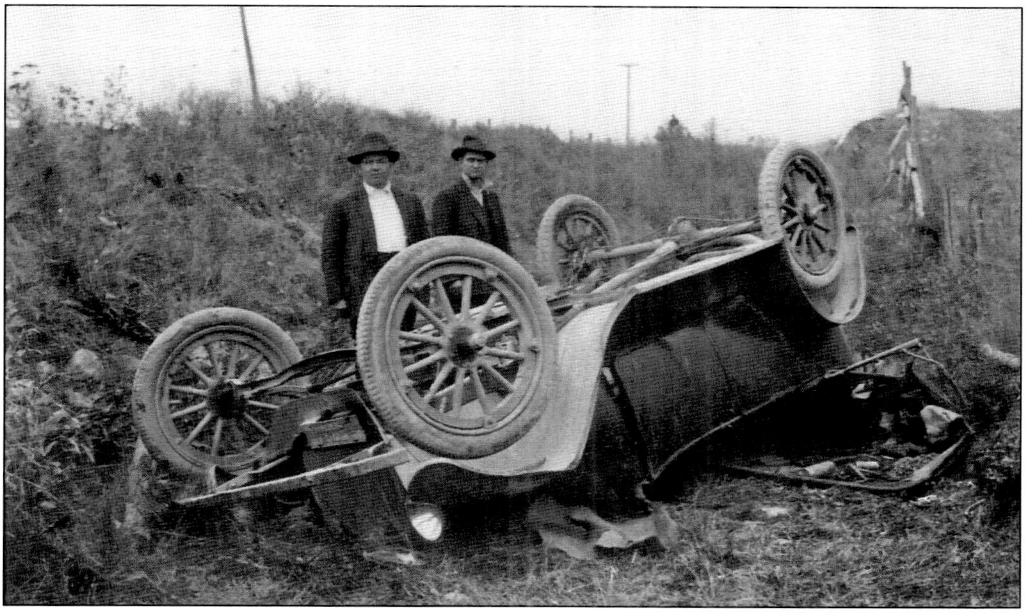

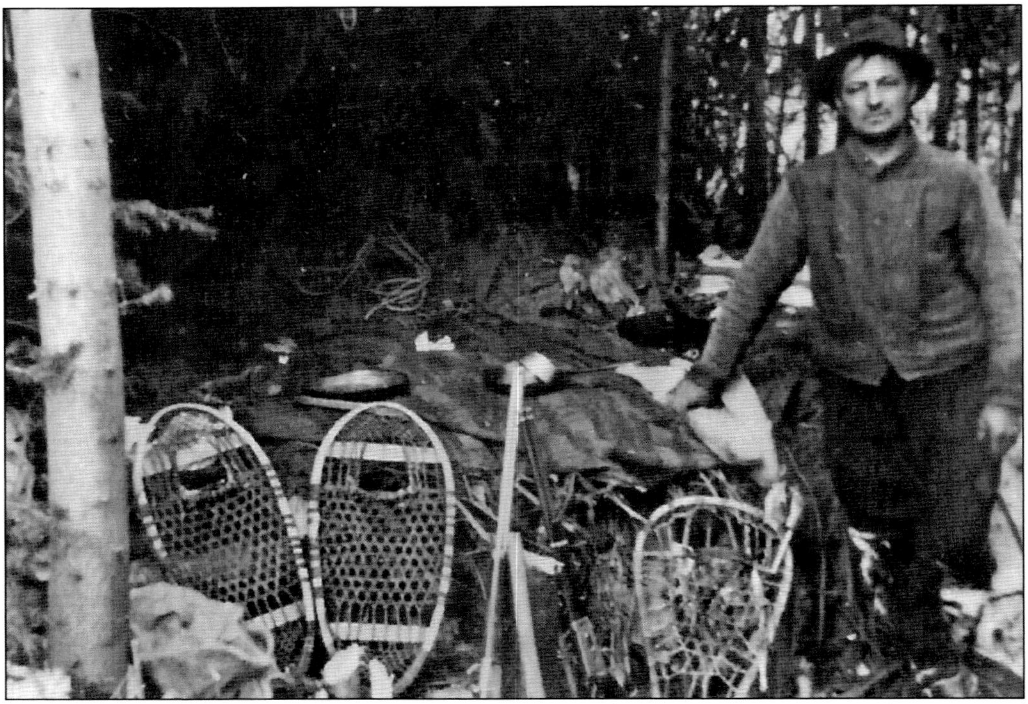

Ray Zeller was a capable man who worked at a variety of jobs in his tenure around Fortine and Trego. Pictured here trapping at Grimm's Meadow, through the years he logged and ran a mill and a hotel. He also made and moved moonshine. In 1995, Zeller's son-in-law, Fred Titchborne, who assisted, recalled that the moonshine "furnished the groceries and the rent so I was doing all right." (Courtesy of Darris Flanagan.)

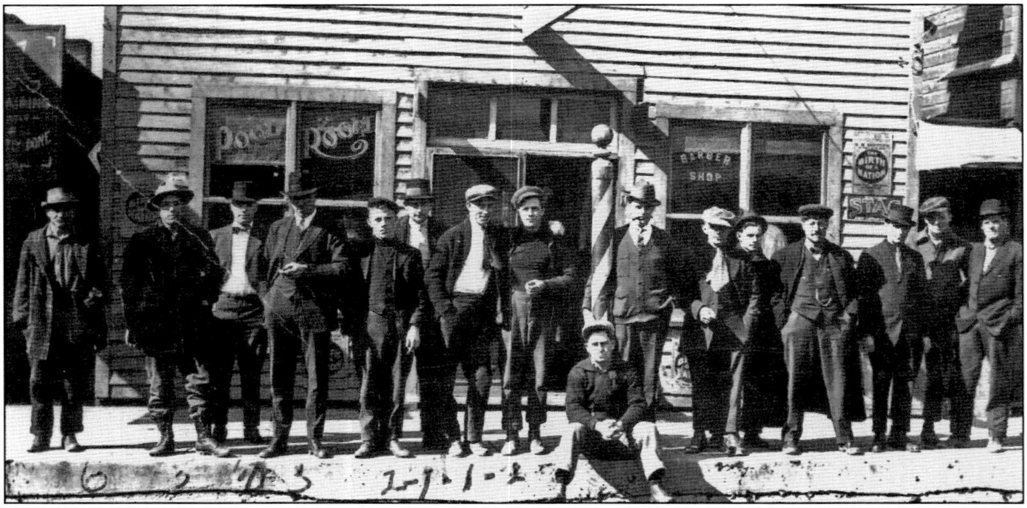

Of these men hanging out in front of the pool hall only Ed Hendrickson is known. He stands in the middle, his arm draped on another man. Hendrickson was chief of police in 1918. Later, during Prohibition, he operated the county road grader. According to Darrell Roose in a 1993 interview, Webb Garey confounded the Dry Squad once by convincing Hendrickson to use his grader to block the road.

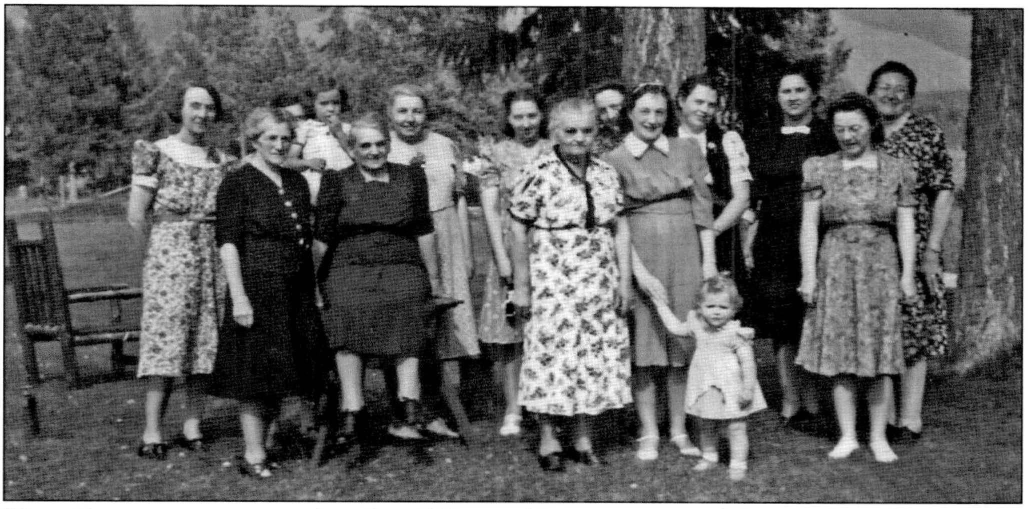

These Fortine women are gathered in 1939, possibly at a meeting of the Good Neighbors or the Home Demonstration Club. Pictured from left to right are (first row) Margaret Weydemeyer, Ina Curtis, Mrs. ? Johnson, Lucretia Larson holding Margaret Larson's hand, and Leota Yoppe; (second row) Mae Keith, unidentified, Marianne Day, Alice Jystad, Marion Johnson, Louise Larson, Marguerite Titchborne, Lillian Baker, and Clara Winkley.

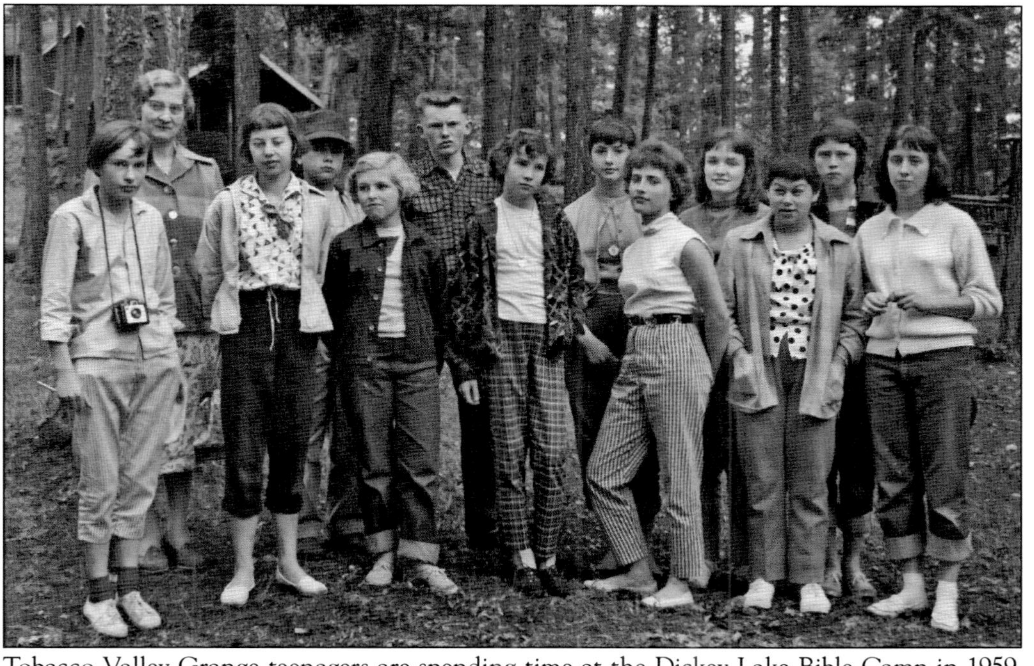

Tobacco Valley Grange teenagers are spending time at the Dickey Lake Bible Camp in 1959. Pictured from left to right are Arlene Weydemeyer, Mary Moses, Aletha Stephanson, Rod Osler, Barbara Kruger, Bruce Weydemeyer, Laura Mustard, Willa Noble, Janet Apeland, Wendy Tripp, Crystal Parker, Julie Parrish, and Kathy Decker.

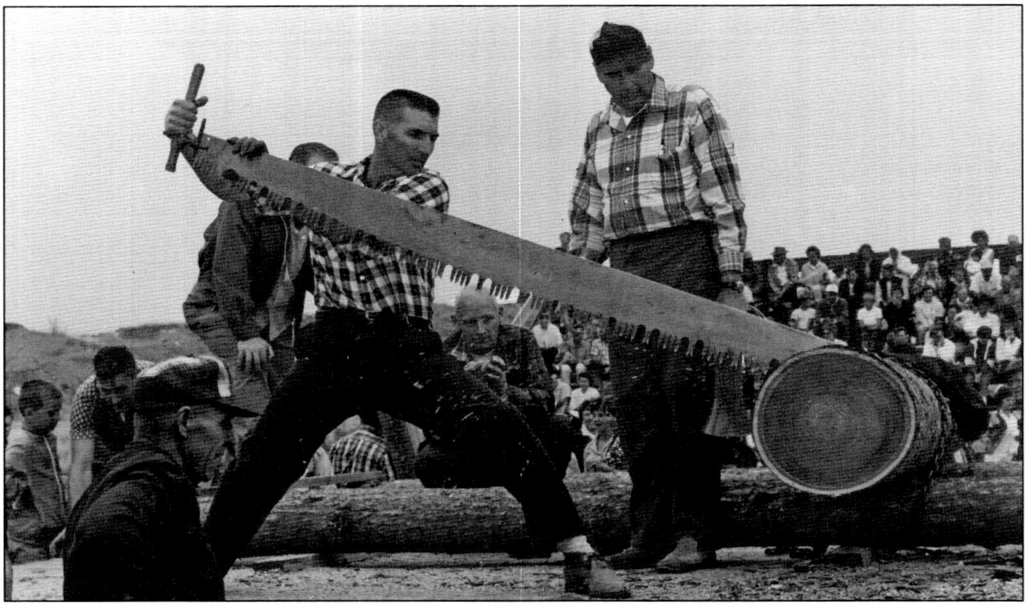

Fred King grew up on Tobacco Plains attending the Iowa Flats School. He became skillful with a crosscut saw and eventually formed a successful logging and road construction operation. He is seen here at the county fair competition in 1967. Don Boslaugh (standing on the right) was the high school principal throughout the 1950s and 1960s. He also partnered up with Marshal James, and they ran a sawmill.

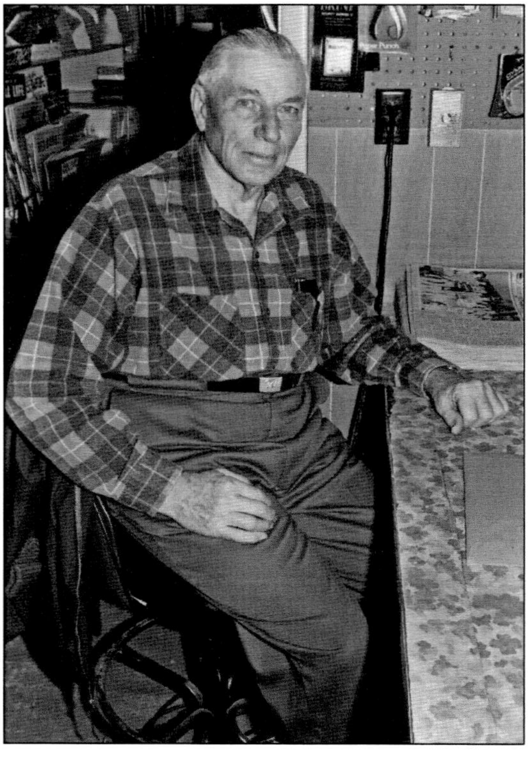

Winton Weydemeyer grew up in Fortine. He attended Montana State University, where he earned a degree in agriculture. Returning to the family ranch, Weydemeyer became active in matters concerning conservation. It is he who was largely responsible for initiating protection for the Ten Lakes Scenic Area as he watched roads being built throughout the Kootenai National Forest.

Ten

All Aboard

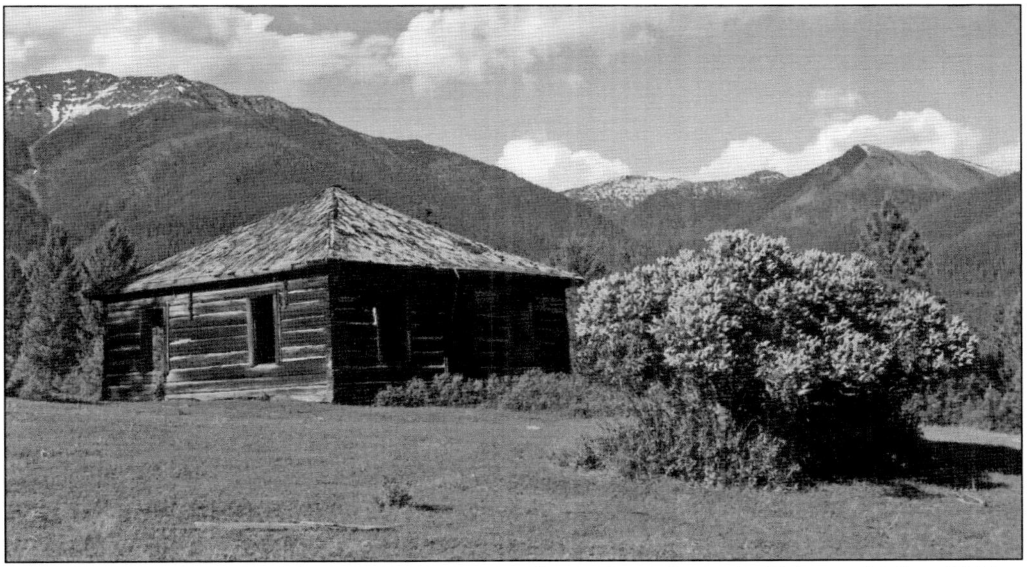

Signs of those who settled this country are in evidence throughout the Tobacco Valley. Old log cabins or rotting foundations with lilac bushes growing nearby are one of the more common reminders. Many homesteaders like the Bendas, who settled on the valley's east side, have passed from the memories of those living here today just as the towns and farms that were inundated by Lake Koocanusa will fade from the collective memory in the future. When Libby Dam was planned and announced and then actually built, it was a difficult thing to comprehend for those who knew the valley in simpler times.

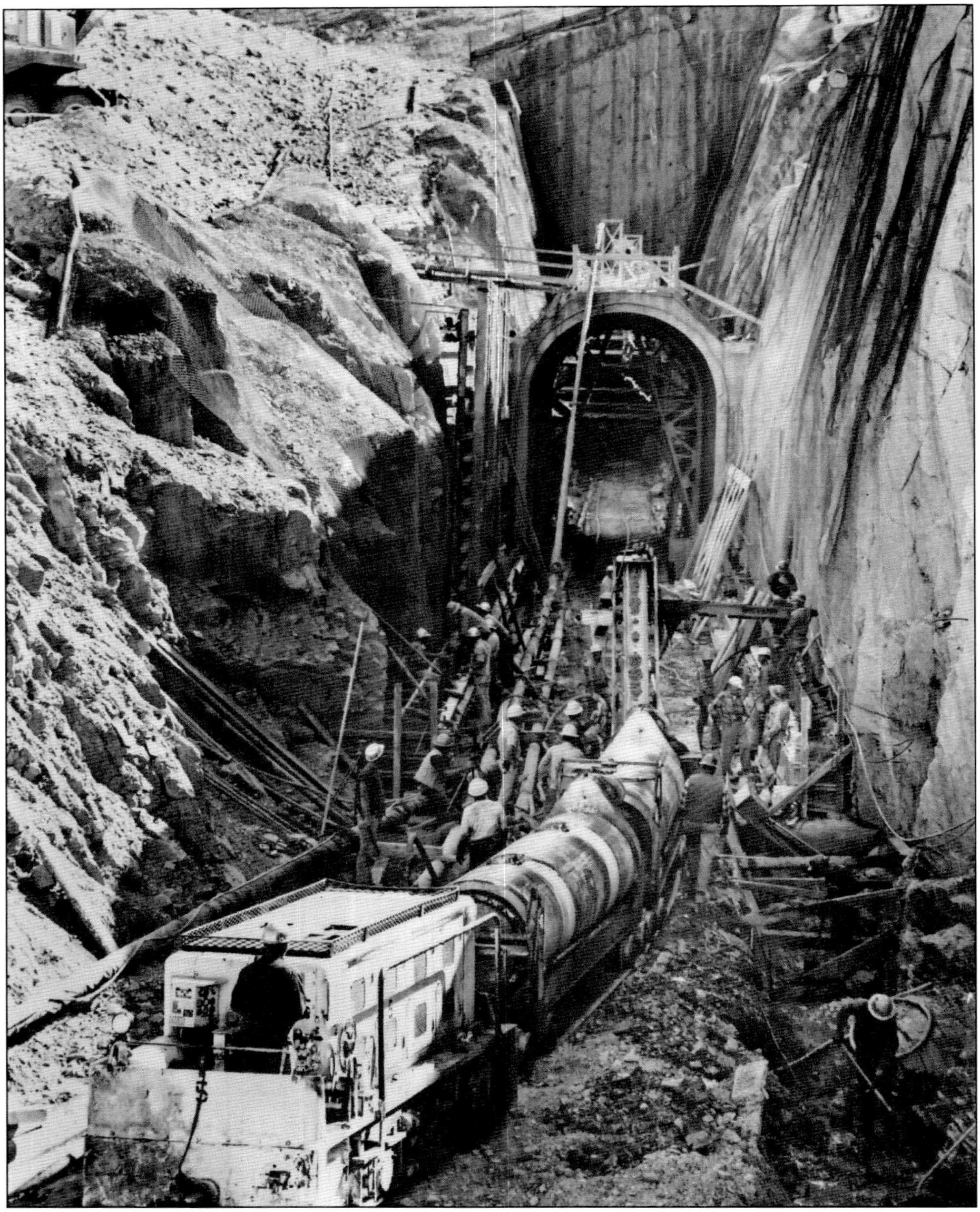

Paramount to the process of building Libby Dam was the relocation of the Great Northern Railroad. There was one practical option, move the line into the Fortine Creek drainage until it ran into Elk Mountain, then excavate a 7-mile tunnel into the Wolf Creek/Fisher River drainage. In 1968, laser-guided machines beginning on either side of Elk Mountain succeeded in drilling a 7-mile hole. During construction, tailings were crushed and used as fill in the 60-mile track relocation effort. Between dam builders and tunnel workers, the economy was flush, with housing demand higher than supply. Part of the deal the Corps of Engineers made with towns like Trego and Rexford was building them new schools to accommodate the influx.

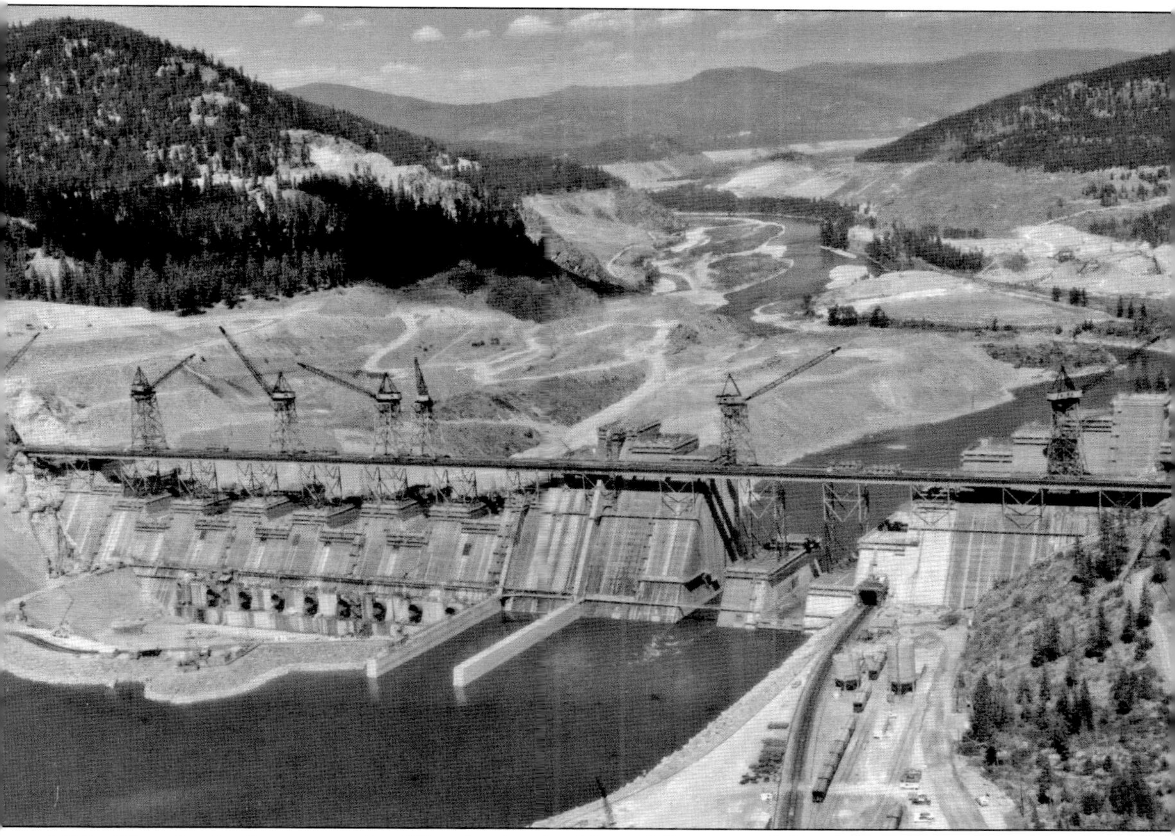

Libby Dam backed water up for 90 miles in the United States and Canada. The edifice rises 420 feet from bedrock, spans 2,900 feet, and was built to withstand a 6.5-magnitude earthquake. Its straight-line construction relies on its sheer weight to hold the water back. Because the interior of the dam was calculated to remain around 45 degrees Fahrenheit, ice was mixed into each batch of concrete to insure structural integrity. Built primarily for flood control and power generation, its water is used 16 more times before reaching the Pacific Ocean. But do not tell that to the fishermen who harvest countless Kokanee salmon from its chilly depths each year. They think it is all there for them. Because of the Libby Dam, the highest and longest bridge in Montana was built.

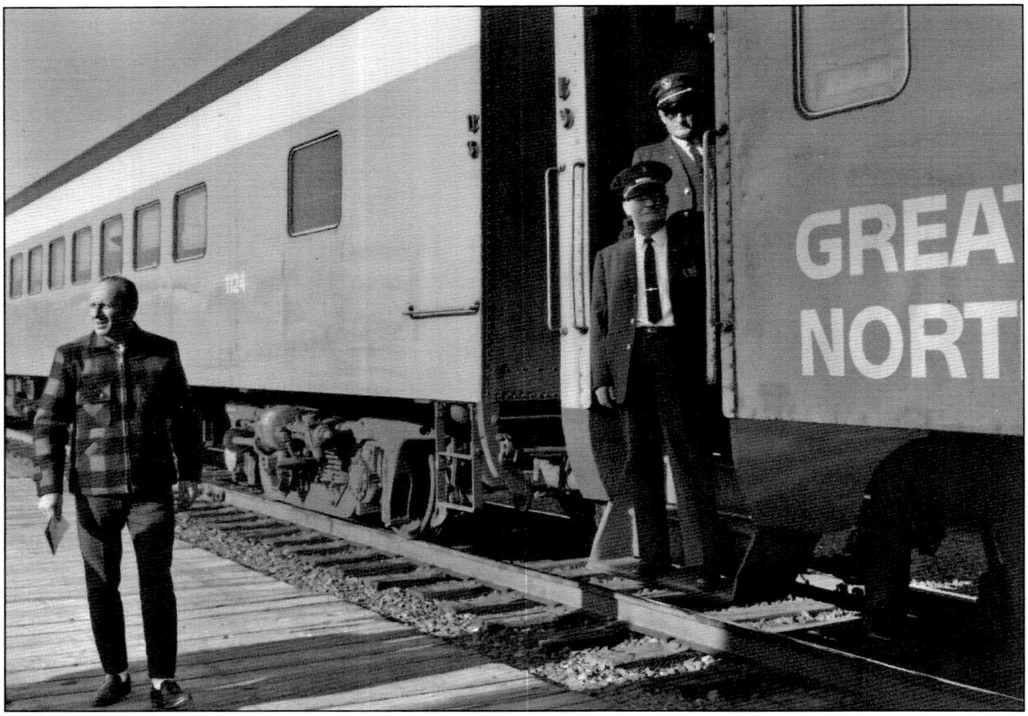

No. 28 was one of the last trains out of Eureka before passenger service was suspended. For 68 years, from 1904 to 1972, Eureka was invigorated by the comings and goings of the *Oriental Limited*, the fast mail train, and serpentine freight trains. Pictured above are, from left to right, depot agent Cliff Vorhees, conductor Marvin "Bud" King, and brakeman Dave Clowers. Below, the *Oriental Limited* glides past the hoodoos along the Tobacco River breaks near its confluence with the Kootenai River.

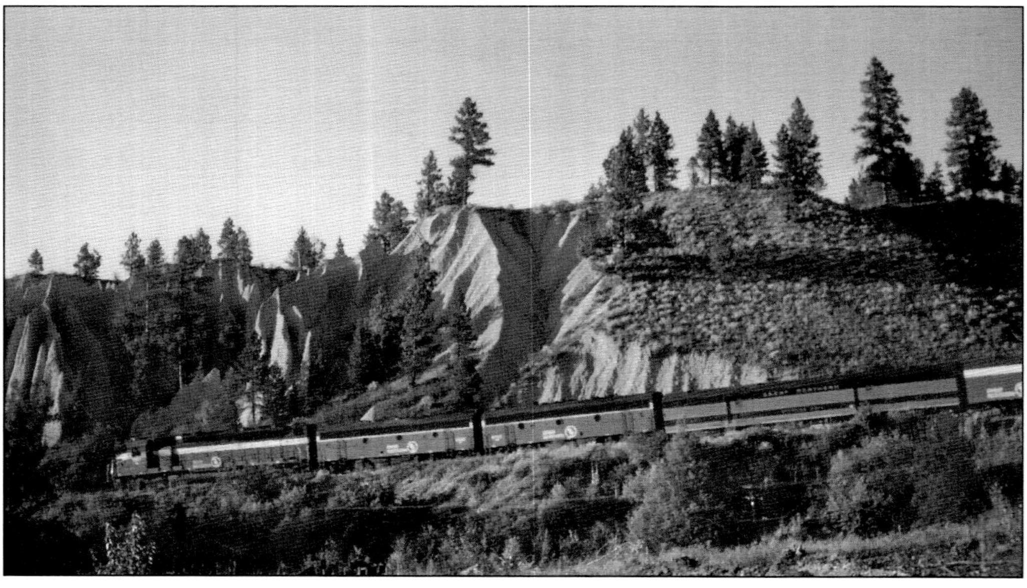

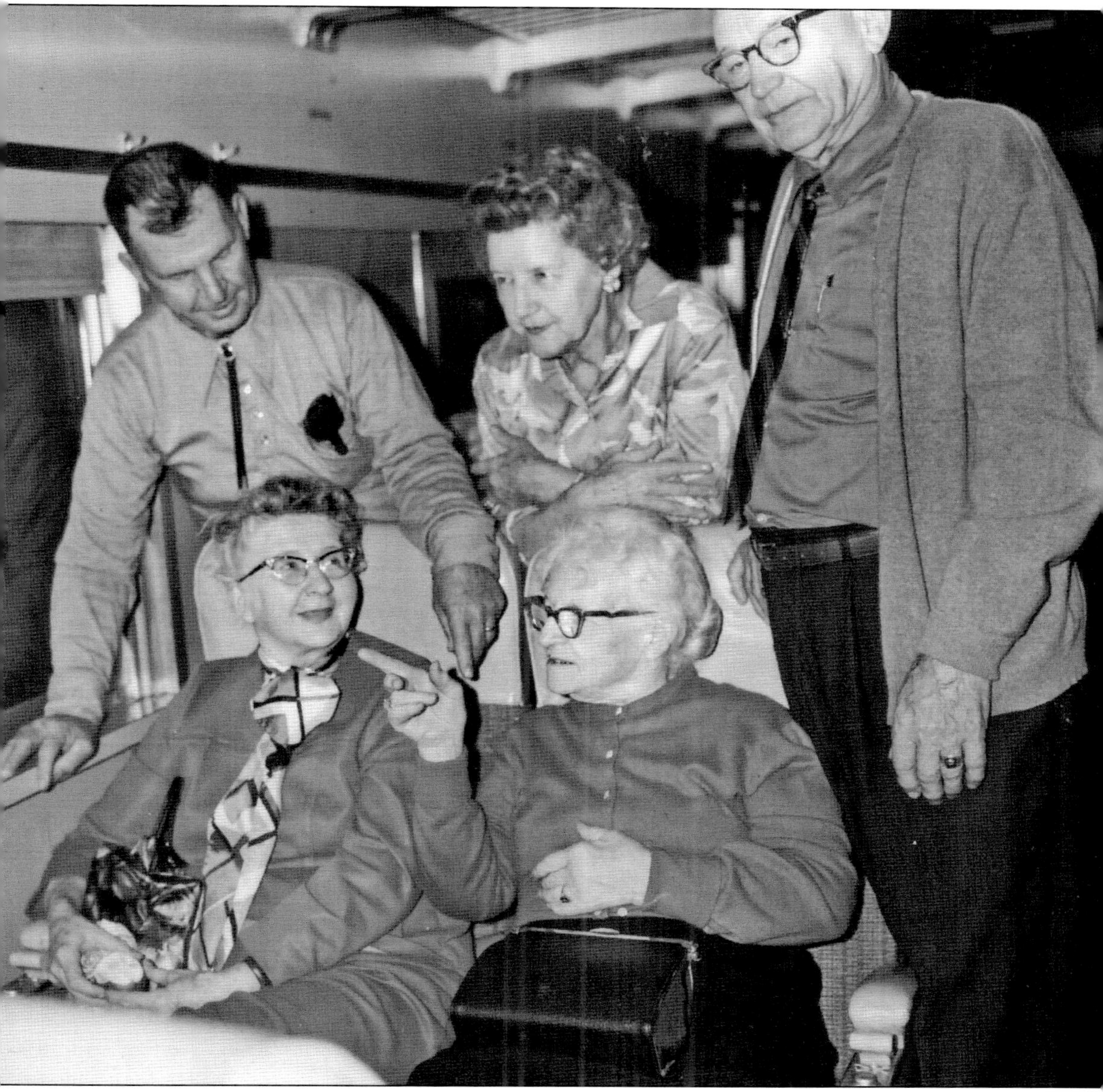

Pictured on the last passenger train out of Eureka are, from left to right, (seated) Clara Brock Fewkes and Alice Beer; (standing) Mr. and Mrs. Harry Velton and Charlie Hart. Clara Fewkes, to whom this book is dedicated, began her tenure in the Tobacco Valley as a nurse at Dr. Fred Bogardus's hospital, ministering to the influenza victims of 1918. Much later, she was one of a handful whose perseverance and dedication has resulted in the Historical Village and the treasures preserved there. To Alice Beer is given the honor of naming the lake created by Libby Dam. Lake Koocanusa is an acronym derived from Kootenai, Canada, and U.S.A.

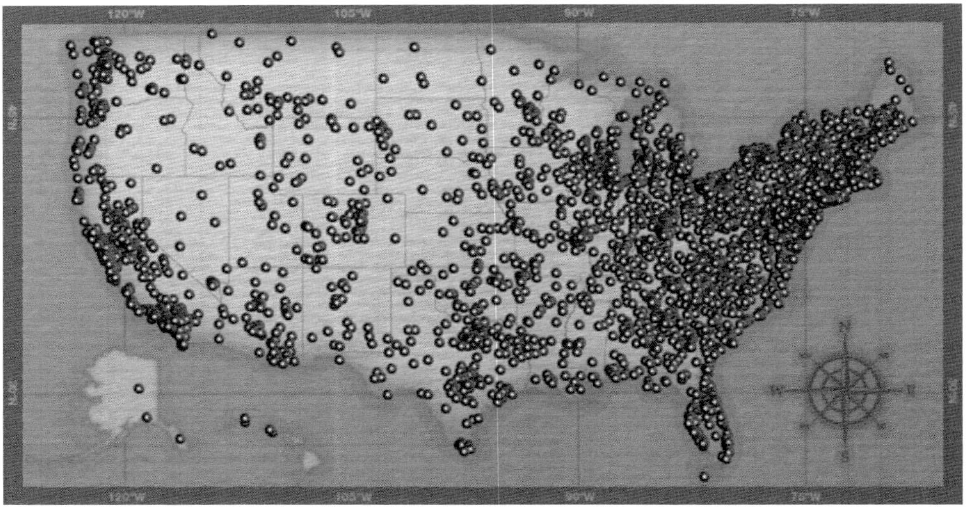